T0334663

Strategic Communications in Russia

This book serves as a reader exploring the scholarly inquiry, professional education, and practice of Russian public relations and advertising in multiple contexts. It examines significant parts of what can be encompassed under the umbrella of strategic communications, including public relations and advertising, rather than investigating all areas of communication in Russia.

Within the context of Russia's history, culture, and ideology, the book begins by tracing the development of communication as a field, as a discipline, and as a social institution in Russia. It then samples current studies in Russian strategic communications, examining this professional specialization's current state and likely future directions. The book's authors are mostly Russians who are experts in their specializations. Chapters are predicated upon the premise that this is an exciting time of great opportunity for Russian strategic communications. However, in Russia, exploiting such opportunities for strategic communications scholarship, education, and professional practice presents challenges within the context of that nation's cultural, historical, and ideological heritage that presently may be unique. The book concludes with a prognosis of the future of Russian strategic communications.

The book is recommended reading for a worldwide audience of strategic communication scholars, educators, students, and practitioners. Such readers will find the book of interest and of unique value because the book will help them to better understand, appreciate, and respect Russian strategic communications, its genesis, and present state.

Katerina Tsetsura is Gaylord Family Professor of Public Relations and Strategic Communication at the Gaylord College of Journalism and Mass Communication, University of Oklahoma, USA.

Dean Kruckeberg is a professor at the University of North Carolina at Charlotte, USA.

Routledge New Directions in PR & Communication Research

Edited by Kevin Moloney

Current academic thinking about public relations (PR) and related communication is a lively, expanding marketplace of ideas, and many scholars believe that it's time for its radical approach to be deepened. **Routledge New Directions in PR & Communication Research** is the forum of choice for this new thinking. Its key strength is its remit, publishing critical and challenging responses to continuities and fractures in contemporary PR thinking and practice, tracking its spread into new geographies and political economies. It questions its contested role in market-orientated, capitalist, liberal democracies around the world and examines its invasion of all media spaces, old, new, and as yet unenvisaged.

The **New Directions** series has already published and commissioned diverse original work on topics such as:

- PR's influence on Israeli and Palestinian nation-building
- PR's origins in the history of ideas
- a Jungian approach to PR ethics and professionalism
- global perspectives on PR professional practice
- PR as an everyday language for everyone
- PR as emotional labor
- PR as communication in conflicted societies, and
- PR's relationships to cooperation, justice and paradox.

We actively invite new contributions and offer academics a welcoming place for the publication of their analyses of a universal, persuasive mindset that lives comfortably in old and new media around the world.

Public Relations, Branding and Authenticity
Brand Communications in the Digital Age
Sian Rees

Paradox in Public Relations
A Contrarian Critique of Theory and Practice
Kevin L. Stoker

Strategic Communications in Russia
Public Relations and Advertising
Edited by Katerina Tsetsura and Dean Kruckeberg

For more information about this series, please visit: www.routledge.com/Routledge-New-Directions-in-Public-Relations--Communication-Research/book-series/RNDPRCR

Strategic Communications in Russia

Public Relations and Advertising

Edited by
Katerina Tsetsura and Dean Kruckeberg

Routledge
Taylor & Francis Group

LONDON AND NEW YORK

First published 2021
by Routledge
2 Park Square, Milton Park, Abingdon, Oxon OX14 4RN

and by Routledge
52 Vanderbilt Avenue, New York, NY 10017

Routledge is an imprint of the Taylor & Francis Group, an informa business

© 2021 selection and editorial matter, Katerina Tsetsura and Dean Kruckeberg; individual chapters, the contributors

The right of Katerina Tsetsura and Dean Kruckeberg to be identified as the authors of the editorial material, and of the authors for their individual chapters, has been asserted in accordance with sections 77 and 78 of the Copyright, Designs and Patents Act 1988.

British Library Cataloguing-in-Publication Data
A catalogue record for this book is available from the British Library

Library of Congress Cataloging-in-Publication Data
Names: Tsetsura, Katerina, editor. | Kruckeberg, Dean, editor.
Title: Strategic communications in Russia: public relations and advertising / edited by Katerina Tsetsura and Dean Kruckeberg.
Description: Abingdon, Oxon; New York, NY: Routledge, 2021. | Series: Routledge new directions in PR & communication research | Includes bibliographical references and index.
Identifiers: LCCN 2020015117 (print) | LCCN 2020015118 (ebook)
Subjects: LCSH: Public relations–Russia (Federation) | Advertising–Russia (Federation) | Strategic planning–Russia (Federation)
Classification: LCC HD59.6.R8 S74 2021 (print) | LCC HD59.6.R8 (ebook) | DDC 659.0947–dc23
LC record available at https://lccn.loc.gov/2020015117
LC ebook record available at https://lccn.loc.gov/2020015118

ISBN: 978-0-367-89392-7 (hbk)
ISBN: 978-1-003-01892-6 (ebk)

Typeset in Bembo
by Newgen Publishing UK

This book is dedicated to those who seek greater understanding, appreciation, and respect among the strategic communications professional community worldwide.

Contents

Illustrations

Contributors

Nelli Bachurina, National Research University Higher School of Economics, Moscow, Russia

Elena Bykova, St. Petersburg State University, Russia

Andrei Dorskii, St. Petersburg State University, Russia

Alexandra Endaltseva, L'École des hautes études en sciences sociales (EHESS), Paris, France

Dmitry Fedyunin, Plekhanov Russian University of Economics, Moscow, Russia

Dmitrii Gavra, St. Petersburg State University, Russia

Julia Gryaznova, National Research University Higher School of Economics, Moscow, Russia

Elena Gryzunova, National Research University Higher School of Economics, Moscow, Russia

Oleg Kashirskikh, National Research University Higher School of Economics, Moscow, Russia

Elena Kaverina, St. Petersburg State University, Russia

Lyudmila Kryuchkovskaya, National Research University Higher School of Economics, Moscow, Russia

Anastasia Kugappi, University of Jyväskylä, Jyväskylän yliopisto, Finland

Irina Kuzheleva-Sagan, Tomsk State University, Tomsk Oblast, Russia

Taisiia Lagutenkova, National Research University Higher School of Economics, Moscow, Russia

Vilma Luoma-Aho, University of Jyväskylä, Jyväskylän yliopisto, Finland

Alexander Mozhaev, National Research University Higher School of Economics, Moscow, Russia

Nikita Savin, National Research University Higher School of Economics, Moscow, Russia

Marina Shilina, Plekhanov Russian University of Economics, Moscow, Russia

Olga Solovyeva, National Research University Higher School of Economics, Moscow, Russia

David Waterman, Gaylord College, University of Oklahoma, USA

Sergey Zverev, National Research University Higher School of Economics, Moscow, Russia

Preface

Despite a growing number of Russian-speaking communication scholars who present at international communication conferences, an increasing presence of several global academic organizations that focus on Russian communication, including the Russian Communication Association (RCA) and the Communication Association of Eurasian Researchers (CAER), and a rising interest in the peer-reviewed scholarly journal, *Russian Journal of Communication*, which is dedicated to studying communication in, with, and about Russia and Russian-speaking communities, no single volume yet offers an organized exploration of scholarly strategic communications inquiry by Russian-speaking scholars. This book aims to fill this void as it systematically presents contemporary thinking in Russian strategic communications, written primarily by Russian-speaking communication academics in English.

The volume you are about to read should not be seen as an all-encompassing comprehensive review of all scholarly work in Russian strategic communications. The goal was neither to cover all areas of scholarly investigation of strategic communications in Russia, nor to have an all-inclusive list of scholars from Russia share their work. Rather, this volume is a reader that explores scholarly inquiry, professional education, and the practice of Russian strategic communications.

We began discussing the possibility of such a volume with strategic communications academicians from Russia several years ago. The journey has not been easy nor particularly speedy. However, we have been able to include timely contributions, which we hope can stand a test of time, from several Russian communication scholars. We also have enriched this volume by adding voices from outside Russia as a few Western scholars have shared their perspective and contemporary thinking about Russian strategic communications. We have included their work to accentuate the differences that Russian and Western scholars in this field might face during their academic discussions at international conferences or in the process of collaboration.

This book is intended to be a catalyst to discussions and dialogues among Russian-speaking scholars/educators, students, and practitioners in strategic communications and their English-speaking counterparts elsewhere throughout the world. Russian scholars, educators, students, and practitioners are eager to participate in a quest for globally applicable theories, normative models of education, and benchmark professional practices. We hope that, after reading this book, English-speaking strategic communications scholars will agree that the Russian strategic communications community can contribute significantly to global discussions, dialogues, and collaborations.

Acknowledgments

This book would not exist without the hard work of many people on both sides of the Atlantic Ocean. A list of all who have helped to publish this volume is truly impressive. First and foremost, many thanks go to our colleagues in Russia, who first proposed the idea for this book a few years ago. Without your enthusiasm and your continuous focus, we would not have been able to complete this work. Next, we want to thank all contributors to this volume: your thoughts and ideas that are presented in this book demonstrate both the depth and the breadth of Russian strategic communications scholarly inquiry, and for that we are truly grateful. We also would like to thank the publisher, Taylor and Francis, as well as the editors and staff members in the United Kingdom and elsewhere in the world for giving us this wonderful opportunity to share the voices of academics who study Russian strategic communications. Finally, we would like to thank our family members, without whom nothing is possible.

Part I

Views on strategic communication(s) in Russia

1 What is (are) strategic communications in Russia?

Dean Kruckeberg

Overview of this book

This book explores Russian strategic communication(s). Many scholars and practitioners use this plural form of the noun communication to describe professional communication applications, which often are theoretically predicated on the social sciences. The term communication (singular) often denotes scholarly areas that are traditionally represented by the humanities, for example rhetoric and linguistics; however, subdisciplines of communication include those that may be applied, for example, interpersonal, group, organizational, health, and intercultural communication. Furthermore, both communication and communications scholars use a range of qualitative and quantitative research methods. Thus, these distinctions can be confusing, often creating contention and debate, and communication and communications frequently are uttered interchangeably, especially in their casual usage by lay people.

The book's ambition

This book's ambition is not to examine all areas of communication and communications. Its table of contents identifies chapters that can be encompassed under the umbrella of strategic communications, for example, public relations and advertising. The text is written in English, and the book's Western publisher has global marketing capabilities. This is by intent. Of course, the book's intended audience includes Russian strategic communications scholar/educators, their students, and that country's strategic communications professionals, most of whom are proficient in English as a second language. However, this volume also is written to attract a wider net of readers, that is, strategic communications scholar/educators, students, and practitioners worldwide who are fluent in English, but who likely are not literate—let alone proficient—in the Russian language. Hopefully, this global audience will find the book of interest and value, helping them to better understand, appreciate, and respect Russian strategic communications, its genesis, and present state. Indeed, with this volume as a foundation and catalyst, the editors and authors hope that strategic communications scholar/educators, students, and practitioners worldwide may wish to participate in a continuing dialogue with their Russian counterparts to understand the role and function of strategic communications in that nation as an area of scholarly inquiry, professional education, and practice.

The book's authors are mostly Russian strategic communications scholar/educators and practitioners who are recognized experts in their specializations. An editor of the book and the coauthor of the concluding chapter is Dr. Katerina Tsetsura, a Russian-American. She is a University of Oklahoma professor who is a globally prominent public relations scholar/educator and a former strategic communications practitioner. Although she has lived in six countries throughout her life, Dr. Tsetsura's heritage is Russian and Ukrainian, and she maintains a continuing relationship with her scholar/educator and practitioner colleagues throughout Russia.

I am an American strategic communications scholar/educator, and I bring an inherently Americentric worldview to this book. Indeed, my greatest contribution may be my worldview that has evolved from an admitted American provincialism and chauvinism to have metamorphosed throughout the years to a profound respect for the Russian people, their heritage, culture, and traditions, as well as to my respect for—if not always total understanding of—many Russian values.

That said, after having made multiple trips throughout Russia during the past three decades, after having working closely with Russians throughout the years, and after having read much about Russia throughout my scholarly career, I frequently question what have I learned from my Russian friends and former students. DeVito (1998) identifies a problem that hinders cultural awareness and sensitivity, that is, the ethnocentrism in which we see others through our own cultural filters and in which we evaluate the values, beliefs, and behaviors of our own culture as being more positive, logical, and natural than are those of other cultures. As an advocate of globalization, I, as an American, realize that Russia is a critically important nation-state in world affairs, and I agree with Giddens (cited in Rantanen, 2002) that globalization today is only partly about Westernization.

Russians are different than are Americans

Decidedly, Russians are different than are Americans—culturally, historically, and ideologically, and Russia's media systems have been and remain different. Kluckhohn (cited in Hazen, 2008, Fall) summarized the Russian national character as a struggle between:

1) warm, expressive expansiveness versus formality, control, and orderliness, 2) personal loyalty, sincerity, and responsiveness versus distrust and conspiratorial mentality, 3) strong identification with the face-to-face groups of

which the individual is a member versus a single tolerated loyalty (upward to people not known personally), and 4) being versus doing or dependent passivity versus ceaseless instrumental "conscious activity",

Hazen (2008, Fall) notes Sinekopova's description of a Russian ethos of a "communal spirit, soul talk, and its complex attitude to the Other" (pp. 456–457). However, Hazen (2008, Fall) warns that a comparative analysis approach to national character has been criticized for its stereotypes and overgeneralizations. Furthermore, it must be remembered that Russia is an exceedingly large, diverse, and complex nation, which citizens represent more than 180 nationalities who reside in 85 regions (in 2014, two regions were added: Crimea and the city of Sevastopol) that extend through 11 time zones. Thus, I have concluded that Americans and Russians are significantly different from one another and that these differences likely won't converge anytime soon. Some, myself included, might argue that they never should.

That said, I disagree with the old Russian proverb (cited in Mezrich, 2015) that says that two bears cannot live in one cave. That is why this book seeks a global audience that can read its text in English. Russian strategic communications as an area of scholarly inquiry, professional education, and practice is important— certainly to Russians, but also to scholar/educators, students, and strategic communications practitioners throughout the world.

Russian strategic communications must be predicated on history, culture, and ideology

Of course, Russian strategic communications as an area of scholarly inquiry, professional education, and practice must be predicated upon and contextualized within that nation's history, culture, and ideology. Such understanding is no mean task and, indeed, can be problematic for non-Russians. It is unlikely that any non-Russian has an entirely accurate perception of Russia. For most non-Russians, a knowledge of Russia's history likely has been relegated to a secondary or tertiary emphasis in their own education in their own nation-state, and their impressions of Russia likely have been influenced by news coverage and political information, including propaganda, that have originated from a range of sources that have been both accurate and inaccurate as well as supportive and nonsupportive of that country.

Certainly, geopolitical and ideological concerns and tensions exist about this country that many throughout the world fear or view as a threat. After the dissolution of the former Soviet Union in 1991, Russia had experienced turbulent times during the 1990s and early 2000s. Today, it is enduring the economic sanctions of the United States and the European Union after its 2014 annexation of the Crimea and parts of Ukraine, as well as for its military involvement in Syria, and certainly because of accusations that it allegedly had attempted to influence the 2016 U.S. Presidential election in the United States. Recent global public opinion and perceived knowledge about Russia certainly have been influenced by other countries' assumptions concerning Russia's political ambitions. Also influential may have been Russia's own considerable efforts in nation-branding to favorably influence perceptions of this nation-state by other nations and their peoples to encourage respect and political advantage in the global arena, as well as to promote foreign investment and tourism. Indeed, this 1,000-year-old country, which is often symbolized as a bear or as a two-headed eagle, has had a long history of nation-branding that has been intended to influence global audiences. Examples include the former Soviet Union's attempts in the 1920s and 1930s to earn revenue for its planned industrialization by branding itself as a desirable tourist destination for wealthy Europeans and Americans; other examples are Cold War communication efforts that had included elaborate displays and powerful videos at Russian airports that had extolled the benefits of a collectivist state. Undoubtedly unknown or under-appreciated by many Westerners, the former Soviet Union had been a major exporter of films and television and radio programs to other countries. Statistics for the 1970s and early 1980s show that the Soviet Union was the largest pur-veyor of broadcast information in the world (Rantanen, 2002). To attract for-eign investment in the 1990s, Russia branded itself as a lucrative and welcoming country in which to do business.

Today, Russia appears to be using the soft power of public diplomacy in its attempt to counter other nations' accusations about this former communist state's alleged empire-restoring imperialism; to address any remaining stigma of a post-KGB police state that, nevertheless, is presumed by other nations to ensure fewer citizen rights and freedoms than are enjoyed in much of the West; and to counter international assumptions about continuing lawless-ness, together with Russia's legacy of historic iconic symbols that include the Kalashnikov rifle. Russia's recent nation-branding appears to rely, not only on showcasing itself, for example by hosting the 2014 Sochi XXII Winter Olympics Games, but also on that country's pervasive use of digital media that appears to be grounded in relationship-management theory. Such nation-branding efforts also have been intended to encourage Russian national unity and citizen pride, while perhaps lessening the influence of indigenous tensions among Russia's diverse citizenry.

Such contemporary political concerns are all the more reason that this book is significant, especially for non-Russian readers. Like bears attempting to live peacefully, ideally with mutual benefit, in a cave, strategic communications scholar/educators worldwide must engage with one another and attempt to understand one another and their respective worldviews. Although it's unlikely that American philosopher and communication scholar John Dewey had ever considered bears living in a cave, he did see communication as an oppor-tunity to enhance society, noting that communication is the means to establish cooperation, domination, and order. He observed that communication is both personally fulling, that is, consummatory, and practical, that is, instrumental, enabling us to live in a world of things that have meaning by our sharing in the objects and arts that are precious to a community. Through communication, meanings are enhanced, deepened, and solidified in a sense of communion (cited in Kruckeberg & Starck, 1988). As Dewey had suggested, communication can address such goals. For this reason alone, Russian strategic communications as an area of scholarly inquiry, professional education, and practice is important to all of us. I would expand Dewey's observations to include both the desire and the potential for a global community.

Succeeding chapters of this book will be predicated upon the premise that this is an exciting time of great opportunity for Russian strategic communications scholar/educators, their students, and that nation's strategic communications practitioners. For example, Tsetsura and Kruckeberg (2009, Summer) said that public relations practitioners in countries in political transition that have emerging capitalist economic systems have been given a unique opportunity that no longer exists where this professionalized occupation has had a much longer tradition. Practitioners in these countries can adopt and/or adapt what has been proven successful and beneficial elsewhere in the world and to reject what has been proven ineffectual or detrimental. In such nation-states, strategic communications in their many applications can evolve quickly, that is, within a highly compressed timeframe. If they wish, these strategic communications professionals can begin with a "clean sheet of paper" that is not scripted from other nations and regions' long professional histories in strategic communications, which have not always been linear and progressive and which sometimes have been proven detrimental to society. Tsetsura and Kruckeberg (2009, Summer) urged these practitioners to build an appropriate body of professional knowledge that is consistent with—although not necessarily indistinguishable from—strategic communications theory and practice that exist in other nations and regions throughout the world. Tsetsura and Kruckeberg (2009, Summer) further recommended that a formalized system of professional education be created and maintained and that professional development must be sought through national and regional professional associations, conferences, seminars, and forums, as well as through continuing education programs.

Russians strategic communications has presented challenges

However in Russia, exploiting such opportunities for strategic communications scholarship, education, and professional practice has presented challenges. Nearly two decades ago, Mast and Keyton (2000, March) stressed that the concept of communication in Russia was new and was not clearly defined; indeed, disciplines in that nation such as sociology, linguistics, cultural studies, management, and psychology were attempting to establish communication's boundaries to distinguish it from their own disciplines. Mast and Keyton (2000, March) noted that Russian scholars used both kommunikatsiya and obsheniye to refer to the American conceptualization of communication. The former, which has become broadly adopted in Russia, was perhaps transferred from the American word communication. However, they observed that obsheniye, which in Russian means communication, was assigned to kommunikatsiya, referring to communications:

> Ease of communicating between two languages probably produced the Russian usage without thought to Russians who still actively use kommunikatsiya to refer to means of communicating and transportation. Those who introduced the terminology and their meanings were probably unaware that they were giving birth to another meaning of the word.
>
> (Mast & Keyton, 2000, March)

In Soviet times, communication was largely considered to be an act or a means of communication and transportation, and the word kommunikatsiya was used primarily in its plural form; however, *obsheniye*, which has the same connotation as the concept of communication in English, translates into English as "common". Mast and Keyton (2000, March) noted that, in the Soviet Union, the word *kommunikatsii* was most commonly associated with mediated communication and public information.

Certainly in some of its professional practices, Russian strategic communications has been influenced by American scholarship and practice. For example, Tsetsura and Kruckeberg (2004) said that the primary difference in the evolution of public relations theory in the United States and its origins in Russia may have been the absence of a communication tradition in the latter country; however, Tsetsura and Kruckeberg (2004) also posited an alternative explanation, that is, women's significant role in the earliest development of Russian public relations. Tsetsura and Kruckeberg (2004) further observed that American public relations and marketing terms have entered the Russian lexicon as these two strategic communications occupations have become part of the Russian social/economic infrastructure. However, Klyukanov and Leontovich (2015) said that it remained to be seen whether Russian communication studies can integrate diverse university curricula such as rhetoric, stylistics, mass communication, media ecology, and public relations. They recommended a dialogical-dialectical approach to conceptualize Russian communication as theoretical meta-discourse and socio-cultural practice.

Acknowledging American domination of communication, Mast and Keyton (2000, March) observed that, after the 1991 break-up of the Soviet Union, U.S. scholars had initiated an introduction to this discipline to their presumed counterparts in Russia. However, Russians' interpretation of communication was often restricted to public relations, journalism, and public opinion research. Mast and Keyton (2000, March) reported an early survey in which Russian professors had indicated that journalism was more commonly associated with communication than were that discipline's other specialized areas. The professors who had responded to that survey identified the most important U.S. communication courses to be (ranked most to least important): Family Communication, Business and Professional Speaking, Organizational Communication, Interpersonal Communication, and Rhetoric and Public

Address. However, those respondents had argued that the best way to introduce such offerings was through Russian professors who could customize these courses, rather than by importing a Western curriculum.

What are the readers of this book, and especially its non-Russian readers, to make of this—particularly as they ponder the future of Russian strategic communications, as they ponder Russian curricula in strategic communications education, and as they conjecture about the continuing evolution of strategic communications professional practice in that nation? How are strategic communications professional occupations in Russia similar to—or different from—the professional practices of those occupations elsewhere in the world, and why do these similarities and/or differences exist? What are the likely research agendas that will guide Russian scholars in their research questions, hypothesis-framing and -testing, and theory-building, and how will these likely influence Russian communication professional practices?

Succeeding chapters of this book will explore some of these questions for Russia, addressing specific areas of strategic communications scholarship, education, and professional practice in which Russians are engaging. However, readers of this book must appreciate that strategic communications may be conceptualized differently in Russia than it is elsewhere, that is, from a Russian worldview that is predicated on that nation's cultural, historical, and ideological heritage. Thus, non-Russian readers' a priori assumptions about Russian strategic communications may not be entirely accurate or even valid; furthermore, other countries and regions' perceived hegemony should not be assumed in Russian strategic communications, despite the examples of external influences to which Tsetsura and Kruckeberg have alluded (2004).

Of course, considerable temptation will exist for non-Russians to make these assumptions. For example, American strategic communications scholarship enjoys global prominence, and U.S. strategic communications education is often emulated elsewhere throughout the world; furthermore, the "best practices" of American strategic communications practitioners are frequently accepted internationally as benchmarks of excellence.

Of course for a variety of reasons, not the least of which is globalization, worldwide comparisons are helpful in examining Russian strategic communications; indeed, such comparisons are essential. However, readers are cautioned about a priori assumptions that may be indicative of their own implicit biases and centricities. Non-Russian readers are urged keep an open mind as they learn about strategic communications as a Russian concept, area of scholarly inquiry, and professional practices and as they examine that country's education models. An initial examination of Russian strategic communications should begin impartially, without a priori assumptions about the superiority of benchmarks, ideal types, and normative models of excellence from elsewhere throughout the world. Furthermore, it should not be assumed that Russian strategic communications scholarship, professional education, and practices are—or seek to become—social, political, economic, and cultural variants or adaptations of what exists elsewhere.

This hardly suggests that the Russian authors of this book are uninformed about—or are resistant to—communication scholarship, education, and professional best practices from elsewhere, nor that universally valid theories, models of education, and professional benchmarks are not achievable or even desirable. Indeed, such universality should be the aspiration of strategic communications scholar/educators and practitioners worldwide. However, this book first seeks to provide a description of Russian strategic communications, that is, its authors will describe strategic communications as a Russian concept and discipline, will analyze Russian theory that has evolved from that concept, and will describe that country's strategic communications education and professional practices. Predicated on those descriptions, examinations, and analyses, the authors will then identify and attempt to determine whether any differences can be reconciled that they have observed between Russian strategic communications and that which had originated and that has evolved elsewhere. Finally, from a global perspective in this book's concluding chapter, a meta-analysis and recommendations for the future of Russian strategic communications will be presented.

To be clear, Russian strategic communications scholar/educators, students, and practitioners assuredly will enthusiastically adopt and/or adapt scholarship, education, and professional best practices from elsewhere throughout the world, given sufficient evidence of their superiority for Russia. Furthermore, it is reasonable to assume that globally applicable theories, normative models of education, and benchmark professional practices may be recognized and agreed-upon through worldwide discussion, dialogue, and collaboration. Russian scholar/ educators and professionals provide evidence that they are eager to participate in this quest for universally valid and applicable scholarship, education, and professional best practices. It also is likely that these Russian scholar/educators and communication professionals can contribute significantly to this global discussion, dialogue, and collaboration.

This book's descriptions, examinations, and analyses of Russian strategic communications must be predicated on a knowledge of the paradigms on which Russian strategic communications exists today: As a concept, if not as a discipline; in its models of education; and in its professional practices. Also, these descriptions, examinations, and analyses must be understood within the context of twenty-first century globalism. Rantanen (2002) observed that Russia has had to reinvent itself politically, economically, and culturally as it has exposed itself to globalization after decades of isolation as part of the Soviet Union. Tsetsura (2009) further noted the lack of a Russian tradition of open and widely shared information. Certainly, the 1917 communist revolution has remained a significant influence on Russians' worldview and in the Russian conceptualization of communication, despite the dissolution of the Soviet Union in 1991. In the words of Marx (1985):

> There are ... eternal truths, such as Freedom, Justice, etc., that are common to all states of society. But Communism abolishes eternal truths, it abolishes

all religion, and all morality, instead of constituting them on a new basis; it therefore acts in contradiction to all past historical experience.

(Marx & Engels, p. 103)

Conclusion

Russia remains Russia—culturally, historically, and ideologically, which confluence has resulted in a Russian worldview that presently may be unique, that is, which has social, political, economic, and cultural dimensions of communication that may be different from those in the United States and elsewhere.

Part II of this book will examine communication as a field, discipline, and social institution in Russia and will outline the history of the development of communication as an institutionalized field and discipline. Part III will explore the development of strategic communications in Russia, examining its current and future challenges. Part IV will sample some current studies in Russian strategic communications, and Part V will conclude this volume with a chapter on the future of strategic communications in Russia.

References

DeVito, J. A. (1998). *Essentials of human communication*. New York: Longman.

Hazen, M. D. (2008, Fall). Thoughts on the development of the communication disciplines in the United States and Russia. *Russian Journal of Communication, 4*(4), 455–475.

Klyukanov, I., & Leontovich, O. (2015). Russian perspectives on communication. In D. Carbaugh (Ed.), *The handbook of communication in cross-cultural perspective* (pp. 29–41). London: Taylor and Francis.

Kruckeberg, D., & Starck, D. (1988). *Public relations and community: A reconstructed theory*. New York: Praeger.

Marx, K., & Engels, F. (1985). *The communist* manifesto. London: Penguin Books.

Mast, Y., & Keyton, J. (2000, March). Communicating about communication: Fostering the development of the communication discipline in Russia. Paper presented at the Annual Meeting of the Western States Communication Association, Long Beach, CA.

Mezrich, B. (2015). *Once upon a time in Russia: The rise of the oligarchs*. New York: Atria Books.

Rantanen, T. (2002). *The global and the national: Media and communications in post-communist Russia*. Lanham, MD: Rowman & Littlefield.

Tsetsura, K. (2009). The development of public relations in Russia: A geopolitical approach. In K. Sriramesh & D. Vercic (Eds.), *The global public relations handbook: Theory, research, and practice* (2nd edition) (pp. 600–618). New York: Routledge.

Tsetsura, K., & Kruckeberg, D. (2004). Theoretical development of public relations in Russia. In D. J. Tilson & E. C. Alozie (Eds.), *Toward the common good: Perspectives in international public relations* (pp. 176–192). Boston: Allyn & Bacon.

Tsetsura, K., & Kruckeberg, D. (2009, Summer). Corporate reputation: Beyond measurement. *Public Relations Journal, 3*(3), 1–8.

2 Russian strategic communications on the global stage

*Vilma Luoma-Aho, Katerina Tsetsura,
and Anastasia Kugappi*

Introduction

Strategic communication is a global phenomenon (Sriramesh & Verčič, 2019), and national borders and legislations are, at best, mere hindrances in the spreading of strategic messages. Yet, strategic communication has cultural differences depending on the region (Holtzhausen & Zerfass, 2015). The increasingly digital environment has further highlighted the impact of strategic communication (Vinogradova, 2013). The current literature on strategic communication relies on research conducted in the context of Western democracies, even though much of strategic communication occurs outside this Western context.

Strategic communication has been referred to as "an umbrella concept embracing various goal-directed communication activities" (Holtzhausen & Zerfass, 2015, p. 3). It is hard to say whether the difference between "strategic communication" or "strategic communications" with an "s" at the end of "communication" is semantic or whether the phenomena that are understood describe different concepts altogether. The Merriam-Webster Dictionary defines "communication" as "a process by which information is exchanged between individuals through a common system of symbols, signs, or behavior" and "communications" as "a system (as of telephones or computers) for transmitting or exchanging information" or "personnel engaged in communicating: personnel engaged in transmitting or exchanging information." Finally, the same dictionary states that "communications, plural in form but singular or plural in construction" can also mean "a technique for expressing ideas effectively" (*Merriam-Webster Dictionary*, 2020, online). The *Encyclopedia of Communication* defines strategic communication as "the study of how organizations or communicative entities communicate deliberately to reach set goals" (Holtzhausen, 2014). Some Russian scholars prefer to discuss strategic communications in the plural form, distinguishing it from the more established form (Paul, 2011). Recall, Chapter 1 explained that this book uses the plural form of the noun communication in its exploration of Russian strategic communication(s), noting that many scholars and practitioners use this plural form to describe professional applications, such as public relations and advertising.

One could argue that, although the practice is not new, strategic communication as a concept is rather newly applied in Russia and is predominantly used to refer to Western strategic communication. This chapter focuses on understanding the differences of strategic communications in Russia in politics and business. Relying on both English- and Russian-language publications as sources, as well as on academic and industry reports, we analyze the definitions of strategic communication(s) (using this intentionally ambiguous spelling) and their uses in Russia. We examine how strategic communication(s) in Russia can be understood in both its political and business contexts. As a result, this chapter offers a comparative table of differences between Western and Russian perspectives on strategic communication(s). This chapter summarizes findings of a study of Russian strategic communication(s), utilizing Russian academic literature and expert interviews of strategic communication(s) professionals in Russia. The chapter asks: What are the differences between the understanding of Western and Russian strategic communication?

Strategic communication: From West to East?

When is communication strategic? Several factors shape how communication can be understood as strategic. These include organizational operations, resourcing, competition, operating environment, risks, innovations, and contracts (Zerfass, Verčič, Nothhaft, & Werder 2018). These are partially visible in the earliest uses of the concept. Strategic communication as a concept stems from a political context: the military. One definition of strategic communication can be found in documents of the U.S. Department of Defense. One document explained that strategic communication:

> focused United States Government efforts to understand and engage key audiences to create, strengthen, or preserve conditions favorable for the advancement of United States Government interests, policies, and objectives through the use of coordinated programs, plans, themes, messages, and products synchronized with the actions of all instruments of national power.
> (U.S. Department of Defense, 2009, p. B-10)

Such strategic communication in U.S. Defense today is under the Global Engagement Center (Toosi, 2017) and centers around the move from one-way influence toward some form of interaction or engagement.

Originating from the West, there has been some hesitation to adopt the concept of "strategic communication," and some Russian scholars are quick to point out the Western origin of the concept (Burlakov, 2016; Vinogradova, 2014; Pashentsev, 2013; Zinovev, 2017).

Overall, Russian researchers consider strategic communication(s) as a set of actions to form and to transfer some ideas into minds of a target audience. Strategic communication(s) is part of a wide range of communication processes, including public diplomacy, public relations, and what is commonly called "information operations" (Burlakov, 2016). This range of processes may be positive or negative and include manipulation, disinformation, and propaganda (Bogdanov, 2017). In the West, most literature on Russian strategic communication(s) focuses on this negative side of propaganda and disinformation. Influence goes beyond politics in Russia, reaching into industries such as journalism and cinematography (Paul & Matthews, 2016).

Table 2.1 illustrates the variety of definitions for strategic communication(s) as understood by Russian scholars. Although the list of these definitions is not comprehensive, they demonstrate a variety of approaches to understanding

Table 2.1 Illustrative examples of definitions of strategic communications in Russia (original in Russian, translated into English)

Context of application	*Illustrative examples of definitions of strategic communications in Russia*
POLITICS, GEOPOLITICS	"In the most general sense, strategic communication is a projection by the state into the minds of national and foreign target audiences of the particular strategic values, interests, and goals by adequately synchronizing diverse activities in all areas of public life with professional communication support" (Pashentsev, 2013, p. 80).
POLITICS, GEOPOLITICS	"Strategic communication is a **strategically coordinated activity that is focused on the management of target audiences** inside and outside the country in order to improve a reputation of the country at the international level" (Vinogradova, 2013, p. 219).
POLITICS, GEOPOLITICS	"Strategic communication in the most general form is a **communication that ensures a development and implementation of a strategy of a social subject with help of special—communicational—recourses, means, tools"** (Gavra, 2015, p. 231).
POLITICS, GEOPOLITICS	"Strategic communication is indented to secure a state policy beyond national borders. **The main object of this impact is a particular target audience**. Such target audience is presented mostly by a political (in the broader context—economic, scientific, cultural, etc.) elite of another state toward which specific actions are taken. The result of the impact is the formation by the target audience of such a system of stable ideas about the actions of another state, which would fully justify these specific actions. As a result, it generates loyalty of a political elite of the state, toward which the actions are aimed, and, consequently, forms an actionable system of a geopolitical control over a chosen territory" (Burlakov, 2016, pp. 9–10).
POLITICS, GEOPOLITICS	"Strategic communications—**a type of information interaction** that implies a targeted sharing of an international position of the nation-state **with specific groups of people** and a counterpropaganda in response to opponents' activities" (Zinovev, 2017, p. 375).

Table 2.1 Cont.

Context of application	Illustrative examples of definitions of strategic communications in Russia
POLITICS, GEOPOLITICS	Strategic communication **is a strategically coordinated activity that is aimed at management of target audiences** inside and outside the country with a purpose to improve a reputation of one's country at the international level, and in case of a political conflict—with a purpose to win an information warfare (Vinogradova, 2014, p. 2).
BUSINESS AND INDUSTRY	Strategic communication **is the focused use of communication** to fulfill a mission of an organization (Gavra, 2015, p. 231).
BUSINESS AND INDUSTRY	"Strategic communications—is one of **management competencies** that determines a competitiveness of an organization and could be achieved with a **help of information technologies...** Strategic communications - an instrument of managerial interaction, as they influence the formation of the economic activity of an enterprise, its corporate culture, values and strategies" (Shchetinina, Dubino, & Dadalova, 2015, p. 182).
SOCIETY AND CULTURE	"Strategic communication—is a way to encourage other people to accept your ideas, policy and actions, that means: to convince friends and allies to be together with you; to convince people who are neutral to choose your side (or at least to continue to be neutral); and, as usual,... to convince enemies and opponents that you have enough power and will **to achieve you are set to accomplish**" (Gavra, 2015, p. 232).

strategic communication(s) in Russia from various subareas and fields, such as political science, business, culture, and society. Despite somewhat different foci, Russian definitions of strategic communication(s) emphasize these elements that are critical for understanding strategic communication(s) from a corporate perspective: the importance of identifying a target audience, strategic values, management, and strategic interaction.

Mostly, strategic communication(s) is understood to be a Western phenomenon. Russian researchers (for example, Vinogradova, 2014) suggested that several factors have contributed to how strategic communication(s) as a concept has developed recently in Russia. In addition to the traditional reasons (national strategies, country image, diplomacy, conflict), new and recent causes include terrorism attacks, cyberdiplomacy, and the more strategic use of communication to achieve political and economic goals (Vinogradova, 2014).

Strategic communications in politics

One could argue that the public sphere is highly controlled in Russia (Snegovaya, 2015), including the planning of social life and political actions

(Overland, 2018). Many sectors work together to establish the central national strategic goals, and, in that sense, much of communication can be defined as strategic. Hence, the division into politics and business is somewhat arbitrary, as many uses of strategic communications combine, including not just these two, but also the entertainment industry.

Combining several authors' views, most agree that, in the political context, strategic communications include a wide range of activities that are connected with the achievement of strategic goals and the synchronization of actions to solve state objectives (Filatova & Bolgov, 2018; Burlakov, 2016; Bogdanov, 2017; Pashentsev, 2013). The main aim remains the improvement of the State's image in the international arena (Bogdanov, 2017). Pashentsev (2013) argued that strategic communication(s) is often used in the context of an international provocation and is seen as a tool of geopolitics confrontation. In this context, the real goal may remain hidden, and the means may remain nontransparent.

Three elements have been suggested for strategic communication in the political context in Russia by Burlakov (2016):

1. A physical presence in a territory of strategic communication(s) application;
2. A creation of some form of communication infrastructure that distributes some power impulses and receives potential responses;
3. A distribution of power impulses that include formulated messages with clear meanings planned to reach a specific target group.

When it comes to political influence in the Russian government and military, a more commonly used concept is information confrontation (Filatova & Bolgov, 2018). Information confrontation is quite similar to strategic communication: "operations and actions of information impact other states in order to achieve goals profitable for themselves while providing protection of their information space against similar actions" (Filatova & Bolgov, 2018, p. 210). Other definitions appear quite alike, and the information confrontation is seen as confrontation that occurs between sides in the use of "special (political, economic, diplomatic, military, and other) methods" that aim to ultimately "influence the information environment of the opponent and defend one's own" desired state (Panarin & Panarina, 2003, p. 20).

In fact, some scholars suggest that strategic communication(s), information warfare, and information operations in the context of politics have identical natures and are used to describe the same actives (Burlakov, 2016; Kolesov, 2010). Information warfare is approached through technology and psychology. Technological information warfare is similar to cyberwar, because it refers to the destruction and sabotage of an opponent's information systems, electronics, and logistics while protecting its own (Khachaturian, 2018). Information warfare in the discipline of psychology can be defined as a way to influence the public and the individual consciousness and subconscious of an opposing party while protecting its own (Khachaturian, 2018). Khachaturian explained:

The concept of "information war" includes two aspects. One is information technology: the destruction and sabotage of information systems of the electronics and logistics of the enemy and the protection of their own communications. This phenomenon is better known as a "cyber war." The second aspect of the information war is the information-psychological one: the influence on the public and individual consciousness and subconscious of the opposing side while protecting one's own population.

(p. 313)

In Russia, political strategic communication is also used when politics are discussed (Zaripov, 2014). Defined in the context of political linguistics, "political communication is focused on propaganda of some ideas, an influence on citizens and countries, stimulating them to a particular political action and accepting particular socio-political decisions among all other points of view in society" (Chudinov, 2012, p. 2). Such definition highlights that, at least in some Russian definitions, propaganda is often associated with political communication.

In sum, Russian literature on strategic communications in politics recognizes it as an effective tool in politics and geopolitics, with its most common goals being the development of a country's image and the achievement of political aims and economic goals. As such, strategic communication(s) in the context of politics is the attempt to influence local and foreign target audiences through a wide range of tactics and channels. Understood this way, much of the political nature of strategic communication(s) relies on one-way communication, where the needs of the audience must be understood, but power still resting with the institutions practicing this strategic communication(s).

Strategic communications in business

Whereas political strategic communication(s) focus on the interplay of several organizations and institutions, strategic communication(s) in the Russian business context often focus on communication on behalf of individual brands or organizations. As such, the concept of strategic communications has mostly been introduced in Russia through the context of modern business communication in the West (Starih, 2012). For businesses, strategic communication(s) aim to achieve a long-term advantage in competition (Gavra, 2015). In the literature, strategic communication(s) is a management competency that determines the competitiveness of an organization that could be achieved with the help of information technologies (Shchetinina, Dubino, & Dadalova, 2015).

In the business context, strategic communication(s) are used to solve a specific business challenge or a strategic initiative, in which communication favorably changes a market situation (Shchetinina, Dubino, & Dadalova, 2015). Russian researcher Tihomirova (2015) emphasized the programmatic character of strategic communications for business: based on a strategy, a program (often large-scale and long-term) is set to achieve the goals of a company by using all communication resources and organizing a *communicative space*, external as well as internal. Moreover, strategic communication(s) involve the development, introduction, and actualization of a system of corporate standards that are targeted at corporate values and that include a regulation of business co-operations for an organization's employees at all hierarchical levels (Tihomirova, 2015).

Some scholars noted that the implementation of strategic communication(s) requires well-organized processes from the business in question, including shared information on the current state of the company and its interactions with stakeholders (Shchetinina, Dubino, & Dadalova, 2015;Tihomirova, 2015). This is especially challenging in cultural settings in which information is typically not transparent or freely shared (Tsetsura & Kruckeberg, 2017). In fact, information-sharing is central for setting the short-term and long-term development goals and for collecting information to achieve these (Shchetinina, Dubino, & Dadalova, 2015).

Russian researchers summarized strategic communication(s) in a business context to be mostly focused around strategic goals of individual businesses, to build on strategic processes that maintain the organization, rely on a combination of internal and external (Shchetinina, Dubino, & Dadalova, 2015). In fact, strategic communication(s) could be performed at different levels: internal and external (Gavra, 2015). Internal strategic communication(s) is targeted at a formation of a certain type of communicative culture that allows the transfer of cultural values from generation to generation of employees and through a hierarchical structure of an organization that allows the implement of more effectively competitive advantages. External strategic communication(s), on the other hand, is focused on creation of an organization's image and reputation as well as a development of an engagement strategy with consumers, partners, competitors, and other stakeholders in the long term (Shchetinina, Dubino, & Dadalova, 2015).

So now, after we have reviewed the differences between the uses of the term strategic communication(s) in the political and business context, we next turn our attention to differences in the understanding of strategic communication(s) uses in the West and in Russia.

Differences in strategic communication(s) between the West and Russia

Public relations and information operations are the most popular communication processes that are used in the organization of strategic communication(s) to support ethical discourse. Ethical discourse means transparent representation of a company's activities, beliefs, and values. To support this ethical discourse, a business needs interaction with stakeholders (Tsetsura & Kruckeberg, 2017). Strategic communication(s) may be used to shape societal and stakeholder attitudes to be more positive to the organization (Vavilova, 2017).

The underlying assumption of much transparency research is that too little transparency contributes to several societal ills, such as weak economic performance, corruption, and bribery (Tsetsura & Kruckeberg, 2017). In this chapter, however, we acknowledge that both extremes of transparency may become tools of strategic communication. Strategic communication can be categorized and understood in its unethical uses and contexts, ranging from strongly transparent strategic overemphasis of certain (for example, unrelated) issues, or fake news to hide others to strategic ambiguity and non-transparency, and withholding information. In that sense, the different uses of strategic communication(s) in the West and in Russia become vivid: the origins of definitions and the context in which they are used will often highlight the particularities.

Table 2.2 summarizes and analyzes the results of the literature review and five in-depth confidential interviews with strategic communication(s) experts in Russia, which were conducted as part of research on strategic communication(s) in Russia (Tsetsura & Luoma-aho, 2019, November) to illustrate differences between the understanding of Western and Russian strategic communication. This table sheds light on how and why misunderstanding in communication between Russia and the West might occur because it demonstrates how perceptions of communication may differ between strategic communicators of the West and of Russia, both in political and in business contexts.

First, *the logic* behind strategic communication(s) in Russia is often broader in range than in Western communication: messages from authorities hold a variety of meanings and follow logic beyond communicating the content of the message. One message can simultaneously serve the purpose of strengthening a political party that might be losing power, building trust among citizens who face an uncertain future, and stabilizing an economy that is under threat. Western communicators are seldom accustomed to analyzing and seeking the different layers of a message. Second, *the order* of delivered information is important. While Westerners might include the most important things first, this is not always the case in Russian communication. In fact, often the most important message comes after a comma and requires readers to conduct a search to extract the important message. Third, as Western communicators often target their messages to specific *audiences*, Russian communicators understand that the same messages can be utilized across audiences and, thus, will need to resonate with internal publics as well.

The next element, *auto-communication*, is related to the previous point. Auto-communication is used in Russia, and it is often strategically planned ahead of time. It becomes central in many messages because, in certain instances, the sources seek communicating with internal publics first and foremost. Hence, auto-communication can become central in external messaging.

Fifth, *the source* also matters in Russia: in fact, paying attention to who delivers a message is just as important, if not the most important feature, in strategic communication as is what's being said. For example, when President Putin speaks, his words should be analyzed and considered carefully by all audiences, internal and external. However, when other officials deliver the message

Table 2.2 The differences between Western and Russian takes on strategic communication

	Typical for Western communication	*Typical for Russian communication*
Logic	Communication by authorities mostly serves citizens' needs.	Communication by authorities is case-specific and may serve a variety of needs (e.g., the needs of a party, citizens, political/economic stability, etc.).
Order	The most important message is said in the beginning and is easy to find.	The most important message might be found in the middle of the text, after a comma (,), and the reader might need to search for it.
Audience	Messages are targeted and mostly serve internal and external audiences separately.	Most external messages need to resonate with internal publics.
Auto-communication	Auto-communication is optional for external messages.	Auto-communication can be central to external messages.
Source	The message is more important than which authority (source) says it.	The authority (source) is just as important as the message itself.
Context	Context plays only a supportive role to the message.	Context and presentation may often define the message.
Probing	Messages are often thought-through before they are presented.	Messages can be tested or probed publicly by various speakers and contexts before they become finalized.
Threats	Low context exists, in which the message is direct and clear and requires minimal analysis.	High-context messages require deep analysis to discover several meanings within different layers, or *the Matryoshka effect* (Tsetsura, 2020).
Transparency	Transparency has intrinsic value.	Transparency is a tool, and non-transparency holds power.
Strategic clarity vs. ambiguity	Strategic messages are communicated clearly.	Strategic ambiguity is central for communication.

(particularly, if the message is controversial or disruptive), the message may not need to be evaluated as being of highest concern.

Traditionally in the West, particularly in the Nordic countries, the media have a high level of credibility. In Russia, trust lies not within the media, but within specific sources of information (for example, individual journalists or public figures). One example is Ivan Golunov, an investigative journalist of a Baltic-based Russian-language media outlet, *Meduza*, who investigated corruption in Russia and who was recently detained by Russian authorities. His arrest created a backlash by several public figures and generated mass protests in the streets of Moscow. The injustice prompted media organizations to condemn the arrest, with three of Russia's most respected newspapers publishing near-identical front pages Monday reading "I/we am/are Ivan Golunov" (BBC, 2019, June 10, online). As a result, Golunov was released from jail, and charges against him were dropped. Other examples of trusted sources of information, according to several communication experts, can be opposition leaders, such as Alexei Navalny. After the mass protests and a rare unification of many public figures in opposition and many leading media outlets in Russia in support of Golunov, President Putin signed the order to dismiss from duties two internal affairs officials, who were the heads of agencies that were responsible for fabricating the case against Golunov (BBC, 2019, June 10, online).

Moreover, *context* is part of the message: where something is said is just as important as what is said. *Probing* is under-utilized in the West, but, in Russia, it serves a central function: for example, when less important officials deliver a message about extreme tax increases (particularly, if the message is controversial or disruptive), that might serve a purpose of testing to how the message might be perceived by the audiences, both internal or external, and what is the range within which the message can be tolerated. This is done strategically ahead of time to enable the real speaker to understand publics and their receptiveness when the real message comes later, when information about the forthcoming tax increases is released.

Furthermore, Russian communication often requires a comprehensive analysis of *threats*, because threats might be built into the message. Threats are often difficult to see in the first round of analysis, because the words are seldom threatening; however, a deeper analysis might reveal what is behind the official statement, such as "We are very disappointed in our Western friends." What kind of consequences will this disappointment lead to? What has already been done?

Transparency is a tool within Russian strategic communications: withholding information or an acknowledgment that the other person holds such information may become an asset, and non-transparency can be skillfully used in back-and-forth arguments on the global arena. Finally, *appearing non-strategic is a strategic choice in itself*: the less that communication looks strategic and planned, the easier it might be to get the desired change to take place via communication.

Conclusion

Of Western origin, strategic communication in Russia has become a modern concept utilized mostly in the context of politics and geopolitics. Russian scholars understand strategic communication to be a collection of different operations, and hence it is often referred to in the plural: strategic communications. Several related concepts are used when influence and communication are discussed, and strategic communication(s) is not necessarily the most common concept among Russian scholars. Despite its origin, several differences exist in terms of how strategic communication(s) is understood in Russia and in the West.

Overall, one of the greatest differences is the understanding of what is considered strategic. In the West, strategic often refers to communication that has a clear aim at what it hopes to achieve. In Russia, strategic aims are not always clearly stated. Strategic ambiguity can, in fact, be seen as a form of strategic communication, in which the desired outcome might be is to confuse audiences. Another major difference is the probing used in official communication: whereas Western communication often relies on polling and surveying citizens, Russian communicators may test ideas on real audiences by widely distributing messages via major news channels and discussing ideas in prime-time TV programs before establishing a final official statement or policy. Moreover, another major difference is the lack of transparency in the whole communication process: it may be of strategic value to withhold information or the source of the message.

Undoubtedly, additional research is needed to better understand the nature of contemporary Russian strategic communication(s). Researchers can investigate how transparency (or non-transparency) can be used in Russian strategic communication(s) practices to achieve certain outcomes. Future studies should also investigate how strategic and non-strategic communication can be better defined and understood. One potential question is whether Russian strategic communication(s) is strategic or opportunistic: Can some Russian communication be simply a result of taking advantage of a particular situation, without reflecting on the overall strategic nature of communication? Or rather, are these opportunities a result of carefully calculated strategy? Finally, as this chapter has explored merely one cultural context, future studies are needed for a more global understanding of strategic communication differences across cultures within Russia. Because Russia is a multicultural society, a future look into specific contexts under which individual cases and messages are crafted might be of value. Finally, understanding strategic intent and impact within a multicultural context of Russia is also needed.

Acknowledgment

This chapter is based on research funded by the implementation of the Finnish Government Plan for Analysis, Assessment and Research (VN TEAS), 2019.

References

BBC. (2019, June 10). Ivan Golunov: Russian newspapers in rare support for charged reporter. *BBC News Online*. Retrieved from www.bbc.com/news/world-europe-48580217.

Bogdanov, S. (2017). Strategicheskie kommunikatsii: Kontseptualnye podxody i modeli dlya gosudarstvennogo upravlenija [Strategic communications: Conceptual approaches and models for public administration, public administration]. *Elektronnyj*

Vestnik [Electronic Vestnik], *61*, 132–152. Retrieved from https://cyberleninka.ru/article/v/strategicheskie-kommunikatsii-kontseptualnye-podhody-i-modeli-dlya-gosudarstvennogo-upravleniya.

Burlakov, V. (2016). Strategicheskaja kommunikatsija kak metod sovremennoj geopolitiki. [Strategic communication as a method of modern geopolitics]. Ojkumena: *Regionovedcheskie issledovanija [Ecumene. Regional Studies]*, *2*, 7–15. Retrieved from https://cyberleninka.ru/article/v/strategicheskaya-kommunikatsiy a-kak-metod-sovremennoy-geopolitiki.

Chudinov, A (2013). *Ocherki po sovremennoy politicheskoy metaforologii [Essays on the modern political Metaphorology]*. Monograph. Ekaterinburg, Russia: Ural State Pedagogical University. Retrieved from http://elar.uspu.ru/bitstream/uspu/5959/1/mon00080.pdf.

Filatova, O., & Bolgov, R. (2018, March). *Strategic communication in the context of modern information confrontation: EU and NATO vs. Russia and ISIS.* Paper presented at the 13th International Conference on Cyber Warfare and Security. Retrieved from https://books.google.fi/books?id=eHpTDwAAQBAJ&pg=PA211&dq=strateg ic+communication+europe&hl=ru&sa=X&ved=0ahUKEwifkMSgwfXhAhUI s4sKHZ_3DC0Q6AEINjAC#v=onepage&q=strategic%20communication%20 europe&f=false.

Gavra, D. (2015). Kategorija strategicheskoj kommunikatsii: Sovremennoe ponimanie i bazovye kharakteristiki [A category of strategic communication: Modern definition and basic principles]. In D. Gavra (Ed.), *Sovremennye tekhnologii biznes kommunikatsij i strategicheskogo PR [Modern technologies of business communications and strategic PR]* (pp. 229–233). Retrieved from https://elibrary.ru/download/elibrary_25449046_ 60796334.pdf.

Holtzhausen, D. R. (2014). Strategic communication. In W. Donsbach (Ed.), *The encyclopedia of communication.* Online. doi: 10.1002/9781405186407.wbiecs106.pub2.

Holtzhausen, D. R., & Zerfass, A. (2015). *The Routledge handbook of strategic communication.* New York, NY: Routledge.

Khachaturian, R. (2018). Strategicheskie kommunikatsii v sovremennom mire: Mediamanipulirovanie (informatsionnye vojny) na primere dopingovyx skandalov 2016. [Strategic communications in the modern world: Media manipulation (information wars) based on the example of doping scandals in 2016]. *Proceedings of the research conference Strategic Communication in the Modern World*, Saratov, RU (pp. 313–316). Retrieved from www.sgu.ru/sites/default/files/textdocsfiles/2018/09/ 04/strategicheskie_kommunikacii_2018.pdf.

Kolesov, P. (2010). Vedenie Soedinennymi Shtatami informatsionnyx vojn. Kontseptsija "strategicheskie kommunikatsii" [Conducting information wars by the United States. The concept of "strategic communications"]. *Zarubezhnoe Voennoe Obozrenie [Foreign Military Review]*, *6*, 9–14. Retrieved from http://pentagonus.ru/publ/vedenie_ soedinjonnymi_shtatami_informacionnykh_vojn_koncepcija_strategicheskikh_ kommunikacij/108-1-0-1581.

Merriam-Webster Dictionary online. (2020). www.merriam-webster.com.

Overland, I. (2018). *Public brainpower: Civil society and natural resource management.* London: Palgrave Macmillan.

Panarin, I., & Panarina, L. (2003). *Vojna i mir [War and peace].* Moscow: OLMA-PRESS.

Pashentsev, E. (2013). Strategicheskaja kommunikatsija Kitaja v Latinskoj Amerike i ee interpretatsija v SSHA, gosudarstvennoe upravlenie [Strategic communication of China in Latin America and its interpretation in USA, public administration].

Electronic Vestnik, 36, 80–98. Retrieved from http://e-journal.spa.msu.ru/uploads/vestnik/2013/vipusk__36._fevral_2013_g./kommunikazionnii_menedjment_i_strategitcheskaja_kommunikazija_v_gosudarstvennom_upravlenii/36_2013pashentsev.pdf.

Paul, C. (2011). *Strategic communication. Origins, concepts, and current debates.* Santa Barbara, CA: Praeger.

Paul, C., & Matthews, M. (2016). *Perspectives: The Russian "Firehose of Falsehood" propaganda model. Why it might work and options to counter it.* Rand Corporation report. Retrieved from www.rand.org/pubs/perspectives/PE198.html.

Shchetinina E., Dubino N., & Dadalova, N. (2015). Economicheskie osnovy formirovanija strategicheskix kommunikatsij promyshlennogo predprijatija [Economic bases of the formation of strategic communication on industrial enterprises]. *Vestnik of BSTU named after V.G. Shukhov, 2,* 181–184. Retrieved from http://webcache.googleusercontent.com/search?q=cache:http://dspace.bstu.ru/bitstream/123456789/479/1/40.%2520%25D0%25A9%25D0%25B5%25D1%2582%25D0%25B8%25D0%25BD%25D0%25B8%25D0%25BD%25D0%25B0.pdf.

Snegovaya, M. (2015). *Stifling the public sphere: Media and civil society in Russia.* National Endowment for Democracy, International Forum for Democratic Studies: Report. Retrieved from www.ned.org/wp-content/uploads/2015/10/Stifling-the-Public-Sphere-Media-Civil-Society-Russia-Forum-NED.pdf.

Sriramesh, K., & Verčič, D. (Eds.) (2019). *The global public relations handbook. Theory, research, and practice* (3rd ed.). New York: Routledge.

Starih, N. (2012). Strategicheskie kommunikatsii: bazovye printsipy proektirovanija [Strategic communications: Basic principles of planning]. *Vestnik of Moscow State University. Journalism, 10,* 2658–3526. Retrieved from https://vestnik.journ.msu.ru/books/2013/2/strategicheskie-kommunikatsii-bazovye-printsipy-proektirovaniya/.

Tihomirova, E. (2015). Kommunikatsija i strategicheskie kommunikatsii [Communication and strategic communications]. *Proceedings of Sankt-Petersburg School of PR: From theory to practice* (p. 49). St. Petersburg: SPGU.

Toosi, N. (2017, February 8). Tillerson spurns $80 million to counter ISIS, Russian propaganda. *Politico.* Retrieved from www.politico.com/story/2017/08/02/tillerson-isis-russia-propaganda-241218.

Tsetsura, K. (2020, May). *The Matryoshka Effect: Understanding high-context and multi-layered strategic communication in Russia.* Paper accepted for presentation at the 2020 ICA pre-conference "Open Communication: A Trans-disciplinary Approach to Strategic Communication in the 21st Century," Melbourne, Australia.

Tsetsura, K., & Kruckeberg, D. (2017). *Transparency, public relations, and the mass media: Combating the hidden influences in news coverage worldwide.* New York: Taylor and Francis/Routledge.

Tsetsura, K., & Luoma-aho, V. (2019, November). *The Matryoshka phenomenon: Strategic communication of Russia.* Paper presented at the public invitation-only conference "Information in the era of hybrid threats" hosted by the European Center of Excellence for Countering Hybrid Threats (HybridCoE). Helsinki, Finland.

U.S. Department of Defense. (2009): *Strategic communication joint integrating concept, Version 1.0.* Washington, DC: The Joint Staff report. Retrieved from www.jcs.mil/Portals/36/Documents/Doctrine/concepts/jic_strategiccommunications.pdf?ver=2017-12-28-162005-353.

Vavilova Z. (2017). Strategichskie kommunikatsii v sovremennom mire. Eticheskij diskurs v upravlenii voprosami: Strategicheskie kommunikatsii v sfere ekologicheskix riskov [Strategic communications in the modern world: Ethical discourse in issue management: Strategic communications in the field of environmental risks]. *Proceedings of the scientific and practical conference, Saratov, Russia* (pp. 403–409). Saratov: Saratov University. Retrieved from www.sgu.ru/sites/default/ files/textdocsfiles/2018/09/04/strategicheskie_kommunikacii_2018.pdf.

Vinogradova, E. (2013, December). K voprosu o rabote s "novymi media" v strategicheskoj kommunikatsii. Gosudarstvennoe upravlenie [To the issue of the work with "new media" in strategic communication. Public Administration]. *Electronic Vestnik, 41,* 218–228.) Retrieved from http://e-journal.spa.msu.ru/uploads/ vestnik/2013/vipusk__41._dekabr_2013_g._/kommunikazionnii_menedjment_i_ strategitcheskaja_kommunikazija_v_gosudarstvennom_upravlenii/vinogradova.pdf.

Vinogradova, E. (2014). Rol strategicheskoj kommunikatsii v mezhdunarodnyx otnosheniakh [Role of strategic communications in international relations]. *International Life, 6,* 111–129. Retrieved from https://interaffairs.ru/jauthor/ material/1085.

Zaripov, R. (2014). Osobennosti metaforicheskogo manipulyativnogo vozdejstvija v politicheskom diskurse [Peculiarities of metaphoric manipulative impact in political discourse]. *Vestnik RUDN, Linguistics, 2,* 145–156. Retrieved from http://journals. rudn.ru/linguistics/article/view/9456/8907.

Zerfass, A., Verčič, D., Nothhaft, H., & Werder, K. P. (2018). Strategic communication: Defining the field and its contribution to research and practice. *International Journal of Strategic Communication, 12,* 487–505.

Zinovev, S. (2017). Strategicheskie kommunikatsii v praktike publichnoj diplomatii Evropejskogo Sojuza [Instruments of strategic communication in a practice of European Union's public diplomacy]. *Young Scientist, 21,* 375–377. Retrieved from https://moluch.ru/archive/155/43685/.

Part II

Examining the historical and contemporary development of communication(s) in Russia

3 The forms and shapes of today's communication as a field, as a discipline, and as a social institution in Russia

Communication development as a result of society's modernization

Oleg Kashirskikh and Sergey Zverev

Introduction

Development of communication as an occupation and as an academic discipline depends on the shape of communication as a social institution. Communication in professional and academic fields becomes more valuable as the level of its integration in society increases–on both systemic and individual levels. As the intensity of communication and the diversification of its channels among individuals, organizations, and societal pillars become stronger, the more diverse is the society and the more autonomous are its political, business, and societal bodies. In their work, Blumler and Kavanagh (1999) defined the decisive influence of the evolution of the social environment on the development of communication as an institution. They believed that these features of exogenous change—modernization, individualization, economization, mediatization, and rationalization—strongly influence the form and content of communicational processes in a society. Various processes, such as social differentiation and specialization, the fragmenting of interests and identities, and proliferating diverse lifestyles in a society, make communication processes more difficult and support "markets for minority media, and may explain the appeal of talkshow explorations of divergent personal and sexual behaviors, conflicts, and aberrations" (Blumler & Kavanagh, 1999, p. 210). Increasing individualization and secularization of society, expressed by an elevation of personal aspirations and reduced conformity to the traditions, is accompanied by the process of consumerization and the expression of self-interest in citizens' preferences. The economization of a society shows through "the subordination of formerly more autonomous" (Blumler & Kavanagh, 1999, p. 210). General rationalization of society happens through the increasing importance of an argumentative method of communication, which is expressed by the systematic gathering of conferences, a quality press, signed columns, analytical journalism, and weekly magazines of news and comment. All that supports the emergence of "the instrumental rationalization of persuasion" relies on the techniques, values, and personnel of (a) advertising, (b) market research, and (c) public relations (Mayhew, 1997, p. 18).

Based on the premise that the professionalization of communication depends on the quality of public institutions, this chapter reconstructs the most significant obstacles that the gradual building of institutions providing interpersonal and organizational communication has yet to overcome. Also, we illustrate how the professionalization of communication has been accompanied by the accumulation of theoretical and practical expertise that are needed to define communication strategically.

The political and economic reforms in Russia as a new structure of the communication industry

During the time of the Soviet political system, there were not sufficient political and economic conditions for civic and commercial communication to develop. To better control citizen's activity, the Soviet authoritative political regime prevented the free exchange of opinions and goods to better control citizens' activity. The modernization of the social structure in Russia began with political and market reforms in the 1990s and is continuing to this day. The rationalization of the minds of the Russian people became possible because of the drop of the ideological limits of the Soviet Era, the commercialization of the media system, and the increased complexity of Russian society backed by a diversity of lifestyles. Today, a wealth of media exists in Russia, including national newspapers, local newspapers, state radio, and commercial radio, as well as satellite and cable television that has become widely available in recent years. Internet growth in Russia had greatly expanded from 2000 to 2010, as the country experienced the largest online growth of any major European country. According to measurement by the World Telecommunications/ICT Indicators Database, 43% of the Russian population were online by March 31, 2011, with an estimated 59.7 million users from among a population of 138.7 million. Russians became the second-largest online population in Europe by mid-2014 (after Germany) and were on course to become the largest online population in the region (International Telecommunications Union, 2011, January 31, p. 6).

The pluralization of the political system and competition among political parties have allowed the emergence of political talk shows, a large number of media-experts, organizational know-how, policy expertise, and speech-writing experts: "communication through the media is an integral part of the interrelated processes of campaigning, cultivation of public opinion, policy-making, and government itself" (Blumler & Kavanagh, 1999, p. 214). Corporate-sector development has initiated the progressive development of the public relations industry in Russia. That industry rose in the beginning of the 1990s, stimulated by international companies that brought their business practices when opening offices in Russia. The new dynamics of market development began gaining momentum toward the end of 2010, when a demand for services from government and from businesses with government input was formed as well as when the boom of social media and the development of new techno-logical platforms spread. An emergence of concerns about corporate reputation and active participation in Russian media (Tsetsura & Chernov, 2009) in its problematization illustrates the increasing role of external communications of businesses, which was directed at understanding. Increasingly more frequently, the media are becoming a place for the discussion of corporate reputation, illustrating the rising importance of the public as a stakeholder. More and more businesses in Russia have realized the growing importance of corporate reputa-tion. This is reflected in the increasing number of corporate publications in the Russian media over the last years (Tsetsura & Chernov, 2009). Public Relations as an academic subject is becoming more popular in Russia each day. Currently, 127 Russian universities are preparing professionals in "Advertisement and Public Relations". Public relations had become accepted as an academic dis-cipline by the Ministry of Education and Science of the Russian Federation at the bachelor's level in 2007 and, in 2010, at the master's level. Russian public relations education standards are oriented toward the European educational standards. According to the new Russian standard, public relations specialists are able to carry out professional activity in public and government structures, in business, and in politics.

Communication as a social institution in Russia: The institutionalization of a public sphere

Communication in a society has an interactive function that allows for soci-etal development based on coordination of common goals and means of their achievement. An institutionalization of communication implies the emergence of long-term channels of cooperation among members of a society as a condi-tion for the development and modernization of that society. To understand the level of institutionalization of communication in Russia, we must define the concept of an *institution*. We do not use the term "institution" as a system that is organized formally, such as a national legislature or courts. Rather, we use it in a more general sense as a certain kind of social organization (for example, media, markets, family) identities or roles. To explain communication as a social institution, we need institutional theory that focuses on interaction-patterns in that society as well as on interrelationships among the state, society, and the market. Hodgson (2004, p. 424) describes institutions as: "durable systems of established and embedded social rules that structure social interactions". Institutions, when perceived as legitimate, must be recognized by most people and acted upon with corresponding behavior, allowing individuals to negotiate "their daily affairs" (Lawson, 1997, p. 187). Institutionalization implies, not only representation, but also cooperation. This means that communication as a social institution highly depends on the development of the public sphere. With the general processes of rationalization and societal differentiation, the state and the market become relatively autonomous societal systems that are characterized by instrumental rationality armed by means of power and money for achieving "concrete goals". However, the public sphere is characterized by communicative rationality, which goal is to strive for a common definition of reality by means of communication. Communication in the public sphere is stressed to achieve understanding, instead of being used instrumentally. The model of the public sphere opposes private and public by interpreting the latter as making public in the sense of making it accessible to debate, reflection, action, and moral-political transformation. Therefore, the public sphere can be seen as "the medium of talk" and "a lifeworld" in which public opinion and cooperation mechanisms can be formed. Critical public debates validate politics, the state, and the market. This ensures the legitimacy of the government and the market, as well as the society's ability to self-perfection and development. The public sphere is viewed as the creation of procedures whereby those affected by general social norms and collective political decisions can have a say in their formulation, stipulation, and adoption: "There may be as many publics as there are controversial general debates about the validity of norms" (Benhabib, 1992, p. 87). The practices that enhance interpersonal communication need the institutional room that can "bridge the gap between self-interest and orientation of the common good, between the roles of client and citizens" (Habermas, 1992, p. 448). The term "institutionalized public sphere" here means the communicative room between a political system and the civil society for setting up a societal and political agenda. The communication proceeds by the active mediation of representative institutions (parliament, political parties) and mass media that affect the public opinion as "interplay between civil society" and "institutionalized decision-making in parliamentary complex" (Habermas, 1992, p. 448); thus, "it puts the state in touch with the needs of society" (Habermas, 1989, p. 31). A civil society that cooperates with political institutions actively through the public sphere is supposed to have the capacity to "self-organize", which means to "develop communicative interactions that support identities" and to "expand participatory possibilities" (Young, 2000, p. 163). In that case, a range of communicative spaces will exist, from small face-to-face discussions to action by social movements and the media (Habermas, 1996). Civil society that is involved in the public sphere is understood as a "venue where ideas and discourses are formed, shaped and contested. Rather than engage in formal negotiation, civil society's role is to mobilize discourses outside the state in unconstrained and perhaps even in strategic ways" (Hendriks, 2006, p. 495).

Under modern conditions, public matters can no longer be the exclusive responsibility of the state. Civil society should become more involved in the governmental process and the realization of market activity. While ways in which civil society can influence the state should be extended, distance should be nevertheless kept among the state, civil society, and the market. This is to prevent corporatist danger: The blurring of responsibilities; the entwining of interests; and the centralization of power. Kooiman (2003) describes modern tendencies of the future model of relationships between the three pillars as: "Interdependence and inter-relationship between the three societal institutions lead toward 'new' structural arrangements: between state and market towards 'public management'; between state and society towards 'political society'; and between state, market and civil society towards 'sustainable society' as examples" (Kooiman, 2003, p. 218). This means that keeping the government, business, and media (as an intermediary) autonomous, while increasing the participatory activity of civil society, promotes: (1) the emergence and development of the public sphere as a space free from manipulation and of instrumental communication to provide understanding and trust; and (2) the increasing importance of communication within the given pillars—primarily political parties, corporate public relations, and nonprofit organizations. The more that communication as a social institution is developed, the more developed is the process of institutionalization of the public sphere. The more that the market, media, and civil society are independent from the state, the more that horizontal connections within the society are able to overcome private, particularistic patterns in communication.

Emergence of the public in Russia

The state of the public is important in understanding the quality of the public sphere as a communication mediator between different individual and societal pillars. Based on Grunig's situational theory, the public can be described in terms of groups' information-processing and information-seeking. Both variables influence groups' communication behavior (Grunig, 1997). The public has higher qualities for fulfilling the integrative function in society when it is capable of intelligent judgment, deliberation, and action. Dewey described qualities the public must have: "to cultivate the habit of suspended judgment, of skepticism, of desire for evidence, of appeal to observation rather than sentiment, discussion rather than bias, inquiry rather than conventional idealizations" (Dewey, 1983, pp. 334–335). Walter Lippmann argued in 1925 that the public exists merely as myth and an idealization as a phantom public (Lippmann, 1993). Sovereign, competent, and capable citizens can be in the mass. In Lippmann's view, public opinion is controlled and manipulated by the elite. Most citizens are unable to cultivate the knowledge and competence that are needed to effectively participate in political and social affairs. Dewey, however, argued that, despite the need to acquire and utilize knowledge, it is not the matter of *omnicompetence* of the public, but rather of proper conditions under which citizens are able to socialize. In Dewey's view, a society is not a sum of "isolated individuals", but have "always been associated together in living" (Dewey, 1927, p. 97). So, to become well informed and communicatively competent, one must use "the ability to judge of the bearing of the knowledge supplied by others upon common concerns" (Dewey 1927, p. 208). To identify the public, Dewey distinguished "static unity of homogenous people" from "heterogeneity and diversity of human experience", therefore highlighting that the importance of communication is decided precisely because "there is a variety and rich set of perspectives". Consequently, the more horizontal connections there are in society, the functionally better constituted is the public. The public forms

Table 3.1 What judgment would you rather agree with?

Variants of answers	1991	1995	1998	2005	2006	2007	2008
People may be trusted	36	24	22	22	26	26	26
To be careful with others	41	76	74	77	72	68	70
Don't know	23	0	4	1	2	6	4

Source: Gudkov, Dubin, & Zorkaja (2008).

through communication of signs and symbols, which requires intensive social interactions and shared experience. Constitution of the public often includes three conditions: the public exists as public expression is available to all; the public's opinions are measured in an opinion poll; and the view of a public can be regarded as an emergent body of those who take a position on an issue through their active participation in deliberative processes. The autonomy of the public is measured by the possibility of intersubjective and mediated communication across lines of difference, which is claimed to be an essential part of a pluralist society. Communication across lines of difference to persuade people to change their minds, that is, any exposure to differing views that does not produce instantaneous compliance, is a valuable component of public opinion formation and a valuable component of constituting the public.

What can be said about the quality/state of the public in Russia, using the stated normative markers? First, it is necessary to point out the high level of interpersonal distrust in Russia, especially because interpersonal communication and shared social practices are only possible in the presence of trust. The main source of horizontal trust is the quality of the institutional and constitutional order. Trust is earned by testing the validity of distrust through participation in elections, freedom of expression, and freedom of the press ("institutionalized distrust") (Offe, 1999). Trustworthy is someone who has made him- or herself known, thus making him or her socially visible ("sozial sichtbar") (Luhmann, 2000, p. 48). Especially through the mediation of representative institutions, collective actors, and the mass media, the truster has the opportunity to validate beliefs, and trust-seeking citizens can build trust by demonstrating their rule-conforming behaviors to others. There will be no possibility to either "monitor" certain politicians and policies or the validity of institutional norms if the public sphere is not constituted by effective political competition, a free press, and a developed net of nongovernmental organizations. The data of Table 3.1 illustrate the constant low degree of trust in others and, at the same time, the constant high degree of trust in the closest people over the last 15 years in Russia. Seventy-three percent of those polled agreed with the judgment that it is impossible to trust anybody today, unless those are the closest people, whereas only 22% disagreed (Gudkov, Dubin, & Zorkaja, 2008, p. 74).

Because of the deficiency of institutionally mediated and generalized interpersonal trust, there is a tendency for communication to be of a "local" and "small scale and short term" nature (Sztompka, 1996, p. 49). As a consequence, citizens "escape into the closed, private world of family, friendship circles and work groups" (Offe, 1999, p. 48), because trust based on belonging compensates functionally for the lack of vertical trust in institutions. Because of the distrust of others and the impossibility to generalize trust, interpersonal communications are mostly limited to like-minded people. Considering these given (imperfect) circumstances, the choice for primordial groups by social reproduction seems to be quite rational: simply, such groups are a more stable sort of ties, seen against the background of the permanent change of institutions and values. Due to institutionally determined distrust, the communicative activity of the Russian people becomes domesticated or localized. The everyday communication of most Russians proceeds among only people of their closest circles: relatives, friends, and neighbors. More than 57% of those polled had very rarely or had never communicated with colleagues and other friends (Gudkov, Dubin, & Zorkaja, 2008, p. 69). In daily dialogues, the majority of Russian citizens communicate only among those in their closest social environment—relatives, friends, especially childhood friends, and neighborhood friends. Over half of those questioned (correspondingly, 57% and 52%) seldom or never communicate with colleagues and other friends in their daily routine. The spatial mobility of Russian citizens is very limited. For example, 61% of the population "practically never" goes to the cinema, and 64% never visit theatres or go to concerts. Communicative activity is limited to visiting and inviting friends (Gudkov, Dubin, & Zorkaja, 2008, p. 70). Dialogue by interests, within the limits of any associations, initiatives, circles, associations, and so forth, is absolutely not significant for the overwhelming majority of adult Russians (Gudkov, Dubin, & Zorkaja, 2008, pp. 67–69). It was ascertained that only from 1 to 3% of adult Russians take part in activities of female, youth, religious, or any other voluntary associations and groups on their own recognition (Gudkov, Dubin, & Zorkaja, 2008, p. 77). However, the narrow and permanent communicative area of Russia's society is mostly like-minded within small "strong ties" groups. The like-mindedness of such groups is reached by the natural aspiration to correspond to prevailing norms to seek the good opinion and approval of others by conforming to the view that prevails in a given group (Noelle-Neumann, 2001). The more homogeneous the group, the less is the probability of communication across lines of difference. However, exposure to conflicting views is sine qua non for the development of communicational competence of citizens, which makes them more informed, tolerant, and reflective. To the extent that people live among homogeneous others in self-selected enclaves, their exposure to dissimilar views may be limited. Mutz believes that, in the context of objective pursuit of the well-known conformism by citizens, exposure to dissimilar views via the media may be more effective: "compared to personal interactions, people have less ability and desire to exercise selective exposure to news media content. With respect to the availability of dissimilar views, the media clearly have an advantage over face-to-face communication" (Mutz & Martin, 2001, p. 99). However, considering the domination of a one-sided point of view in the majority of the Russian media, formation of the public is significantly more complicated. Research indicates that the ability of Russians to identify tradeoffs is highly limited "where the provenance and reliability of information is obscure and advocacy without tradeoff cues is the norm in Russian media discourse" (Mickiewicz, 2005, p. 356). Hauser points out that narrowing the vocabulary of the public in the case of the monopolization of the public sphere through the power of media leads to prepotency of the terms that serve the interests of the elite and make it difficult for ordinary citizens to "discern their own interests apart from those of the vested" (Hauser, 2007, p. 335).

The level of formation of communication as a social institution can be measured by citizens' ability in critical and contextual thinking. These communicative abilities are seen as the quality of feedback between the society on one side and the state and market on the other. Development and modernization of the country generally depends on the quality of the requirements and expectations laid out by its society. The higher the communicative competence (political and citizen competence) of citizens and their level of critical thinking, the more likely is the increase in the quality of decision-making on political and business levels in the interests of social development. The existing institutionally determined difficulties to transcend "the private" into "the public" do not allow Russian society to become a heterogeneous communicative space. The emergence of such communicative spaces may be expected in places where a more complex societal structure is able to engender new social roles and the need exists to communicate them in the course of identity formation. Simultaneously, the conservation of a flat social environment, structured on the principle of *implicit* belonging and determined through inner-cultural homogeneity, does not change the manner of treating publicity and communication with others.

Media system in Russia

Media system classification in Russia is generally possible based on the model proposed by Hallin and Mancini. They classify media systems based on four key dimensions: (a) the degree and nature of state involvement in the media; (b) the degree of political parallelism, which is the extent to which the media are linked, formally or informally, with parties and other political institutions; (c) the degree of professionalism in journalism, as measured by the independence of journalists and their adherence to articulated standards of practice, including a commitment to public service; and (d) the degree of mass dissemination of news content (Hallin & Mancini, 2004). Based on these dimensions, what does the situation with media system creation in Russia look like?

The mass media are now experiencing the political "kolonisierung" from the Russian state. The state is the owner of "Channel Russia" and is the major shareholder of ORT—the two most popular national television stations. The second-largest shareholder of mass media is the state-owned Gazprom. This company owns several of the most influential newspapers and the third largest national television station, NTV. Thus, state presence in television extends to all of the three largest national television stations, which broadcast throughout the entire country. As a consequence, the informational policy of most mass media has often a one-sided character. Even though there seldom is direct prohibition of single programs or publications, the financial dependence of many television stations and the press functions as leverage. Another aspect of journalism in Russia is the political attitude of owners. This trend correlates with the tendency for an expansion of political control on powerful business groups. For that reason, journalists often consider themselves, not as "challengers of the political status quo", but rather as "political players". Therefore, some experts argue that journalism loses reliability and the Russian citizen loses "information to meaningfully debate political issues or participate in civic life" (Oates, 2007, p. 1288). Furthermore, the cancellation of life programs from news and informational broadcasts on TV deteriorates the quality of investigation journalism. Regional mass media display a high level of clientelism in relation to the owners of regional mass media and the government:

> Owners rely on the government's goodwill for continuing smooth operation of their publications, and underpaid staff-level journalists depend increasingly on financial resources that only wealthy local elites can provide. The harsh economic climate contributes to this dependency, as most publications—the Regional being something of an exception—are unable to gain revenue through alternative channels that would allow escape from dependency on powerful patrons. The government's close relationship with area businesses helps ensure this dependency.
>
> (Lowrey & Erzikova, 2010, p. 284)

The relatively "high" place of the mass media in the trust list of Russian citizens should not be misleading regarding its importance as a public sphere and as a means of communication. The reflection patterns of Russian citizens on mass media production give evidence of the inability and inexperience of the former to use mass media as analytical sources of personal opinion-making. According to surveys, TV news should "lead", rather than "describe" (Oates 2007, p. 1296). In the opinion of the majority of Russian citizens, the mass media should not fulfill an informational, but rather an inspirational, function (Oates, 2006, p. 165). The mass media are not usually perceived as a source of information or as a kind of representation, but rather as a source of entertainment. Such attitudes are proven to be true by respondents' answers that give evidence about their reflexive inability by understanding the sharp deterioration of the freedom of speech in the mass media over the last ten years: 40% of Russians who were polled believe the present informational policy of the mass media to be true, as opposed to only 6% who believe that this was the case in the 1990s. Moreover, 47% of Russians are assured that the present authority in Russia in no way threatens the freedom of speech and restrains the activity of independent mass media. Only 27% believe that this was the case in the 1990s.

Many researchers and experts share the opinion that the Russian state tries to restore the centralized system of media control by the government, engaging in the series of activities for centralization of the media control (Koltsova, 2006). The current media system in Russia generally is not an effective channel of political representation. Specifically, it is not a space for communications which agenda is defined from the bottom, meaning by civil society. Oates said, "Russia provides a communications paradox in that there is so much information and so little democracy" (Oates, 2013, p. 12). Diversity of media has been developed, yet the media have not established themselves as objective or balanced. Becker notes that diversity is relatively well-tolerated in some sectors (such as print), but not in key broadcast outlets (Becker, 2004).

Status quo of communication's theory and practice in Russia

Donsbach, in his work "The Identity of Communication Research", talks about communication as an academic discipline, concluding that communications still lack identity:

> "Communication" as the object is much too broad; almost everything in life involves communication. Moreover, not everything that deals with aspects of media communication is, in my view, communication research. For instance, research on psychological deformations as an effect of violent media content is still psychology and research on the causes of media concentration is still economics ... not communication.
>
> (Donsbach, 2012, 22)

The two most-known methodological approaches constitute the disciplinary identity of modern communication science: psychology-based communication research, when explaining media exposure with mood management or processes of persuasion with the elaboration likelihood model or priming; and sociology-based research, when describing the patterns of personal interaction or the social gratifications of media use (Donsbach, 2012). Formation of the disciplined identity of communications in Russia happens completely differently. While in the Western world, the communication discipline includes a wide range of sociological and psychological theories; in Russia, it is a domain of philologists and journalists. The official name for communication as a discipline in official documents of the Russian Ministry of Education is still "mass media and informational-library conduct". There is still an active inflow of journalists to the Russian communications industry. Journalists became the base of staff formation in the Russian public relations industry at the beginning of its formation. Leontovich points out the theoretical narrowness of the disciplinary identity of communication in Russia, which in the United States and in other Western countries communication study is a well-developed field, but in which the linguistic aspects of discourse are largely ignored. In Russia, on the contrary, there is a strong preference for linguistics, whereas communication study is still at an early stage of its development (Leontovich, 2008).

Focusing on *linguistics*, instead of *communication*, is a consequence of weakness of communication as a social institution. While *linguistics* reflects primarily on problems with reading and talking in interpersonal relationships, *communication* focuses on problems of interactive relationships in the context of all of the complexity and interdependence of societal systems: state, market, and society. The importance of communication as a way of public interaction initiated the development of Western disciplines that are associated with public speech, group discussions, and argumentative forums that corresponds with one of the most important communicative functions of influencing others in public and private discourse. Instead, the understanding of communication was classified in the USSR and in modern Russia as a philological study. Hazen points out the direct link between society's acceptance of the practical importance of communication and the growing application of communication theory and research to applied fields such as health, law, organizational behavior, and conflict resolution (Hazen, 2008, p. 470). A disciplinary narrowness of communication as a subject caused the weak development of the theoretical foundation of communication studies in Russia. Because communication is rarely viewed as a *social process* in Russian education, communicative paradigms such as systems theory, social constructionism, social constructivism, cognitive psychology, and critical theory are rarely encountered in the education programs. In Russia, these theories still remain in the domain of sociology. Their affiliation with the discipline of communication does not become common knowledge when the disciplinary identity of communication is still limited by journalistic and linguistic knowledge. Typically, the most popular subjects in the area of communication are marketing communication and advertising. In fact, communication as a discipline is most often represented by marketing communication and advertising, especially when discussing the relationship between corporate and academic spheres. A complete dominance of instrumental communication (marketing, advertising) in the Association of Communicational Agencies in Russia (Russian public relations organization) in partnership with academic institutions is typical. "Advertising and marketing communication" in Russia is the most common equivalent of communication education, together with linguistics and "librarianship". There is a significant lack of popularity and representation of public relations and closely related neighboring communicational disciplines, such as: crisis communication, internal communication, government relations, corporate social responsibility, and health communication. Professionalization of these areas of communication implies recognition of social and political pluralism, specifically a priori conflict in Russian society as freedom of expression of one's opinion as a right for autonomy. We consider public relations practice and its professional education as processes that assist making communication to be a social institution much more than are marketing communication and advertising, because, to gain more social significance for corporations, at the other end of two-way communication is not only the need to see the client but also the citizen as a stakeholder. Thus, development of public relations is one of the most important indicators of communication modernization, which is based, not only on technologies (communication technologies in Russia are generally on the same level as are Western standards), but primarily on the changes in the public structure: modernization, individualization, economization, mediatization, and rationalization. Thus, it is necessary to examine the problem of the professionalization of public relations in Russia as at a practical field of emancipation of communication as a practical activity.

Theoretical and practical issues of communication are tightly interrelated. Watching the development of the market of professional services in Russia, one can draw a parallel with the tendencies of development of communication as an academic discipline that were described earlier. To estimate the level of professionalism in public relations, it makes sense to turn to the conceptualization of professionalism in public relations that was formulated by Yang and Taylor. The authors define public relations as fundamentally

> a profession of relations, and it is through building and maintaining relationships, and facilitating communication among different social actors that the profession of public relations contributes to the accumulation of social capital and supports the existence of democratic processes in a society.
> (Yang & Taylor, 2013, p. 257)

The authors believe that public relations is a profession, rather than a practice, and identify five criteria for its professionalization: higher education, professional associations, codes of ethics and systems of accreditation, responsibility to ethical information flows in society, and organizational allocation of resources to public relations (Yang & Taylor, 2013, p. 258). At the same time, an EBOK (European Public Relations Body of Knowledge) Delphi study identified four main characteristics of public relations that are typical in Europe: managerial, operational, educational, and reflective. Under "reflective tasks of public relations", the authors mean "continuous adjustment of corporate decision processes to society's changing norms and values" (Signitzer & Prexl, 2008, p. 9). Therefore, the question of professionalism in public relations is more often understood by looking at an organization from a societal view. Hence, public relations in general not only maintains "relations with the public(s), but creates a platform for public debate and, consequently, a public sphere" (van Ruler & Vercic, 2005, p. 256). This implies that, the more professional are the public relations activities, the more they become a component of the interactive relations among the state, market, and public and the more they become part of the public sphere. Such understanding of professionalization in public relations presupposes a "societal approach", in which public relations contributes to a free flow of information and serves a "democratic function" (van Ruler & Vercic 2005, p. 257). Sriramesh and Vercic (2003) point out that public relations tends to be one-way propaganda in societies which political systems do not possess institutionalized public discussions. Thus, when examining public relations professionalization in Russia, we shall focus on the interrelationship between civil society and the market to understand how much corporate communication contributes to the public sphere.

A critical analysis of the Russian public relations industry is presented in a 2014 report by the Russian Public Relations Academy (Russian Academy of Public Relations, 2014). In particular, the report notes that, despite Russian public relations following all global development trends, it is still impossible to overcome "specific conjunctures" of the regional character: general educational standards, as well as professionalism and service quality evaluation methods, are missing, and information disclosure protocols and clear ethical standards are missing. The lack of a developed system of industry periodicals supports informational isolation of individual members, prevents integrative processes in the industry, and promotes "balkanization" and "provincialization" (formation of "local activity standards"). The report states difficulties associated with building relationships with businesses under the condition of "client's incomprehension of the factual PR services for the client's primary activities". Additionally, the opacity of a significant number of actors in the market undermines the public relations industry's reputation and credibility. Corporate reputation of the market actors remains undemanded. In fact, corporate reputation is often interpreted as a "necessary evil the company has to face because of external pressures" (Tsetsura & Chernov, 2009, p. 56). This example illustrates that Russian civil society often is not considered as a stakeholder or as a partner. In this sense, it is typical for the importance of corporate reputation for Russian companies to grow significantly when they plan to enter international markets, in which the public (civil society) is much more demanding and competent than in Russia (Tsetsura & Chernov 2009, p. 56). Tsetsura and Chernov claim that "Russian corporate mentality hardly recognizes the doing-good-for-the-sake-of-doing-well philosophy" (Tsetsura & Chernov, 2009, p. 60). When it comes to a relationship with society, instrumental awareness prevails, that is, the awareness of short-term financial benefits. The report of the Russian Public Relations Academy also highlights the clear relationship between problems with the constitution of the public relations industry in particular as well as general problems in Russian society: The lack of a developed civil society leads to the lack of a formulated demand for communication management of "public relations". To create demand for "public relations", there must be at least an interested "public" that is ready to protect its own rights, that is, without building relationships, no public social institution can function. Among other obstacles to professionalizing the public relations industry in Russia, authors of the report listed immaturity of business and political culture, as well as political engagement of the media and its clear affiliation with the state.

Conclusion

The development of communication in its theoretical and practical spheres depends on the extent to which communication is institutionalized in a society as a form of cooperation, interaction, and mutual understanding. The importance of communication as a social institute depends primarily on the rationalization of social development. To become socially and politically important, communication needs to be a public process. The institutionalization of the public sphere in Russia—communicative spaces emerging from small face-to-face discussions, social movements, and the media—is facing major difficulties because of the low levels of institutional and interpersonal trust. The atomization of Russian society—the prevalence of primordial communicative activities and lack of shared experience—does not allow the formation of a unity of language symbols, nor identification of symbolic instruments, that are required for proper mutual understanding and participation in social, political, and economic life: "Lack of mediating structures coincides with the lack of 'tools' with which to understand the transformation" (Oushakine, 2000, p. 1006). Developing autonomy of the largest societal pillars—government, market, and society—is experiencing significant difficulties:

> The pattern of interactions between business and the state does not correspond to bargaining in a market-like environment of multiple and changing buyers and sellers. Rather, it is consistent with a patrimonial system where favors are distributed in reward for loyalty.
>
> (Rutland, 2006, p. 90)

At the same time, civil society in Russia is subordinated to the state as a consequence of a lack of political competition and open criticism. Due to the narrowing of the public sphere and actors' unequal rights, the conflict resolution process is structured hierarchically: in communication's theory and practice, the instrumental approach dominates, orienting on results and not mutual understanding. As a consequence, communication as a discipline cannot obtain autonomy in education, being unable to overcome the traditional association with disciplines such as journalism and advertising communication. The lack of demand for argumentative, empathetic communication within Russian society induces difficulties with the constitution of the public relations industry, which popularity depends on the level of citizens' interest in the public justification of actions undertaken by the market and the state. With an absence of this particular interest, Russian society does not offer itself as an equal partner (stakeholder) to the market, which deprives the latter from stimuli to invest in corporate reputation. The society is not interested in the market, and the market treats down the society: the lack of equality devaluates the importance of interaction and communication. Recognition and further strengthening of communication in practice and in academia will depend on the strengthening of horizontal and "weak" ties within Russian society. The more that civil society has an opportunity to influence the formation of a political and economic agenda, the more that communication will be defined strategically as a platform for relationships among the state, market, and the public.

References

Becker, J. (2004). Lessons from Russia: A neo-authoritarian media system. *European Journal of Communication*, *9*(2), 139–63.

Benhabib, S. (1992). Models of public space: Hanna Arendt, the Liberal tradition, and Jürgen Habermas. In C. Calhoun (Ed.), *Habermas and the public sphere* (pp. 73–98). Cambridge, MA: MIT Press.

Blumler, J. G., & Kavanagh, D. (1999). The third age of political communication: Influences and features. *Political Communication*, *16*(3), 209–230.

Dewey, J. (1983). Education as politics. In J. A. Boydston (Ed.), *The middle works of John Dewey, vol. 13, 1921–1922* (pp. 334–335). Carbondale, IL: Southern Illinois University Press.

Dewey, J. (1927). *The public and its problems.* New York: Henry Holt.

Donsbach, W. (2012). The identity of communication research. *Signo y Pensamiento*, *31*(60), 18–29.

Grunig, J. E. (1997). A situational theory of publics: Conceptual history, recent challenges and new research. In D. Moss, T. MacManus, & D. Vercic (Eds.), *Public relations research: An international perspective* (pp. 3–48). London: International Thomson Business Press.

Gudkov, L., Dubin, B., & Zorkaja, N. (2008). *Post-sovjetskij chelovek i grazhdanskoje obshestvo* [Post-Soviet person and civil society]. Moskow, RU: Moskovskaja shkola politicheskih issledovanij [Moscow School of Political Research].

Habermas, J. (1992). Further reflections on the public sphere. In C. Calhoun (Ed.), *Habermas and the public sphere* (pp. 421–461). Cambridge, MA: The MIT Press.

Habermas, J. (1989). *The structural transformation of the public sphere: An inquiry into a category of bourgeois society.* Cambridge, MA: MIT Press.

Habermas, J. (1996). *Three normative models of democracy.* In W. Benhabib (Ed.), *Democracy and difference: Contesting boundaries of the political* (pp. 21–30). Princeton, NJ: Princeton University Press.

Hallin, D. C., & Mancini, P. (2004). *Comparing media systems: Three models of media and politics.* Cambridge: Cambridge University Press.

Hauser G. A. (2007). Vernacular discourse and the epistemic dimension of public opinion. *Communication Theory*, *17*(4), 333–339.

Hazen, M. D. (2008): Thoughts on the development of the communication discipline in the United States and Russia. *Russian Journal of Communication*, *1*(4), 455–475.

Hendriks, C. M. (2006). Integrated deliberation: Reconciling civil society's dual role in deliberative democracy. *Political Studies*, *54*(3), 486–508.

Hodgson, G. M. (2004). *The evolution of institutions: Agency, structure and Darwinism in American institutionalism.* London: Routledge.

International Telecommunications Union. (2011, January 31). *World telecommunications/ICT indicators database.* New York: United Nations Statistical Division.

Koltsova, O. (2006). *News media and power in Russia.* Abingdon, UK: Routledge.

Kooiman, J. (2003). *Governing as governance.* London: SAGE Publication.

Lawson, Tony (1997). *Economics and reality.* London: Routledge.

Leontovich, O. (2008). Intercultural communication theory in Russia: Present and future. *Vestnik of the Russian Communication Association.* Retrieved from http://www.russcomm.ru/eng/rca_biblio/l/leontovich01_eng.shtml.

Lippmann, W. (1993). *The phantom public* (1927; repr.). New Brunswick, NJ: Transaction.

Lowrey, W., & Erzikova, E. (2010). Institutional legitimacy and Russian news: Case studies of four regional newspapers. *Political Communication, 27*(3), 275–288.

Luhmann, N. (2000). *Vertrauen: Ein mechanismus zur reduktion der sozialen komplexität.* 4 Auflage (Lucius & Lucius Stuttgart).

Mayhew, L. H. (1997). *The new public: Professional communication and the means of social influence.* Cambridge, UK: Cambridge University Press.

Mickiewicz, E. (2005). Excavating concealed tradeoffs: How Russians watch the news. *Political Communication, 22*(3), 355–380.

Mutz, D., & Martin, P. M. (2001). Facilitating communication across lines of political difference: The role of mass media. *American Political Science Review, 95*(1), 97–114.

Noelle-Neumann, E. (2001). *Die Schweigespirale.* München: Neuauflage.

Oates, S. (2006). Where is the party? Television and election campaigns in Russia. In K. Voltmer (Ed.), *Mass media and political communication in new democracies* (pp. 130–144). New York: Routlege.

Oates, S. (2007). The Neo-Soviet model of the media. *Europe-Asia Studies, 59*(8), 1279–1297.

Oates, S. (2013). *Revolution stalled: The political limits of the Internet in the Post-Soviet sphere.* Oxford: Oxford University Press.

Offe, C. (1999). How can we trust our fellow citizens? In M. Warren (Ed.), *Democracy and trust* (pp. 42–87). Cambridge: Cambridge University Press.

Oushakine (2000). In the state of post-Soviet aphasia: Symbolic development in contemporary Russia. *Europe-Asia Studies, 52*(6), 991–1016.

Van Ruler, B., & Vercic, D. (2005). Reflective communication management, future ways for public relations research. In P. J. Kalbfleisch (Ed.), *Communication yearbook 29* (pp. 239–273). Mahwah, NJ: Lawrence Erlbaum Associates.

Rutland P. (2006). Business and civil society in Russia. In A. B. Evans, Jr., L. A. Henry, & L. M. Sundstrom (Eds.), *Russian civil society. A critical assessment* (pp. 73–94). New York: M.E. Sharpe.

Russian Academy of Public Relations. (2014). *Sostoyanie natsional'noj industrii obschestvennyh svyazej* [State of the national industry of public relations]. Report. Retrieved from http://pracademy.ru/files/upload/1e/16/RAOS-2014-%D0%B4% D0%BE%D0%BA%D0%BB%D0%B0%D0%B4.pdf

Sriramesh, K., & Vercic, D. (2003). A theoretical framework for global public relations research and practice. In K. Sriramesh & D. Vercic (Eds.), *The global public relations handbook: Theory, research, and practice* (pp. 1–22). Mahwah, NJ: Lawrence Erlbaum Associates, Publishers.

Signitzer, B., & Prexl, A. (2008). Corporate sustainability communications: Aspects of theory and professionalization. *Journal of Public Relations Research, 20*(1), 1–19.

Sztompka, P. (1996). Looking back: The year 1989 as a cultural and civilizational break. *Communist and Post-Communist Studies, 29*(2), 115–129.

Tsetsura, K., & Chernov, G. (2009). Constructing corporate reputation in the Russian media. *Russian Journal of Communication, 2*(1/2), 46–65.

Yang, A., & Taylor, M. (2013). The relationship between the professionalization of public relations, societal social capital and democracy: Evidence from a cross-national study. *Public Relations Review, 39*(4), 257–270.

Young, I. M. (2000). *Inclusion and democracy.* Oxford: Oxford University Press.

4 The history of the development of public relations as an institutionalized field and as a discipline in the post-Soviet space

Nelli Bachurina

Introduction

Communication as a science and as a formal educational standard in the post-Soviet countries is difficult to discuss because the countries differ so much economically and politically. Russia, which is the core of the post-Soviet states and the country to which several other countries of the former Soviet Union have strong economic and political ties, is of particular interest in the institutionalization of communication; however, the development of communication in Russia may differ from that of other post-Soviet countries.

Although a Communication Studies degree is not yet offered by Russia institutions, several communication areas have been developed, even during the Soviet era. The key factor for uniting the post-Soviet countries is the Russian language, which some republics of the former Soviet Union recognize as an inter-ethnic/national language. Since Soviet times, the linguistic and philological branches of communication have been developed the most (Matyash, 2002, 2003; Matyash & Beebe, 2003; Kashkin, 2014; Vasilik, 2004).

In the post-Soviet countries, some communication disciplines first appeared with the transition to democracy at the state level. Public relations (PR) is one such discipline (Matyash, 2004). The study of the history of public relations education in Russia is influential because the education system, itself, is the context that forms a certain way of thinking about communication.

For example, Tsetsura (2003, 2004), Azarova and Shishkin (1998), Azarova (2003), Shishkina (2002), Moiseeva (1997), Bocharov (2007), Chumikov and Bocharov (2009), Kuzheleva-Sagan (2006a), and Shilina (2011) have paid much attention to the development of public relations in Russia. Nevertheless, far less attention has been given to the history of public relations as a discipline in Russia, particularly in how it is affected by the Soviet past and by globalized education. Thus, this chapter analyzes the history of public relations education in Russia through the prism of patterns of Soviet ideology, the country's social-cultural evolution, and a multicultural and global context.

This research has these questions:

R.Q1: How have Soviet sociocultural traditions and practices influenced development of public relations education in current Russia?

R.Q2: How does the multicultural and global context influence public relation education in post-Soviet Russia?

Knowledge of the history of public relations education in Russia will be useful for comparative studies that can identify trends of public relations higher education development in other post-Soviet countries. Taking Russia as an example, this study determines the specific development and content of communication education in countries that have joined the path of democratic society not so long ago. The article also can be useful to international public relations educators and researchers.

Literature review

Several well-known Western and Russian scholars have been researching the history of Communication Studies in the Soviet and post-Soviet Russia (Matyash, 2002, 2003; Matyash & Beebe, 2003; Beebe, Kharcheva, & Kharcheva, 1998; Tolstikova-Mast & Keyton, 2002; Bergelson, 1998; Zassoursky, 2005, 1996; Vasilik, 2004).

Olga Matyash, former president of the Russian Communication Association and a famous proponent of the introduction of communication studies as a formal educational standard in Russia, undertook a systematic and integrated study of the genesis of communication in Russian higher education. Matyash (2003) described the history of communication as a discipline in Russia that had resulted from Russia's sociocultural characteristics and behavioral patterns. Beebe and Matyash (2003) have identified several characteristics of Russian communication instruction that have been determined by the country's history: (1) a Russian cultural intellectual tradition that emphasizes conceptualization and broad philosophical understanding versus a pragmatic approach; (2) an economic structure and principles that have created little incentive for developing customer-oriented communication skills; (3) a different ideological and philosophical tradition; (4) a different public speaking tradition: speaker-centered versus audience-centered; and (5) a cultural and educational tradition of text analysis versus speech interaction and language-in-use analysis.

Beebe, Kharcheva, and Kharcheva (1998) conducted a study on the role of speech communication in post-Soviet education in Russia and found that:

> the lower value placed upon oral communication competency in Russia, may be explained, in part, by the generally lower value that has been historically assigned to free expression of opinion and thought. The value that is placed upon teaching or using effective communication principles and skills may be one index of a society's commitment to democratic ideals.
>
> (p. 270)

Thus, communication studies were developing in the Soviet Union in a limited form, and the change of the country's political system became a catalyst for new branches of communication studies to emerge.

With the collapse of the Soviet Union and with Russia turning toward a democratic society, the institutionalization of public relations as a discipline began that was based on Soviet higher education traditions and the system of relationships between people that had formed throughout the years of "building" socialism. Public relations as a sphere of institutional activities began forming at the end of the 1990–1991 timeframe.

Much research has been done in public relations history, both by Russian and international scholars. A majority of the Russian scholars have preferred to periodize this history. They indicate these features to identify the historical stages of Russian public relations: sociocultural determinants, organizational communication features, and a state of research in public relations (Azarova & Shishkin,1998); a development level of public relations institutions (Shishkina, 2002); major institutional milestones in public relations development (Moiseeva, 1997); and a complex of socioeconomic, political, and other aspects of the country's development (Shilina, 2011).

Some Russian scholars argue that the history of public relations began in ancient Russia. Public relations proto-forms are presented in books by Bocharov (2007), Pochekaev (2007), and Medinskiy (2010).

International scholars have also made a significant contribution to the conceptualization of some issues of public relations institutionalization in Russia. However, most of these studies were made at the beginning of the 2000s and were based on surveys of public relations practitioners in the major cities (Moscow and St. Petersburg) of Russia (Guth, 2000; Clarke, 2000; McElreath et al., 2001).

Recognized international scholars whose interests have focused on historical and contemporary aspects of institutionalization of public relations in Russia include Tsetsura (2003, 2004) and Erzikova (2013). Tsetsura (2003) presented a development of public relations education and industry from their early institutionalized forms. She noted that, due to the absence of a communication tradition in Soviet and post-Soviet Russia, public relations institutionalization in Russia differs significantly from that of the United States (Tsetsura, 2003). Tsetsura stressed the need for a geopolitical approach to the development of public relations because of the specifics of public relation practices in different areas of Russia. She called them "metaregions" that are "geographically, politically, and economically different and culturally diverse" (Tsetsura, 2003, p. 302). In 2004, Tsetsura examined the state of public relations education and the industry in Russia in the early 2000s. She also reviewed public relations textbooks that were used by Russian scholars and educators in the late 1990s–early 2000s (Tsetsura, 2004). Erzikova (2013) studied the effects of globalization on the processes of the institutionalization of the Russian public relations industry. The author noted a contradiction between Western principles of public relations and their use in Russia, which were due to substantial sociocultural differences. As a result, Russian public relations practices were an "interweaving" of foreign and domestic approaches and seem "de-centered" in relation to the conceptualization of global processes.

Few studies have examined the specifically historical aspects of public relations institutionalization as an academic area in Russia. Chumikov and Bocharov (2006) reviewed historical facts of the institutionalization of public relations as a discipline in Russia through their chronological description of public relations trade journals, professional events, and student and professional competitions in the public relations sphere. Krivonosov et al. (2010) provided one of the successful attempts of periodization of public relations education in the Russian academic literature. The authors gave the following overview of the Russian "PRology" (science of public relations):

1. 1990–1995—The stage of vulgar knowledge, "Black's era".[1] Literature on business communication and imageology (studies of image-making) prevails.
2. 1995–1999—Pre-institutionalization. Prevalence of the U.S. model of public relations education and practice, "Pocheptsov's era". Introduction of European public relations theory (the French public relations school), thanks to the works of T. Lebedeva[2] (Lebedeva, 1996).
3. 2000–2001—Primary PRology institutionalization. The first serious academic studies, Ph.D. theses in public relations. Introduction of translations of high-quality foreign public relations textbooks, thanks to "Image-Contact" PR Agency (Moscow).
4. 2002–2003—The stage of secondary institutionalization. Subsequent development of applied research. The processes of "secondary vulgarization" of PRology, such as the emergence of popular science literature for "dummies" (Krivonosov et al., 2010).

This periodization is limited by the only parameter that was considered as the key factor for the selection of these stages—the state of public relations academic publishing and research activities in Russia. To create a holistic view of Russian public relations education, these aspects are important: the impact of educational reform in Russia and Russia's participation in the Bologna Process and the outcomes of the influence of foreign academic schools on the Russian public relations academy.

Although some studies have addressed the development of public relations education in Russia, their findings must be updated, taking into account the Soviet past and ongoing changes in globalized higher education.

Method

This study uses an historical-descriptive approach, including an analysis of historical facts about public relations education in Russia, the latest reports of Russian professional public relations associations, current curricula of Russian institutions, descriptions of advertising and public relations degrees from the official websites of Russian universities, and the Russian bibliographic database of academic publications—eLibrary.[3]

Discussion

Genesis of post-Soviet public relations education

The beginning of public relations as a professional activity in Russia occurred in the late 1980s and early 1990s, when the first representatives of international public relations agencies and specialized departments in companies appeared in Russia. Public relations as a discipline in Russia emerged in the early 1990s. The Moscow State Institute of International Relations first offered the specialty "Public Relations" in 1991. In 1993, the St. Petersburg State Electrotechnical University offered the Public Relations Degree (a five-year curriculum). In 1996, the State Educational Standard of Higher Professional Education in Public Relations was approved by the Russian Federation Ministry of Education. In the first half and in the middle of the 1990s, the first academic public relations departments appeared in Russian universities, including in the regions. They were formed under departments of social sciences and humanities, as well as in mass media and journalism departments, and rarely were they under departments of business and public administration. The first educators of the public relations discipline in Russian universities were journalists, political consultants, and teachers from social and human sciences departments. Initially, higher education in public relations in Russia was oriented toward business (marketing focus) or journalism (communication focus) (Tsetsura, 2003). In the same region, there were universities with one or both focuses (Tsetsura, 2003). Political public relations got the greatest development in the academy and in professional practice, due to a high demand for political consulting in the late 1990s and early 2000s in Russia. During that time, public relations practices were lacking compliance with professional ethical standards. Paid public relations publications in the mass media, known as *zakazukha*, were widespread (Tsetsura, 2003). During the initial stage of the institutionalization of public relations, the concepts of public relations and propaganda were synonymous. This led to the term "black PR" to denote manipulative techniques that were used mostly in political campaigns (Tsetsura, 2003). Within the framework of higher education, paid training and coursework in public relations became popular. They were organized by foreign public relations agencies at first and then by domestic political public relations consultants.

In September 2001, there were more than 60 public relations programs (as cited in Tsetsura, 2003, p. 304). By the mid-2000s, higher education in public relations became standardized.

In 2003, Russia joined the Bologna Process that was a turning point for higher education in public relations. Within the Bologna Treaty, for the next seven years Russian educational programs in public relations experienced several methodological changes to align national curricula to the world standard of a two-level degree system of training. The modernization reform of the higher education system under the influence of the Bologna Process has increased continuity with European academic traditions, thanks to intensified exchanges. During the first decade of the 2000s, the Russian academic and professional public relations community actively established relations with Western partners from Europe and the United States. Moscow and St. Petersburg's leading universities were inviting public relations professionals and scholars from abroad (Tsetsura, 2003). As a result of these academic exchanges, Russian scholars formed their commitment to the European or to U.S. public relations schools.

In 2003, the Russian Federation's Ministry of Labor and Social Development approved qualification characteristics of public relations practitioners. The Russian National Classification of Occupations of Employees added the following types of occupation: Public Relations Deputy Director, Chief of the Public Relations Department, Public Relations Manager, and Public Relations Specialist. In the mid-2000s, these specializations (minors) of public relations degree programs were introduced: public affairs and public relations in commercial and non-commercial organizations. Establishing the Association of Public Relations Educators (APRE) in 2005 was one of the important advancements in the institutionalization of public relations as a discipline. In 2006, the Russian Association of Public Relations (RAPR) (n.d.) created the "Committee of Education". Presently, the Committee aims to drive development of educational methods in public relations in Russian higher education institutions that are relevant to industry needs (RAPR, n.d.).

In 2008, 140 universities nationwide offered public relations degrees. The final stage of implementation of these reforms for transition to the two cycles of higher education qualification (Bachelor's and Master's level) within the Bologna Process ended in 2010. Instead of the previous independent five-year specialist's separate degrees in "Advertising" and in "Public Relations", the Ministry of Education and Science approved an integrated or "joint" degree "Advertising and Public Relations". The first admission to an Advertising and Public Relations undergraduate program was in 2010. After the adoption of a two-level degree system, Russian curricula's structure and number of courses became compatible to those in Europe and in the United States. The introduction of a doctoral program (PhD degree), as it is understood in Western countries, is still under consideration.

The year 2013 was the first year when Russian universities offered graduate programs in public relations. Mainly, those were graduate programs of universities in Moscow and St. Petersburg. In 2019, the total number of undergraduate Advertising and Public Relations programs in Russia was 278, according to vuzoteka.ru's website (http://vuzoteka.ru, n.d.). Throughout Russia thus far, a graduate degree has been offered in about ten Russian universities, few of which are located in the regions. The names of graduate programs vary and are flexible, for example, "Integrated Communications", "Strategic Communication in Public Relations and Advertising", and "Government relations".

In recent years, there has been a decline in the number of applicants for Advertising and Public Relations programs in Russia (Solovey, 2013). This can be explained by the demographic decrease in the university-age population in the 1990s and by the small number of graduate programs in public relations today. Meanwhile, cooperation with foreign universities continues in Russia. Since 2013, the Moscow State University has participated in the European Communication Professional Skills and Innovation Programme (ECOPCI) project. In 2014, the Higher School of Economics (HSE) hosted a conference in Moscow with representatives of the Chinese universities that offered public relations programs. Russian universities are opening new specializations that are associated with the latest trends in the public relation industry, such as a concentration in "Communications in Digital Environment" within the Advertising and Public Relations undergraduate program at the Higher School of Economics.

Development of the structure and key elements of the curriculum

The system of higher education is regulated by the Federal State Educational Standard (FSES) (2010), which is approved and administered by the Ministry of Education and Science of the Russian Federation. As part of the modernization of higher education in the Bologna Process, there was a consistent change of several generations of the Federal State Educational standard (first, second, and third generations).[4] Each succeeding standard was more advanced than was the previous one and gave more academic freedom to universities. Standards of the first and second generations that were adopted in 1997 and 2000, respectively, contained a list of compulsory courses in curriculum, with little flexibility (15–30%) with selective courses within the part of the curriculum known as a "regional component".

Transition to third-generation standards and the introduction of "integrated", in a literal sense, combined "Advertising" and "Public Relations" as a new stage in the history of public relations education in Russia.

The main differences of the third-generation standards are as follows:

* competences as learning outcomes are the basic parameter of education effectiveness evaluation;
* degree programs have *a modular structure* (a module is a combination of parts of a discipline or disciplines that is responsible for the development of a competence);
* the flexibility with selective courses in the part of curriculum is about 50% (for the Bachelor's Degree program).

The innovation of advertising and public relations undergraduate programs that are based on the third-generation standards lies in four mandatory modules, containing core (foundational) courses: "Kommunikologiya" (Communication Science), "Integrated Communications", "Management", and "Marketing".

According to the developers, the modules may include these disciplines: "Kommunikologiya" module—"Theory of Communication", "Theory of Mass Communication", "Sociology (or Psychology) of Mass Communication"; "Integrated Communications" module—"The Basics of Advertising", "The Fundamentals of PR, Copywriting", "Below-the-line Promotion", "History of Advertising and PR"; "Management" module—"Project Management", "Management of Advertising and PR Departments Activity", "Fundamentals of Planning Advertising and PR-Campaigns", "Media Planning Fundamentals"; "Marketing"—"Analysis of Object Promotion", and "Market Research and Situation Analysis"[5] (according to FSES for Advertising and Public Relations Bachelor's degree).

The Russian course design is *object-centric* (for example, studies in phenomena, institutions, and processes) (Kryaklina, 2012). In U.S. universities, foundational courses are aimed at applied knowledge; however, in Russia, the studied *objects* may not be connected to practice but rather are very broad, abstract, and theoretical (see the titles of disciplines earlier in this chapter).

Analyzing the Advertising and Public Relations undergraduate programs of universities in different regions of Russia, I have calculated the average cumulative number of credits per course for each of the four modules and then have placed the names of the modules in credit-number decreasing order: "Kommunikologiya" (22, 6), "Marketing" (16, 5), "Integrated Communications" (12, 5), and "Management" (11). Disciplines of these modules are the basis for any official Advertising and Public Relations undergraduate program in Russia. The ratio of a number of credits for each module displays the priorities in learning outcomes. As the analysis shows, Russian Advertising and Public Relations programs give preference to communication and marketing disciplines. Because the new "joint" degree has included advertising since 2010, the number of public relations disciplines has decreased. The program has become truly multidisciplinary.

Despite the elements of novelty in the third-generation standards, Advertising and Public Relations undergraduate programs are similar to the ones of previous years. An extensive list of disciplines that are mandatory for the first year of study has remained unchanged (general knowledge courses: Sociology, Political Science, Philosophy, History, Psychology, Economy, and Foreign and Russian languages). This makes the current programs an inherent part of the Soviet traditions of "classical higher education". In support of this, descriptions of today's advertising and public relations programs on university websites comprise such expressions as "preparation of generalists …", "variety of courses", as "classic education in humanities".

Thus, the solidity of public relations programs in Russian universities has been retained since their introduction, but they have become more multidisciplinary in their content. This has resulted in a number of internal contradictions in the understanding of the nature of public relations education, which combines communicative activities that are different in their scope and character.

The integrated program: Complexity and reasons for merging

The "integrated" Advertising and Public Relations program is not a purely Russian phenomenon. For instance, DePaul University in the United States offers a Public Relations and Advertising degree as well as do universities in Spain, which have a degree in Advertising and Public Relations that is official nationwide (Xifra, 2007). In addition, various Western universities also offer degrees in Integrated Marketing Communications that include communication degrees.

Meanwhile, Russian scholars believe that the merging of degrees, once autonomous, has both advantages and disadvantages. In particular, one disadvantage is that the wide field of professional activity has led to more loosely defined content components, that is, modules of the curriculum. This, in turn, has made it more difficult to clearly identify the professional skills of graduates (Kryaklina, 2012). A division into the four modules of disciplines does not have any analogues in Western practice and seems controversial. For example, which of the three modules "Kommunikologiya", "Integrated Communications", or "Management" should comprise, for example, a Corporate Communications course; how should interdisciplinary relations of the module disciplines be presented with one another in the process of learning and teaching? Precisely because of the lack of the answers to these questions in the Russian academic community, the general education program is multidisciplinary, but not interdisciplinary. Zavodchikova (2010) wisely noticed that "... lack of understanding the links, that curricula have, affects the understanding of the profession as a complex" (p. 128).

Moreover, despite the fact that Advertising and Public Relations graduates have well-rounded knowledge, they are far inferior to their foreign peers in terms of applied knowledge in both advertising and public relations. Therefore, chasing fundamental and multidisciplinary education prevents the students from acquiring practical knowledge and skills. In my observation, students value less the courses that are too abstract and theoretical.

The collapse of the Soviet Union has inevitably turned Russia into a part of the global educational arena. Integration of Russia into the European arena for higher education, thanks to the Bologna Process, has led to the country's adoption of a common framework of transferable and comparable degrees. As a consequence, it has reduced the overall number of degree programs in Russian universities.

Kazakova and Feoktistov (2012) noted that the current state of the market for public relations in Russia has become an important cause for the merging of once-autonomous degrees into a single "Advertising and Public Relations" degree. The market has not yet generated a more-or-less distinct demand for public relations practitioners. Many regions completely lack examples of public relations practice, with no professional public relations agencies whose functions are performed by advertising agencies (Kazakova & Feoktistov, 2012). According to the report on public relations in the Russian regions for 2013 that was written by the Russian branch of the Association of International Communications Consultancy Organizations (AICCO), few agencies provide only public relations. Even when agencies declare public relations service, they, in fact, conduct a complex of services in marketing communication and advertising (Consulting Companies in Public Relations, Annual Report of Consulting Companies in Public Relations, 2013). The report also demonstrates the most common specializations of public relations practice among members of the AICCO in Russia in 2013. They are presented here in descending order by popularity (demand): (1) corporate communication (including areas of reputation, corporate social responsibility, media relations, and philanthropy), (2) crisis communication, (3) marketing communication, (4) digital communication, (5) communication research and analysis, (6) public affairs and government relations, (7) internal and employee communications, (8) cross-related and other, (9) territory branding, (10) financial communications and investment relations, and (11) political communications (Consulting Companies in Public Relations, Annual Report of Consulting Companies in Public Relations, 2013, p. 50).

Recently, there has been a significant decline in the popularity of political public relations, which was in high demand in the early stages of the institutionalization of Russia public relations. The current substantial demand in marketing communication (in third place, according the report) fits well with the content of the current Advertising and Public Relations program, where marketing issues take significant part.

Development of research in public relations

The public relations school at St. Petersburg State University, headed by Marina Shishkina, is one of the best known in Russia. It is based on these principles:

- Communicative, information basis of public relations
- Priority in studying information basics of public relations practitioners' daily activity
- Description of PRology as a basic academic discipline
- Standardized system of academic categories
- Recognition of the existence of public relations as a particular social institution in its continuous development (Krivonosov et al., 2010, p. 8).

The St. Petersburg school has developed the system of academic categories of PRology (the science of public relations). Here are a few PRology terms: "publicity capital", "social communication", and "public relations as engineering activity". Publicity capital is image capital or reputation capital (as cited in Krivonosov et al., 2010). Social communication is an activity defined by the system of social standards and assessments, samples, and rules of communication, accepted in a given society (Krivonosov, 2010). According to Shishkina (1999), "public relations as an engineering activity" or a technological ("socio-engineering") approach is required for theoretical justification, because any public relations practice represents development and implementation of specific technical solutions for the design, for example, of public relations campaigns, image creation, or transformation of public opinion. The basic knowledge of public relations includes technological knowledge, a variety of techniques, and social technologies (Shishkina, 1999). Pellenen (2005), Makarevich (1999), and Poverinov (2000) have also contributed to the conceptualization of the "technological" approach to public relations. Pellenen (2005) divided all public relations technologies into management, publicity-type, and communication. Makarevich (1999) said the technological approach considers public relations as management technologies and the technologies of influencing people. Poverinov (2000) noted that the technological or applied approach manifests itself when public relations is presented as a tool for the implementation of certain tasks. In fact, the technological approach is a pragmatic approach to public relations, the downside of which is that its perception is limited to purely technical aspects. Meanwhile, as of December 2019, 535 articles from among 4,949 available on *eLibrary* with the word "public relations" (and other ones synonymous to public relations) in their titles also included the word "technology". For comparison, 24 articles in the same sample had the word "strategic" in the titles. Thus, in this sample of works available on *eLibrary* for 1991–2019, the number of articles dealing with technical aspects of public relations prevails over the number of articles in which, for example, public relations is seen as strategic communication. The analysis of Advertising and Public Relations undergraduate curricula has also shown an interest in the "technological" approach of Russian educators, which is reflected in the titles of these courses: "Effective Communication Technologies", "Election Technologies", "Public Opinion Management Technologies", and "Public Relations Technologies".

As for publication activity of Russian scholars in public relations, their articles, unfortunately, are rarely visible in the international arena because of their poor proficiency in academic English or their inability to meet the requirements of the international academic journals.

Publishing of articles on public relations in Russian academic journals is not simple as well. The Russian Communication Association (RCA) has worked on making achievements of Russian communication scholars known to the international public for several years. The RCA's official journal, *Russian Journal of Communication* (published by Routledge–Taylor & Francis), has already gained recognition in the Western academic community due to the dedicated work of the Association.

There are still no specialized journals in public relations in the Russian language. Therefore, Russian scholars publish their articles in journals having a cross-disciplinary focus or that specialize in journalism, linguistics, philology, economics, or sociology, such as *Vestnik of Moscow University (Series: Journalism), Vestnik of Public Opinion, Medi@lmanah, Mediaskop, Information Society, Journal of Sociology and Social Anthropology, Society. Environment. Development.*

Since 2013, a peer-reviewed journal, *Kommunikologiya*, which is not yet included in the list of VAK[6]-approved scholarly journals, has been issued in Russia. VAK-approved journals are considered to be the leading academic journals in Russia. Meanwhile, these journals are also called "controversial" because of VAK's ambiguous selection requirements. In addition, most journals listed by VAK are not indexed in international bibliographic databases. However, they are included in the Russian electronic database *eLibrary.ru*, which provides data on the impact factor called Science Index (RINTS)[7] for journals, authors, and organizations.

The analysis of scholarly publication dynamics on public relations is the best way to characterize the state of research. I have used the databases of *eLibrary* and *the Science Index (RINTS)* to find articles, dissertations, and books that mention the word "public relations" (and other words synonymous with public relations) in keywords and titles.

As a result, the Russian *eLibrary* and *Science Index (RINZ)* has displayed the following data: the number of dissertations in 1991–2003—36; in 2004–2008—122; in 2009–2013—79; in 2014–2019—167; the number of articles in 1991–2003—32; in 2004–2008—324; in 2009–2013—1,116; in 2014–2019—3,477; the number of textbooks in 1991–2003—59; in 2004–2008—247; in 2009–2013—362; and 2014–2019—333.

Therefore, the mid-2000s saw a significant increase in Russian public relations scholarship. Presently, there is a decrease in publications compared with that period, indicating that a deeper consideration of challenges and advancements in the profession and science of public relations has occurred.

Features of public relations research in post-Soviet Russia

Localization of academic discussion

One of the features and, at the same time, challenges of public relations studies is that many Russian scholars have low interest in international publications. They prefer to publish their articles in Russian-language journals. Another reason for localization is that only the universities in the major cities subscribe to international databases of academic publications that would motivate faculty members to publish articles in foreign journals. A degree of autonomy (localization) of Russian scholars is reflected in their references. The majority of references are in the Russian language only. Moreover, the structure and volume of the articles by Russian scholars often do not comply with requirements of international journals. Of course, all of these factors make it practically impossible for the international public to become familiar with Russian scholarship in public relations.

Prevailing philosophical understanding of public relations and high level of theorization

Kuzheleva-Sagan (2005a, 2006b), Savrutskaya (2008), and Klyagin and Shipunova (2013) pay particular attention to the sociophilosophical understanding of public relations and its conceptualization. Research in public relations that has been undertaken by Russian scholars often has represented a simple description of Western theories (Zaitsev, A., 2013a; Zaitsev, A., 2013b). One of the most debatable issues of Russian public relations research remains, *"How to define PR?"*. Kuzheleva-Sagan (2006b) explains this as the Russian intellectual and philosophical tradition that focuses on "learning of universal laws of 'mysteries of life' and is strong in its conceptualizing and abstractive features" (p. 113).

Interpretative approaches rather than objective worldview

Highly theorized and descriptive articles by Russian public relations scholars are a direct consequence of the lack of cooperation between the academic community and public relations practitioners. Quantitative methods based on surveys of public relations practitioners are normal for Western public relations scholars. Russian public relations scholars prefer qualitative methods because of their long-time commitment to conceptual, rather than applied, research.

Multitude approaches from social sciences versus communication's methodological paradigm

Because Russian scholars came to public relations from different areas of the social sciences and because communication studies has not been a part of formal Russian higher education, the methodology of public relations research is extremely multidisciplinary. As a result, communication theory approaches are less applied by Russian scholars than are those in the social sciences. Basically, Russian scholars use a multitude of methods from, for example, sociology, political science, linguistics, and philosophy. The methods of these studies are usually used: culture studies (Borisov), sociology (Fedotova, Shishkina), communication (Zverintsev, Pocheptsov), and conflict management (Vuima, Lukashev, Ponidelko, Olshevskiy) (Shelep, 2013).

Old models for understanding of public relations prevail in Russian academic discourse

At present, a strategic perspective on public relations is significantly underestimated in Russian academic articles, compared to that in Western countries where it has become prevailing in the academic and professional spheres. The purely Russian "technological" approach to public relations is quite widespread domestically, despite the fact that it corresponds to the old model of public relations, that is, the press agentry/publicity model. The situation gets worse in terms of the progress of Russian public relations in higher education due to "obsolete" ideas that sometimes appear in the curricula. Thus, public relations' relatively young age in Russia has prevented a high level of research. Today, the Russian academic school of public relations has certain "teething" problems that are inherent in the transition period of the country that it is expected to overcome someday.

The impact of the Soviet past on contemporary public relations higher education

Centralized public relations curriculum and centralized communication between the state and a university

The Soviet past is a complex set of ideas that is an integral part of Russian culture. Describing the development of communication in Russia, Beebe and Matyash (2003) have rightly observed: "… the present is shaped by the past" (p. 15). Contemporary higher education in Russia has inherited elements of the Soviet system of education. It is characterized by such features as centralized management, flow-cluster-type organization of the educational process, and government regulation and control. The significant changes in the structure and content of the higher education system in post-Soviet Russia are primarily the result of government reforms that have occurred within the past more than 20 years. A contemporary Advertising and Public Relations curriculum can be called *centralized,* because of the government's key role in its design. The Ministry of Education and Science of the Russian Federation states that the educational program should include compulsory and elective (selective) courses. For example, according to the existing curriculum of the Advertising and Public Relations undergraduate program of the Altai Academy of Economics and Law, elective disciplines account for 34.6%, which is half less than the number of compulsory disciplines. As a result, course selection has been limited and constrained by the government regulation.

The centralized communication between the state and universities from the Soviet legacy is consistent with the system of values of Russians. Professor Yasin wrote that the system of values of Russians is "more inclined to the order, hierarchy and less to rights and freedoms of the individual" (as cited in Yadov, 2009, p. 19). In this context of a hierarchy-based organizational structure of a university, that is, a "knowledge-transmitting approach" in teaching (Matyash, 2003), a centralized curriculum is accepted by Russians with tolerance due to sociocultural practices and traditions that have been left from Soviet times.

An institutional inertia of public relations education in regions of Russia

A distinctive feature of post-Soviet countries, according to political analysts, is a radical gap between the major cities and provinces (Yadov, 2007). Moscow and St. Petersburg are the leading centers of public relation education (Tsetsura, 2003). For example, about 20 universities in St. Petersburg offer Advertising and Public Relations degrees. Substantially regional universities offer a lower quality of public relations education than do some universities in the major cities of Russia. In opinion polls, Moscow and St. Petersburg are usually considered more pro-Western cities. Institutional development in Russian regions is mostly affected by Soviet traditions, values, and attitudes. The phenomenon of inertia of institutional development in the major cities and on their peripheries has been called "Mexicanization" in sociology, similar to that of the life of Mexican peasants, most of whom live like hundreds of years ago, whereas most of the population of Mexico is Americanized (Yadov, 2007).

Today, regional universities are facing many difficulties that Moscow and St. Petersburg universities have already experienced. Limited employment and an insufficient number of well-trained teachers specializing in public relations are current challenges that regional universities are facing today. The majority of the faculty in the regional universities have a social sciences, journalism, or philology background. The absence of rotation leads to the fact that the faculty has already educated several "generations" of public relations practitioners. Another problem is insufficient involvement of public relations practitioners in the teaching process, due to their lack of enthusiasm to educate students. The difference in access to different education opportunities and the amount of financial resources available for universities in the major cities and regions is striking. For example, Advertising and Public Relations programs in leading Moscow universities provide courses taught by guest lecturers, visiting scholars from Europe and from the United States, international exchange programs, grants, conferences, and internship in the offices of international agencies such as BBDO and Ogilvy. These opportunities are not available to Advertising and Public Relations students in the regions.

The quality of applicants and their geographical distribution throughout universities in Russia also increases the gap between higher education in the major cities and the regions. Students with high USE scores[8] apply to the leading universities in Moscow and St. Petersburg. Upon graduation, they usually stay in those cities due to more employment opportunities than in the regions from where they come. Thus, the gap between the level of public relations education in the regions and in major cities of Russia ("Mexicanization") is a typical example of institutional inertia. The higher education system in Russian regions shows inhibited institutionalization due to universities' weak academic connections with those in the major cities and throughout the rest world. There is a high probability that regional universities will maintain the academic traditions of the old school of public relations for some time.

Multidisciplinary nature of advertising and public relations curriculum

Academic standards of Soviet education assumed that a graduate would be a person with high morals. The intelligent educational tradition in the Soviet Union implied the inclusion of a curriculum having a wide range of liberal arts and social sciences disciplines, prompting the belief among foreigners that they could discuss any topic with a Russian. Since the Soviet period, the fundamental nature of education has become a sign of the quality of higher education. The Soviet principles of higher education that were reflected in public relations curricula of the 1990s included a wide range of liberal arts and social sciences disciplines, in addition to public relations and communication-related courses. The same refers to current Advertising and Public Relations curricula that, in addition, becomes more diverse in curricular content. Consequently, a solid foundation of general knowledge courses and the multifaceted content of the curriculum are consistent with Soviet beliefs of what constitutes the best academic education.

Ethical controversy in the scholarship and practice of public relations in Russia

The old understanding of public relations as one-way communication can be observed in the post-Soviet Russian public relations practice and academy. On one hand, modern public relations practice in Russia has become noticeably more civilized than in the early 2000s. On the other hand, some books and university website descriptions of public relations sometimes contain a completely distorted and outdated understanding of public relations as a tool of propaganda and public opinion manipulation. Unfortunately, the booming business literature that has catchy titles, such as *PR: White and Black: Technology for Hidden People Control*, misleads even more. One reason for the existence of early interpretations of public relations is the ethical controversy in understanding what public relations is. Kuzheleva-Sagan (2005a) noted that some Russian scholars consider that, "in the situation of severe political and economic competition, ethical public relations is not in demand" and accuse others of "over-idealization and 'sterilization' of students views of PR" (p. 85).

Thus, the existence of a large gap between the standard of public relations in the classic sense (in Russia, this is the Black Public Relations definition) and the actual practice of public relations in Russia leads to a double standard that has been caused by the collision of values of civilized society with values of the transition society that is modern Russia.

Social values and beliefs of the Russian academic community as representation of historical legacy

Institutionalization of public relations as an academic field is determined by daily human interaction. Greif (1997) indicated that "current values are a product of current behavior and past values" (p. 31). In the post-Soviet societies, a combination of "old" communist values and "new" capitalist values is most pronounced (Kyriazis & Zouboulakis, 2005). Shtompka (2001) supposed that the combination of traditional and modern values is typical for transition economies, calling this phenomenon "cultural trauma of the transitional period". Matyash (2003) highlighted some "old" behavior models of Russian educators, such as a "status-oriented" approach to teamwork and "social passivity". I would emphasize a few more, one being *traditionalism (orientation on the past)*. The process of leaving the past and meeting the requirements of a new day has been painful for Russian educators. For example, conservative behavior manifested itself in 2008 in the discussions of the state standard for a third generation of the Advertising and Public Relations program.

Academicians showed an intent to leave the former discipline titles the same as they were before, because they "have been established in terms of terminology" (Fedotova, 2008, p. 16). In fact, the result of this collective traditionalism is disappointing and counterproductive. The comparison of current Advertising and Public Relations undergraduate curricula of the different Russian universities has made clear a uniformity of titles of general knowledge and core courses, despite the fact that the third-generation standards provide a list of mandatory courses just with approximate titles (Solovey, 2010).

Another behavioral pattern that influences the structural changes of Russian society in general and the institute of education in particular is the *priority of human development over professional development*. In hindsight, the academic tradition of the priority of moral qualities over professionalism was inherited from the Soviet era. Today, students' personal qualities still value more than their knowledge gained. Weak professional skills are forgiven and justified. Thus, the old modes of thinking among Russian educators contradict rational ideas and healthy competition in the civilized public relations market.

Due to the reasons mentioned earlier, it seems that the institutional development of public relations education is determined by the logic of "path-dependence". Nee and Cao (1999) considered "path-dependence" as "the mechanisms that reproduce and perpetuate core features of the preexisting social order" (p. 800). The "preexisting social order" indications concerning public relations education in Russia include the following: critical role of the government in curriculum design; the inhibited institutionalization of public relations education in the regions; Soviet standards to the content of higher education; and the outdated understanding of public relations and old mental models among public relations educators and practitioners.

Genesis of public relations education in Russia in the multicultural and global context

The trend towards internationalization of education in the late 20th–early 21st centuries has been observed almost everywhere, including in Russia. The fall of the Iron Curtain made possible free and open communication and intensified international communication, including in the field of higher education.

At the initial development stage of public relations as an academic field, the Russian developers have adapted their educational programs under the U.S. model:

> The first Russian university-based degree program in public relations was established in 1993 at the St. Petersburg State Electrotechnical University. Modeled on the undergraduate degree program at Towson State University in the United States, it was approved by the Russian Ministry of Higher Education.
>
> (Azarova, 2003)

A great help in launching of the first public relations program in the Moscow State Institute of International Relations (MSIIR) in 1991 was provided by U.S. universities, private foundations, and government agencies such as the United States Information Service and PRSA (Guth, 2000). The Russian first course of study in public relations at the MSIIR was based on U.S. textbooks, granted by PRSA (Ewing, 2005).

Textbooks by Cutlip, Center, and Broom (2000) *Effective Public Relations*, and Newsom, Turk, and Kruckeberg (2001) *This is PR: The realities of public relations* had become the most popular ones for instruction among Russian educators in early 2000s.

The U.S. contribution to development of public relations education in Russia has been significant, but the ideas of the European school have also been recognized by Russian scholars. The commitment to U.S. or European school of public relations is most evident in academic discussion of Russian scholars about "What is PR?". For instance, Golubkov (1994) defined public relations as a part of marketing activities, while Yakovlev (1995) defined it as "a management activity, related to establishing of favorable (harmonious) relations through communications between the organization and the social environ-ment (the public)". In fact, the above-mentioned perspectives demonstrate the "selling" (known as the functional perspective) and "socializing" (known as the relational approach) approaches to understanding of public relations (Shelep, 2010, p. 74). Business- or communication-oriented departments in public relations in Russian universities reflect one of these perspectives (Tsetsura, 2004). Moreover, Russian scholars have close associations of "selling" (func-tional perspective) and "socializing" (relational perspective) approaches with U.S. and European public relations schools, respectively. T. Lebedeva (2011), described the European public relations as follows: "In Europe, public relations has always been seen as a tool for fostering a climate of confidence, consensus in the society" (p. 18). Bentele (2004) underlined the difference between the European and U.S. schools of public relations in following way: "…what impact or which function all organizational activities of all public relations departments of all organizations and all public relations firms in a society have on society seems to be a typical European question rather than an American one" (p. 488). Krivonosov (2010), a representative of the St. Petersburg school of public relations, said: "Russian public relations is … closer to the European public relations: I do believe that it is humane and humanistic, not a common 'maid of business', as it is preached across the ocean".

The continuity of the European and Russian schools of public relations is clearly recognized in Russian academic literature. However, the fact that U.S. scholars have never denied a social orientation of public relations often has been unseen by Russian scholars. For example, Newsom, Turk, and Kruckeberg (2001) considered public relations as professional activity in which public goals prevail over personal ones.

Thus, Russian scholars have these stereotypical judgments about public relations: the values of humanism associated with the period of Enlightenment relates to Europe and the materialistic view of public relations refers to the values of the United States. The "socializing" perspective of public relations has been reflected in courses in current Advertising and Public Relations curricula, which comprise, for example: "Social Advertising and PR", "Social Engineering in the Area of Public Affairs", and "Social Problems in the Mass Media". In scholarly studies, the "socializing" approach also appears as follows: from the 1,099 articles for 1991–2014 with the word "public relations" (and other words that are synonymous to it) in the titles on *eLibrary*, 444 articles include the word "social". This is three times more than, for example, the number of articles within the same sample containing word "management". Thus, in Russian public relations education and research framework, the social aspect of public relations is relevant.

The foundations for ideological continuity between Russian and the European schools of public relations were laid in the late 1990s and early 2000s. Thanks to the efforts of T. Lebedeva, French textbooks of public relations became available at the end of the 1990s in Russia. Moreover, the names of Phillip Buari, Zhak Segela, and Zhan-Pier Boduan became recognizable brands for public relations practitioners. Among well-known public relations textbooks by French authors in Russian are Boduan's (2001) *Management of Company's Image: PR: The Object and Mastery* and Buari's (2001) *Public Relations or Strategy of Trust*.

France and the Russian regions of Southern Ural, Perm, and Kaliningrad have joint projects in public relations education. They include lectures by distinguished French public relations scholars and practitioners, summer schools, workshops, and internships for Russian educators in France and training program for Russian government officials.

The humanistic tradition of European public relations has been brought to Russia by Buari's *Public Relations or Trust Strategies* as well as Black's *Public Relations: What Is It?* Black's definition that public relations "…is art and science of achieving harmony by means of mutual understanding, based on the truth and complete information awareness" is considered a "classic" one. The book *Public Relations: What Is It?* became the first textbook translated into Russian that was available in the country (Black, 1989).

Among the "classic" definitions of public relations and the most cited by Russian scholars are by Rex Harlow, the International Assembly of National PR Associations in Mexico, Public Relations Society of America (PRSA), British Institute for Public Relations (IPR), Webster's New International Dictionary, and L. Matra, European Confederation of Public Relations (CERP) (Kuzheleva-Sagan, 2005b).

In addition to an historical continuity of the Russian academy with the European school of public relations, Russia's integration in the European arena for higher education within the Bologna Process has reinforced student and professional exchanges. Fedotova (2008) expressed the Russian educators' enthusiasm for the participation of Russia in the Bologna Process as follows:

> The uniformity of academic disciplines is among other things required for exchanging students in Russia, or to the maximum in the European

environment. In the future, we'll need a list of majors, programs, and discipline names that will be uniform with Europe.

Throughout this time, however, Russian public relations scholars and practitioners have begun to realize that Western examples cannot always be applied to the Russian reality. In practice, specific forms are distant from Western standards for public relations. Erzikova (2013) described the process of adaptation of Western public relations in Russia thus: "Western 'ways of doing PR' have infiltrated Russian PR field, simultaneously changing it and mutating under the field's influence" (p. 252).

Critical analysis of Western theories and definitions of public relations has played an important role in the establishment of the identity of the Russian public relations school. Kuzheleva-Sagan (2005a) indicated that several studies contained the analysis of Russian scholars' attitudes to "classical" Western definitions of public relations. As a result, Kuzheleva-Sagan (2005a) identified three approaches: "pragmatic" (definitions are too altruistic, naïve, not applicable in practice); "compromise" (tolerance to classic definitions); "altruistic" (classic definitions applicable in practice). In this context, she stated that:

> neither deep pragmatism, nor conscious conformism …, nor deliberate idealization and "sterilization" of views do not correspond to the objectives of higher public relations education, aimed at its own researching and professional positions, on the basis of broad and deep knowledge in the field of social, life and formal sciences …
>
> (p. 85)

Gradually, Russian educators have given their preference to national public relations cases studies. If, in the 1990s, Russian educators preferred textbooks by Western authors (Black, 1989; Newsom, Turk, & Kruckeberg, 2001; Boduan, 2001; Buari, 2001), from the early 2000s, they stared to trust Russian textbooks (Ignatiev, Beketov, & Sarokvasha, 2002; Chumikov, & Bocharov, 2006; Krivonosov, Shishkina, & Filatova, 2010).

Thus, a multicultural and global context as the background for the development of public relations education in Russia has contributed to the adaptation of Western public relations theory to the Russian reality in specific way. The influence of the European (particularly, French) public relations schools was more intense. History has proven that Russia has continually demonstrated a desire to become a "European country". On the one hand, the commitment of the Russian public relations academy to the European "socializing" approach to public relations is evident by factual academic links, with some European countries and joint area of higher education within the Bologna Process. On the other hand, Russians' affinity with the European school of public relations is partly determined by stereotypical judgments about the European understanding of public relations from "the humanistic perspective" only.

The formation of a national public relation school in Russia is a consequence of opposing forces, including globalization and differentiation that have affected the higher education sphere. The reliance on the national differences of Russian public relations scholarship has been an important condition to find out its own identity. The inertial or inhibited institutionalization of public relations in post-Soviet Russia becomes evident in its efforts to catch up to the countries that have advanced public relations practice.

Meanwhile, to become a recognizable member of the world academic community, Russian scholars must free themselves from misunderstanding, national stereotypes, and outdated notions and must keep up with global changes in public relations theory, ceasing a commitment to a particular country or continent approach. For internationalizing the Russian public relations curriculum, domestic scholars should learn not only from one part of the world (Toth & Aldoory, 2010).

Conclusion

The genesis of the institutionalization of public relations as a discipline has been based on an historical analysis of the processes in Russian higher education, in particular the accreditation of a university degree; textbooks and books publishing; and formation of a national academic school.

The functioning of the public relations education system in post-Soviet Russia is a path-dependent process. This study has emphasized specific characteristics of the national higher education system and their relationship to the Soviet past. As an outcomes of the Soviet legacy, these characteristics explain the inertia of the institutionalization of public relations in Russia: centralized communication between the state and universities; traditions of "classical higher education" realized in the Advertising and Public Relations program; in some cases, an outdated understanding of public relations; and the gap between the quality of higher education in Russian regions and that of the capital cities.

However, the influence of both European and U.S. schools has had a significant impact on the evolution of public relations in post-Soviet Russia. Due to global integration, the geopolitical, cultural, and, to some extent, stereotypical thinking, European public relations traditions correspond more closely to Russian social values. As a result, the identity of Russian public relations education is a blend of Western and Russian approaches. The old understanding of public relations as press agentry and the lack of agreement on professional ethical questions in the academy and in the public relations industry are indications of the still young stage of public relations as a practice and a discipline in post-Soviet Russia.

Due to multicultural influences, critical thinking of Western experience, and the ongoing demand for marketing public relations in Russia, the emergence of the Advertising and Public Relations program has been a logical consequence. It remains unknown whether this "joint" program will continue or becomes just a trend in education. The multidisciplinary, eclectic nature of the program and its increased focus on marketing and communication disciplines create unique conditions for the development of integrated communication in Russia, in which a special role should be strategic public relations.

While U.S. and European scholars consider integrated communication as "encroachment" on public relations' territory (Grunig & Grunig, 1998; Gruning & Gruning, 1991; Lauzen, 1991; Hutton, 2010; Hallahan, 2007), the idea of combining marketing (advertising) and public relations functions through the introduction of a unified degree did not cause a long-lasting dispute in the Russian academic community. Thus, the development of integrated communication as a discipline and a practice has favorable chances in Russia. The first step in this direction was the first admission to an Integrated Communication Master's degree program at the Higher School of Economics in 2013.

Thus, the historical legacy and a specific multicultural and global context have contributed to the current state of public relations education in Russia. The state of the public relations discipline represents a mix of new and old and global and local sociocultural traditions and practices that incorporated, in a literal sense, an "integrated" Advertising and Public Relations degree.

Notes

1 Sam Black was a British theorist of public relations, whose *Public Relations: What Is It?* (Black, S., 1989) was translated into Russian in the early 1990s in Russia. Thus, the textbook became widely recognizable among pioneers of and firstcomers into Public Relations in Russia.
2 Tatyana Lebedeva is a professor of Moscow State University and a well-known Russian pioneer of international public relations and advertising. In Russia, she popularized European Public Relations (especially French PR theorists) through collaborative publishing projects for academia.
3 eLibrary is the largest digital library of scholarly publications in Russia. The platform eLibrary.ru was established in 1999 and is administered by the Ministry of Education and Science of the Russian Federation. It is a free public tool for the measurement and analysis of publication activities of scholars and organizations.
4 Special terminology of the Ministry of Education and Science under the higher education reform in Russia.
5 The choice of suggested disciplines for these modules is up to the universities, and the titles of the disciplines may also vary.
6 Higher Attestation Commission (VAK) is a national government agency that sets standards for the awarding of advanced academic degrees.
7 The Russian Science Citation Index is a national information and analytics system that has accumulated more than 2 million publications by Russian authors, as well as information about citing of these publications obtained from over 3,300 Russian magazines. The Science Index (RINTS) is integrated with eLibrary. Some publishers, for various reasons, do not provide information to the RINTS. For this reason, the system provides approximate data for a number of publications.
8 The Unified State Exam (USE)—an exam in secondary schools held in a centralized way in the Russian Federation. It simultaneously serves as a school graduation exam and as an entrance examination in higher education institutions.

References

Azarova, L., & Shishkin, D. (1998). Potencialnaya potrebnost v specialistah po svyazyam s obshchestvennostyu: opyt-ehmpiricheskogo-issledovaniya [Prospective demand for practitioners of public relations: Experience of empirical research]. *Chelovek v kontekste kultury*, 102–111.

Azarova, L. (2003). Public relations higher education—A Russian experience. *Higher Education in Europe, 28*(4), 495–498.

Beebe, S., Kharcheva, M., & Kharcheva, V. (1998). Speech communication in Russia. *Communication Education, 47*(3), 261–273.

Beebe, S., & Matyash, O. (2003). Making global links with Russian communication educators: Establishing networks between Russian and non-Russian communication educators and researchers. Electronic conference proceedings: *Communication and culture in a networked world*. World Communication Association 17th Biennial Conference. Stockholm, SE: Haninge.

Bentele, G. (2004). New perspectives of public relations in Europe. In B. van Ruler & D. Vercic (Eds.), *Public relations and communication management in Europe: A nation-by-nation introduction to public relations theory and practice* (pp. 485–496). Berlin: Walter de Gruyter.

Bergelson, M. (1998). Publichnaya kommunikaciya kak problema socialnogo partnerstva v sovremennoj Rossii [Public communication as an issue of social partnership in contemporary Russia]. Conference proceedings: *Grazhdanskoe obshchestvo: Perspektivy razvitiya*, 115–124.

Black, S. (1989). Блэк C. *Pablik rilejshnz: chto ehto takoe? [Public relations: What is this?]* Moscow: Modino-press.

Bocharov, M. (2007) *Istoriya pablik rileyshnz: nravy, biznes, nauka [History of public relations: Customs, business, science]*. Moscow: RIP-Kholding.

Boduan, J. (2001). *Upravlenie imidzhem kompanii pablik rilejshnz predmet i masterstvo [Management of company's image. PR: the object and mastery]*. Moscow: Infra-M.

Buari, F. A. (2001). *Pablik rilejshnz ili strategiya doveriya [Public relations or strategy of trust]*. Moscow: Infra-M, Imidzh-kontakt.

Consulting Companies in Public Relations, Annual report of Consulting Companies in Public Relations (2013). Retrieved from www.akospr.ru/wp-content/uploads/2014/01/ACOS_GO_2013_A4-prew.pdf.

Chumikov, A., & Bocharov, M. (2006). *Svyazi s obshchestvennostyu. Teoriya i praktika [Public Relations. Theory and Practice]*. Moscow: Delo.

Chumikov, A., & Bocharov, M. (2009) *Aktualnye svyazi s obshchestvennostyu. [Topical Public Relations]*. Moscow: Yurayt.

Clarke, T. (2000). An inside look at Russian public relations. *Public Relations Quarterly, 45*(1), 18–22.

Cutlip, S. M., Center, A. H., & Broom, G. M. (2000). *Effective public relations.* Upper Saddle River, NJ: Prentice-Hall.

Erzikova, E. (2013). Shaken, not stirred: Western public relations practices in Russia. *Russian Journal of Communication, 5*(3), 252–263.

Ewing, M. (2005, October). Russia's father of public relations shares insight and inspiration with U.S. college students. *Public Relations Tactics, 12*(10), 22.

Federal State Educational Standard of Higher Professional Education for undergraduate degree in Advertising and Public Relations authorized by the Ministry of

Education and Science of Russian Federation in 2010. [Official document]. (2010). Retrieved from www.edu.ru/db-mon/mo/Data/d_10/prm221-1.pdf.

Golubkov, E. (1994). *Marketing: Slovar [Marketing: Dictionary]*. Moscow: Ekonomika, Delo.

Greif, A. (1997). On the interrelations and economic implications of economic, social, political, and normative factors: Reflections from two late medieval societies. In J. N. Drobak & J. V. C. Nye (Eds.). *The frontiers of the new institutional economics* (pp. 57–84). San Diego, CA: Academic Press.

Fedotova, L. (2008). Novyj standart: vozmozhnaya pravka [The new standard: A possibility of modification]. *Mediaskop, 2*, 13–18.

Grunig, J., & Grunig, L. (1991). Conceptual differences in public relations and marketing: The case of health-care organizations. *Public Relations Review, 17*(3), 257–327.

Grunig, J., & Grunig, L. (1998). The relationship between public relations and marketing in excellent organizations: Evidence from the IABC study. *Journal of Marketing Communications, 4*(3), 141–162.

Guth, D. (2000). The emergence of public relations in the Russian Federation. *Public Relations Review, (2)*26, 191–207.

Hallahan, K. (2007). Integrated Communication: Implications for public relations beyond excellence. In E. L. Toth (Ed.), *The future of excellence in public relations and communication management* (pp. 299–336). Mahwah, NJ: Lawrence Erlbaum Associates.

Hutton, J. (2010). Defining the relationship between public relationship and marketing. In R. Heath (Ed.), *The Sage handbook of public relations* (pp. 509–523). Thousand Oaks, CA: Sage.

Ignatiev, D., Beketov, A., & Sarokvasha, F. (2002). *Nastolnaya ehnciklopediya public relations [Handbook of Public Relations]*. Moscow: Alpina-pablisher.

Kashkin, V. (2014). Russian communication studies: A semi-clandestine science. *Russian Journal of Communication, 6*(1), 89–92.

Kazakova, E., & Feoktistov, V. (2012). Public relations are phenomenon of 20th Century. *Proceedings of International Scientific and Applied Conference of Topical Issues of Social Sciences and Humanities: Part 5* (pp. 31–33). Penza: Social Technologies & Philology.

Klyagin, S., & Shipunova, O. (Eds.). (2013). *Filosofiya kommunikatsii: problemy i perspektivy. Monographiya. [Philosophy of communication: Challenges and perspectives. Monograph]*. Saint-Petersburg: Izdatelstvo politekhnicheskogo universiteta.

Krivonosov, A. (2010). Onlayn-konferentsiya Alekseya Dmitrievicha Krivonosova. [Online conference with A. D. Krivonosov]. Retrieved from www.raso.ru/conferences/conference166.html.

Krivonosov, A., Shishkina, M., & Filatova, O. (2010). *Osnovy teorii svyazej s obshchestvennostyu.* [Basics of public relations theory]. Saint-Petersburg: Piter.

Kryaklina, T. (2012). Integrirovannaya tekhnologiya proektirovaniya osnovnykh obrazovatel'nykh programm bakalavrov [Integrated technology of basic bachelor degree programs design]. *Vestnik Altayskoy akademii ekonomiki i prava, 3*, 128–131.

Kuzheleva-Sagan, I. (2005a). Aktualnost filosofskoj verifikacii fenomena pablik rilejshnz [The urgency of philosophical verification of public relations phenomena]. *Vestnik Tomskogo gosudarstvennogo universiteta, 286*, 84–89.

Kuzheleva-Sagan, I. (2005b). Problema mnogoobraziya ponyatiynoy sfery pablik rileyshnz [The issue of the variety of public relations definitions]. *Vestnik Tomskogo gosudarstvennogo universiteta, 286*, 89–96.

Kuzheleva-Sagan, I. (2006a). Aktualnost rekonstruirovaniya genezisa pablik rilejshnz i osnovaniya dlya klassifikacii istoricheski versij PR [The urgency of reconstruction of public relations genesis and foundations for classification of historical versions of PR]. *Vestnik YuUrGU. Seriya Sotsial'no-gumanitarnye nauki, 8*(63), 17–20.

Kuzheleva-Sagan, I. (2006b). Osnovnye issledovatelskic paradigmy v sfere teorii kommunikacii socialno filosofskij aspekt [Major research paradigms in the sphere of communication theory: Sociophilosophical aspect]. *Vestnik TGPU. Seriya: Gumanitarnye nauki, 7*(58), 106–117.

Kyriazis, N., & Zouboulakis, M. (2005). Modeling institutional change in transition economies. *Communist and Post-Communist Studies, 38*(1), 109–120.

Lauzen, M. (1991). Imperialism and encroachment in public relations. *Public Relations Review, 17*(3), 245–255.

Lebedeva, T. (1996). *Iskusstvo obolshcheniya. Pablik rilejshnz po-francuzski. Koncepcii. Praktika [The art of enticement. Public Relations in French. Concepts. Practice].* Moscow: Izdatelstvo moskovskogo universiteta.

Lebedeva, T. (2011). Tatyana Lebedeva otvetila na voprosy almatinskikh studentov. [Interview of Tatyana Lebedeva with students from Alma-Ata]. Retrieved from www.blogpr.ru/node/3297.

Makarevich, E. (1999). *Obshchestvennye svyazi kak instrument sotsial'nykh izmeneniy. [Public relations as a tool of social changes].* (Doctoral thesis, Institut molodezhi, Moscow, RU). Retrieved from https://dlib.rsl.ru/01000242403.

Matyash, O. (2002). Communication studies and their role in a changing Russia. *Proceedings of the Russian Communication Association International Conference: Communicating Across Differences, Vol. 2* (pp. 171–174). Pyatigorsk, RU: Russian Communication Association. Retrieved from http://www.russcomm.ru/eng/rca_biblio/m/matyash04_eng.shtml.

Matyash, O. (2003). The challenges of establishing a new discipline: Introducing communication studies in Russian higher education. Paper presented at the National Communication Association Convention, Miami Beach, FL.

Matyash, O. (2004). Plyuralizm kak sostoyanie i printsip razvitiya sovremennogo kommunikativnogo znaniya. [Pluralism as condition and development of contemporary knowledge of communication]. *Proceedings of the Russian-U.S. scientific school and seminar* (pp. 6–8). Moscow, RU: Print Media. Retrieved from http://www.russcomm.ru/rca_biblio/m/matyash09.shtml.

Matyash, O., & Beebe, S. (2003). Kommunikativnoe obrazovanie v Rossii: istoriya i sovremennost' [Communicative education in Russia: Past and present. Siberia. Philosophy. Education]. *Sibir'. Filosofiya. Obrazovanie, 7,* 60–76.

McElreath, M., Chen, N., Azariva, L., & Shadrova, V. (2001). The development of public relations in China, Russia, and the United States. In R. L. Heath (Ed.), *Handbook of public relations* (pp. 665–673). Thousand Oaks, CA: Sage Publications.

Medinskiy, V. (2010). *Osobennosti natsional'nogo piara. PRavdivaya istoriya Rusi ot Ryurika do Petra. [Specificity of national public relations. Truth story of Russia: From Ryurik to Peter the I].* Moscow: Olma Media Grupp.

Moiseeva, V. (1997). Razvitie rossijskogo rnka svyazej s obshchestvennostyu [Development of Russian market of public relations]. *Marketing i marketingovye issledovaniya v Rossii, 5,* 6–15.

Nee, V., & Cao, Y. (1999). Path dependent societal transformation: Stratification in hybrid mixed economies. *Theory and Society, 28*(6), 799–834.

Newsom, D., Turk, J., & Kruckeberg, D. (2001). *Vse o PR. Teoriya i praktika pablik rileyshnz [This is PR: The Realities of Public Relations].* Moscow: Konsaltingovaya gruppa imidzh kontakt, Infra-M.

Pellenen, L. (2005). Tekhnologicheskie aspekty pablik rileyshnz [Technological aspects of Public Relations]. *Vestnik YuUrGU. Seriya Sotsialno-gumanitarnye nauki, 7*(47), 147–149.

Pochekaev, R. (2007). *Istoriya svyazey s obshchestvennostyu [History of public relations].* Saint-Petersburg: Piter.

Poverinov, I. (2000). *Pablik rileyshnz kak mekhanizm garmonizatsii sotsialnoy sredy [Public Relations as a tool for garmonization of social sphere].* (Doctoral thesis, Mordovskij gosudarstvennyj pedagogicheskij institut im. Meevseveva, Saransk, RU). Retrieved from https://dlib.rsl.ru/01000282562.

RAPR (Russian Association of Public Relations). (n.d.). *About RAPR's Committees.* Retrieved from www.raso.ru/about.php.

Savrutskaya, E. (2008). Filosofskiy vzglyad na problemy kommunikatsii v mire [Philosophy perspective on communication issue worldwide]. *Vestnik Nizhegorodskogo gosudarstvennogo lingvisticheskogo universiteta im. N.A. Dobrolyubova, 2,* 140–152.

Shelep, I. (2010). Utopiya Dzhejmsa Gryuniga: k voprosu ob ehvolyucii PR modelej v 20-veke [Utopia of James Grunig: The issue of evolution of PR models in 20 century]. *Vestnik Nizhegorodskogo universiteta im. N.I. Lobachevskogo. Seriya Sotsialnye nauki, 2*(18), 70–76.

Shelep, I. (2013). K voprosu o raznoobrazii podhodov k issledovaniyu problematiki pablik rilejshnz [The issue of a variety of approaches to topic of public relations research]. *Vestnik NGTU im. R.E. Alekseeva. Seriya "Upravlenie v sotsialnykh sistemakh. Kommunikativnye tekhnologii", 4,* 68–74.

Shilina, M. (2011). Genezis rossijskih svyazej s obshchestvennostyu: aktualnye aspekty. [Genesis of Russian public relations: Topical aspects]. *Mediaskop,* (2), 22–31.

Shishkina, M. (1999). Svyazi s obshchestvennostyu v sisteme socialnogo upravleniya [Public relations within social management system]. (Doctoral thesis, Saint-Petersburg, St. Petersburg State University, RU). Retrieved from https://dlib.rsl.ru/01000253412.

Shishkina, M. (2002). *Pablik rileyshnz v sisteme sotsialnogo upravleniya. [Public relations within social management system].* Saint-Petersburg: Pallada-media and SZRTs Rusich.

Shtompka, P. (2001). Kulturnaya travma v postkommunisticheskom obshchestve (stat'ya vtoraya) [Cultural trauma in post-Communism society (second article)]. *Sotsiologicheskie issledovaniya, 2,* 3–12.

Solovey, V. (2010). Primechaniya k onlajn konferencii s Valeriem Solovej [Notes of online conference with Valeriy Solovey]. Retrieved from www.apco-ru.ru/index.php/konferentsiya-v-d-solovya.

Solovey, V. (2013). Osnovnye tendencii razvitiya obrazovaniya v oblasti reklamy i svyazej s obshchestvennostyu [Major trends in development of advertising and public relations education]. Materials of Sessions of Educational and Methodological Unity. Moscow State Institute of International Relations. Retrieved from www.mgimo.ru/files2/y03_2013/7102/solovei_13_02_20.pdf.

Tolstikova-Mast, Y., & Keyton, J. (2002). Communicating about Communication: Fostering the development of the communication discipline in Russia. Collected research articles. In I. N. Rozina (Ed.), *Theory of communication and applied communication: Bulletin of the Russian Communication Association, Issue 1* (pp. 119–134). Rostov-on-Don: Institute of Management, Business and Law Publishing.

Toth, E., & Aldoory, L. (2010). *A first look: An in-depth analysis of global public relations education.* College Park, MD: University of Maryland.

Tsetsura, K. (2003). The development of public relations in Russia: A geopolitical approach. In K. Sriramesh & D.Vercic (Eds.), *Global public relations handbook. Theory, research and practice* (pp. 301–319). Mahwah, NJ: Lawrence Erlbaum Associates,

Tsetsura, K. (2004). Russia. In D. Vercic (Ed.), *Public relations and communication management in Europe* (pp. 331–346). Berlin: Mouton de Gruyter.

Vasilik, M. (2004). Nauka o kommunikatsii ili teoriya kommunikatsii? K probleme teoreticheskoy identifikatsii [Science of communication or theory of communication? The issue of theoretical identity]. *Collected research articles: Aktual'nye problemy teorii kommunikatsii*, 4–11.

Vuzoteka Online. (n.d.). *Bachelor degree program of "Advertising and Public Relations" in Russia*. Retrieved from http://vuzoteka.ru/вузы/Реклама-и-связи-с-обществен ностью/42-03-01.

Xifra, J. (2007). Undergraduate public relations education in Spain: Endangered species? *Public Relations Review, 33*(2), 206–213.

Yadov, V. (2007). Teoretiko-konceptualnye obyasneniya «postkommunisticheskih transformacij» [Theoretical and conceptual explanation of «post-Communist transformaitons»]. *Rossiya reformiruyushchayasya, 6*, 12–23.

Yadov, V. (2009). O russkom natsionalnom mentalitete, v kakoy mere on skazyvaetsya v povedencheskikh praktikakh i kak my issledovali problemu [Russian social and cultural patterns, what its effect on behavioural patterns and how we have researched the problem] (pp. 15–29). In V. Yadov (Ed.), *Vozdeystvie zapadnykh sotsiokulturnykh obraztsov na sotsialnye praktiki v Rossii*. Moscow: TAUS.

Yakovlev, I. (1995). *Pablik Rileyshnz v organizatsiyakh [Public Relations in organizations]*. Saint-Petersburg: Petropolis.

Zaitsev, A. (2013a). R. Burkart: PR-dialog i konsensus-orientirovannye svyazi s obshchestvennostyu [PR dialogue in consensus oriented public relations]. *Obshchestvo: Politika, Ekonomika, Pravo, 4*, 28–31.

Zaitsev, A. (2013b). Dialogicheskaya model svyazej s obshchestvennostyu Dzh Gryuniga i sovremennost [Dialogic model of public relations of James Grunig and the present]. *Vestnik KGU im. A. N. Nekrasova, 3*, 84–88.

Zassoursky, Y. (1996, July). *Zhurnalistskoe obrazovanie v Rossii [Journalism education in Russia]*. Address to the Speech Communication Association Research Colloquium, Moscow, Russia.

Zassoursky, Y. (2005). Mediasistemy 21 veka i novaya filosofiya zhurnalistskogo obrazovaniya [Media systems in 21 century and new philosophy of journalism education]. *Informatsionnoe obshchestvo, 1*, 36–39.

Zavodchikova, N. (2010). Posledovatelnaya sistema razvitiya navykov professionalnoj aktivnosti bakalavrov specialnosti "Reklama i svyazi s obshchestvennostyu" [Sequential system of development skills for professional activity of bachelor with "Advertising and Public Relations" Degree] (128–133). *Proceedings of 5th international scientific and applied conference of higher education for PR practitioners: Theory and practice*. Yekaterinburg, Russia.

Part III

The academic and professional development of strategic communications in Russia

Examining current and future challenges

5 The Russian Professional Public Relations Standard

Julia Gryaznova

Introduction: The mission of the Russian Public Relations Professional Standard

Existence of the Russian Public Relations Professional Standard is evidence of public relations' professional maturity in Russia. The Russian public relations industry has developed intensively since the late 1980s. By early 2010, there was an understanding of the necessity to formulate the Russian Public Relations Professional Standard. This professional standard enables public relations practitioners and educators:

- To determine the content and prospects for the development of the profession
- To develop a professional community that is united by a common vision of its professionalism
- To determine the competencies and specialist knowledge that are demanded of practitioners to perform all public relations professional functions
- To work with organizational staff in recruiting, assessment, grading, and providing advanced training
- To identify specific requirements for practitioners in different types of organizations within the public relations industry
- To provide reference points for practitioners' professional trajectories and education
- To provide career guidance for students and young professionals and to provide those who discontinue their education with certain reference points to choose an alternative occupation
- To help universities determine the curricular content of professional education, helping to create education programs and standards

The professional standard as a collective product

For these tasks to be accepted by the professional community, the Russian Public Relations Professional Standard must represent the collective work of its member. In 2014, the Russian Public Relations Association (RPRA) initiated the development of the Russian Public Relations Professional Standard for its public relations specialists. The organizational work was conducted by a working group of nine RPRA members, and about 100 key professionals and experts in the public relations industry performed the substantive work. More than 2,000 Russian public relations specialists participated: professionals in public relations agencies, in-house specialists in business corporations, and those in government agencies and non-profit organizations, as well as professors of communication disciplines at universities. More than 30 open discussions were held during a three-year period. Moreover, a permanent online discussion was organized, and the Russian Public Relations Professional Standard was piloted in corporations as well as in education programs.

The public relations specialist professional standard structure

The development of the Russian Public Relations Professional Standard was conducted simultaneously with the State Program of Russian Federation for Professional Standards Development. Since 2012, the need for professional standards has been accepted both by Russian professional communities and the Russian Ministry of Labor, the latter which has developed a common methodology and structure for professional standards that are based on references of the International Labor Organization (ILO). Accordingly, in the course of developing its own professional standard, RPRA made use of the form of the professional standard that was proposed by the Russian Ministry of Labor. The structure of the professional standard contains:

- A description of general characteristics of public relations activity
- A public relations industry trend forecast for the next three to five years
- A public relations profession outline (by identifying basic functions/ processes of labor)
- Details about each of these labor functions
- Description of knowledge and competencies that are required to perform each of these labor functions

General characteristics of public relations

It is commonplace to consider public relations as a strategic function, that is, as a type of management, along with production, finance, sales, and human resource management. This focus is also held by the Russian Ministry of Labor. In its *Classifier of Economic Activities*, the Ministry considers Public Relations Activity to be a subclass of Counselling for Management. Having accepted public relations as a type of management, this description is the basis for the Russian Public Relations Professional Standard: The fundamental task of public relations is strategic management for the communication environment to increase public and information transparency and the organization of processes that promote social changes and development through creation and maintenance of:

- Reputational and social capitals
- New sustainable public relations
- Collective values
- Effective tools of communication that generate new knowledge, meanings, ideas, and projects
- Ensuring accessibility to information and its credibility

Public relations industry trend forecast for the following three to five years

To create a professional standard, surveys and discussions among experts have allowed us to identify key public relations industry trends, which helps build the standard with orientation to the near future and in consideration of rapid changes in the profession. We included the following trends in formulating the public relations standard:

- Convergence of public relations with other management techniques and activities, as well as the growth of the strategic role of public relations
- Increasing demand for crisis communications, which is caused by both global economic instability and accelerated information transfer, which have made information crises more frequent and crisis communications an integral part of public relations professional activity
- Rise in the differentiation of target groups and communication tools, with increased attention to communication campaign targeting
- Increasing demand in establishing trust and open interactions among the state, businesses, and society, including the strengthening of corporate social responsibility and communication management of companies' social activity
- Rising importance of internal communication as a crucial part of business processes and increased demand for internal communications development services
- Strengthening of local and regional players, with increasing communication activities that are accompanied by public interest in the local agenda
- Information environment systematization and the emergence of new measurement capabilities and information context analytics
- Development of public relations efficiency evaluation methods, including public relations corporate activity results in the Key Performance Indicators (KPIs)
- Increasing information scope and intensified competition for attention, resulting in the growing popularity of such forms as "packaging" of information, visualization, and storytelling

- Development of integrated communications that combine traditional and new communication channels as well as various types of communication tools
- Development of digital and mobile communications, with the emergence of new tools and platforms for social interactions
- Institutionalization of the industry due to the generational change toward public relations management, with the transfer of management responsibilities from business owners to salaried professional managers
- Realization by the Russian Public Relations Society of the particular place of the public relations specialist, with the increasing comprehension and acceptance of the public and corporate functions of public relations

The public relations profession outline (through basic functions/processes of labor)

The most difficult task of creating a professional standard is the definition of the key processes (*labor functions* in the terminology of the document of Russian Ministry of Labor). Our discussions have led us to a collective agreement on the six basic processes of public relations activity:

- Development of human capital and self-organization
- Communication strategy design
- Information analysis
- Project management
- Organization of public communications—implementation of communication strategy
- Content creation

Having identified the basic labor functions in public relations, the Russian Public Relations Association compared this list with the structure of principles in the core of *The Global Standard of the Communication Profession* (Global Alliance for Public Relations and Communications Management, n.d.) that had been developed by the International Association of Business Communicators (IABC) (Table 5.1). This standard was developed at approximately the same time as was the professional standard of the Russian Public Relations Association, which members saw the direct benefit of including strategy and analytics to the list of basic functions (principles, in terms of IABC).

After analyzing the meanings behind each of the principles of *The Global Standard of the Communication Profession* (Global Alliance for Public Relations and Communications Management, n.d.), as well as each professional function of the Russian Public Relations Professional Standard, RPRA saw that its vision of the principles of the public relations profession was very close. In almost every labor function, the standard of the Russian Public Relations Association requires adherence to business ethics. Context and engagement are included in functions such as information analysis, communication strategy

Table 5.1 IABC principles

Generalized labor functions in PR (RPRA)	Principles for the communication profession (IABC)
Development of human capital and self-organization	Ethics
Communication strategy design	Consistency
Information analysis	Context
Project management	Analysis
Organization of public communications - implementation of communication strategy	Strategy
Content creation	Engagement

Source: www.globalalliancepr.org/news/iabccodeofethics

design, and content creation. Compared with the IABC standard, the Russian Public Relations Professional Standard puts more emphasis on the managerial aspect, as well as on human capital of public relations professionals. The IABC standard is more focused on the ethical aspect of public relations, which is a reference point for the near future for the Russian public relations industry.

Development of human capital and self-organization

The Russian Public Relations Association categorized the labor function as development of human capital and personal self-organization, which speaks not only for the public relations specialist's need to have certain personal competences and to be engaged in his/her own personal development but also as parts of public relations work, which fulfillment must be of concern both to the public relations practitioner and the employer. Moreover, it is at universities where future professionals must learn the competence of self-organization. In recent years, the question of what is more important for public relations careers—soft skills or hard skills—has become a key issue, both on the labor market and in public relations professional education. When the Russian Public Relations Association developed the professional standard, its members understood that public relations is simultaneously a creative profession, a profession in which communications with partners and clients occupy a significant place, and a profession that changes rapidly. Consequently, the main resource is the professional himself or herself, that is, the human resource. In 2016, the Russian Public Relations Association conducted an opinion poll of employers from communication agencies, corporate public relations departments, and recruiters. The poll confirmed that soft skills in public relations are primary in making decisions on employment and career promotion. Employers are paying more attention to personal competencies, understanding that they, themselves, will teach the necessary technologies and methods; however, the new employees must have the necessary personal competencies for training and collective work. In many cases, the absence of significant personal competencies (for example, the ability to cooperate, the ability to establish trust, and resistance to stress) has prevented a practitioner from career advancement, despite extremely high levels of professional competence, that is, hard skills. This makes us place soft skills in the core of communication vocational education.

But development of human capital and self-organization is not only the maintenance of soft skills, such as the management of personal resources (for example, energy, health, time) and stress resistance. Thus, we have also included:

• Creation and implementation of personal long-term development strategy
• Observation of ethical rules in relations with partners, clients, colleagues, and audiences
• Participation in professional community activities

In addition to the development of human capital and self-organization, the Russian Public Relations Association also has included in the public relations standard a list of personal competencies that are necessary to perform labor functions. These include:

• Willingness and ability to learn continuously
• Sense of responsibility
• Ability to pay attention
• Ability to work "in the flow"
• Reflexivity
• Interpersonal communication skills
• Appreciation of beauty
• Proactive initiative
• Openness to change
• Stress resistance
• Ability to be an "antenna person" who can capture the signals of change and transform them into action
• Ability to work in conditions of uncertainty and multitasking
• Ability to build trust
• Ability to establish interpersonal relationships and to create communities
• Ability to formulate thoughts succinctly and clearly
• Strategic thinking
• Systems thinking

While creating this list, we proceeded from an analysis of public relations practice, but also relied on the model of Goleman (2013), which says a modern leader must possess three types of capital:

• Capital of internal (personal) resources
• Capital of human trust and relationships
• Capital of collective understanding, attention, knowledge.

The Goleman model and the model of the Russian Public Relations Professional Standard, in the section, Personal Competences and Development of Human Capital, are quite close, that is, the Professional Standard lists competencies like many of the competencies that Goleman's model identifies for a leader.

Design of communication strategy

The second labor function is the development of communication strategy, which is directly related to the strategic aspect of public relations and its growing importance. Our description of the development of communication strategy is not unusual, except that the Russian Public Relations Professional Standard emphasizes the need for a close connection between communication strategy and business strategy in its orientation of public relations strategy for business results. Also, the Russian Public Relations Professional Standard pays particular attention to the implementation of communication strategy in an organization's activities, as well as the measurability of public relations results and the demonstration of public relations efficiency for the organization.

Information analysis

Studies of the public relations market show that information analysis is increasing, which public relations professionals realize is a critical competence that provides efficiency (Comcowich, 2016, December 15; Peddy, 2016, June 27). Information analysis is associated with the personalization of communication, the role of big data in communication planning, and clients' growing demand for measured effectiveness of public relations. As a result, we note the extension of analytics units within public relations departments and agencies. Analytics becomes an instrument of communication between the client and the agency or an organization's public relations department. Public relations activity, itself, is becoming more connected to mathematics and computer programming. The Russian Public Relations Professional Standard represents all of this in the labor function, information analysis.

Project management

Project management is fourth in our list of labor functions. The content of this function includes nothing specific for public relations; rather, this is the same project management that is used in engineering, science, and industry. Project management is extremely important. Mastery of its technologies and its logic (which is normal for other divisions of a company or for a client's business) allows public relations to coordinate with other company divisions by synchronizing with other business processes, thereby elevating the practitioner's status from that of distributing press releases, copywriting, and organizing events to that of manager. Working on the Public Relations Professional Standard, we engaged with experts from clients as well as experts from the public relations industry. Client experts identified a problem with dialogue and cooperation with public relations professionals because most of these practitioners did not use project management technologies. At the same time, traditional technologies of project management are undergoing a radical transformation that is associated with these changes:

- The employer chooses the employee, but the employee also chooses the employer
- Financial motivation no longer works; rather, interesting work is the key motivation for employee
- An unmotivated employee is inflexible, uncreative, and irresponsible
- Findings about consumers quickly become outdated
- Almost all communication today is crisis communication
- Higher-level values, such as CSR, are important to consumers.

As a result, management systems including project management are forced to adopt:

- Horizontal structures
- Self-managed teams
- A partnership with customers
- Measurability of goals
- Transparency of processes
- Orientation on the values of self-development and improvement of the world

Content creation

One of the trends in recent years has been the predominance of content. Interesting content is everything for communication. However, at the same time, content is no longer only text. Now, we have to create multimedia content using text, photos, videos, and infographic formats. Therefore, it is not enough for public relations practitioners just to write well; rather, practitioners must be able to write targeted texts. Also, the ability to just write also is inadequate; public relations practitioners must be able to create photo-, video-, and infographic content and to create this content, if not in real time, then very quickly.

Organization of public communications—and implementation of communications strategy

This is the most extensive unit of the PR standard, which includes all implementation of the public relations project:

- Tactical planning of events within the communication strategy implementation framework

- Definition, description, and analysis of stakeholders and the communications environment for strategy implementation
- Planning and maintaining the organization's communication system
- Communication's content elaboration
- Management of interaction with the mass media
- Organizing direct communications
- Organizing interaction with professional communities, experts, analysts, competitors, partners, and suppliers of the market's infrastructure
- Arranging business-to-business (B2B) and business-to-consumer (B2C) interaction
- Organizing public events and presentations of different scales
- Communication support of external and internal events
- Organizing digital communications
- Arranging crisis communications
- Communication effectiveness measurement
- Organizing interaction with government bodies, that is, government relations (GR)
- Organizing interaction with shareholders, financial analysts, banks, and other capital market participants, that is, investor relations (IR)
- Sustainable development of the organization
- Organizing interaction with the staff and partners, that is, internal corporate communications

The Russian Public Relations Professional Standard implementation

The Public Relations Professional Standard has been implemented in the Russian public relations industry. Already, the Professional Standard has been placed into the core of more than a dozen university educational programs, as well as in corporate training/retraining programs. The Russian Public Relations Association has created its educational on-line course, which is in great demand in Russia. The Professional Standard is actively used for assessment of professional competencies, for which we have developed an online form where public relations professionals can pass both personal assessment and group assessment (department in the university, public relations department in a corporation, and in public relations agencies). Finally, the Professional Standard has been repeatedly used as a matrix for the creation or development of in-house public relations departments.

References

Comcowich, W. (2016, December 15). PR leaders predict increased & more effective media analytics in 2017. *Media Measurement News,* 3 Retrieved from https://glean. info/pr-leaders-predict-increased-effective-media-analytics-2017/.

Global Alliance for Public Relations and Communications Management (n.d.). *The Global Standard of the Communication Profession.* Retrieved from www.globalalliancepr. org/news/iabccodeofethics.

Goleman, D. (2013). *Focus: The hidden driver of excellence.* New York: Harper Collins.

International Association of Business Communications (n.d). The global standard of the communication profession. Retrieved from www.iabc.com/global-standard-2/.

Peddy, G. (2016, June 27). Why is PR measurement so important? *The Holmes Report.* Retrieved from www.holmesreport.com/agency-playbook/sponsored/article/ why-is-pr-measurement-so-important.

6 Modern scientific knowledge of public relations and its objective-subjective field

Irina Kuzheleva-Sagan

Introduction

This chapter is an abbreviated version of one part of my monograph, *Scientific Knowledge of Public Relations (PR): A Philosophical Analysis,* which was published in Moscow several years ago (Kuzheleva-Sagan, 2011). The Russian Communication Association (RCA) awarded that volume "the best book on communication studies of the 2013–2014 academic year" from among those nominated in the category, "Organizational, professional, and business communication and public relations" (http://ifiyak.sfu-kras.ru/news/item/610-itogi-knizhnogo-konkursa-luchshaya-kniga-po-kommunikativnyim-naukam-i-obrazovaniyu-2013-2014-akademicheskiy-god, n.d.).

The foundation of the monograph is the philosophical and theoretical research I did in the beginning of the 2000s. Initially, the research was not meant to be "philosophical and theoretical". At that time, I had rather practical problems to solve. They were connected with launching a new major in public relations at Tomsk State University. At the time, I had a PhD in pedagogics. Naturally, the first question that occurred to me was "How to *teach* public relations?" However, further communication with my colleagues at countless regional and national conferences and seminars on public relations revealed that the real questions were "*What is* public relations?" and "*What is modern scientific knowledge* of public relations?*" There is no way one can teach something without any systematic conceptualization of the subject, but building a system of knowledge of public relations appeared to be impossible, because the range of views on the essence of the phenomenon was too broad. The variety of definitions of public relations was seen as the main obstacle to developing a unified theory of public relations or PRology (that term was coined by Shishkina, 1999). However, I believed that any lecturer in the sphere would want to have something like a "Mendeleev's table" in his or her disposal that could help to communicate and to consistently explain already existing scientific facts, ideas, and social practices, as well as to predict the appearance of new phenomena.

I concluded that a universal typological "Mendeleev's table" representing a unified model of modern knowledge of public relations could be developed, first and foremost, within philosophy, more specifically, within ontology and gnoseology, the latter which is the philosophy of knowledge and cognition. I had to deal with fields of philosophy and social and humanistic scientific knowledge that were absolutely new to me to apply them to the theory of public relations. As a result, in 2008, I finished and defended my doctoral dissertation (Grand PhD), *Onto-gnoseological and philosophical and methodological grounds for scientific knowledge of public relations.*

It took me several years to complete my research, as I had to be a lecturer, a manager, and a public relations practitioner at the same time. However, I found a positive aspect to that length of time, which proved that the strategies I had chosen as the methodological grounds for my research were efficient and viable. They allowed me, not only to propose my own understanding of the existing variety of the conceptual field and its practices, but also to predict its further development. These methodological grounds turned what seemed to be an obstacle on the way of creating a unified theory of public relations into a natural breeding ground that was necessary for conceptualization. The results of my research provided answers to these questions:

- Why is there not (cannot be there) a single and universal definition of "public relations"?
- Why do altruistic definitions of public relations matter, even though they do not reflect the real (often manipulative) public relations practice?
- Why cannot scientific knowledge of public relations (as well as its practice) have a one-and-only "true" history?
- What is the specific character of public relations as one of High-Hume (humanities) technologies and the object of public relations studies?
- How can a model of modern public relations studies be presented?
- (And many other valid questions)

Of course, all the answers to these questions are connected with the issues of scientific knowledge of public relations that I propose in my book are open to discussion. However, they are not in contradiction with one another other within my research, *Onto-Gnoseological and Philosophical and Methodological Grounds for Scientific Knowledge of Public Relations* (2009).

This chapter proposes a variant of constructing a general model of the objective-subjective field of scientific knowledge of public relations (PRology) as one of the contemporary techno-sociohumanistic scientific disciplines that focus on studying general mechanisms of constructing and functioning of various types of sociotechnical objects that are aimed at developing corresponding individual and public consciousness (so-called High-Hume technologies).

Problematization of the theme

Modern science is both the result and the source of technologization as a global process that involves all spheres of life within a society that concerns all areas of scientific knowledge, including social sciences and humanities. Modern scientific knowledge in the social sciences and humanities is not only becoming better equipped, but includes a new type of scientific disciplines that represent joint technological sociohumanistic knowledge. The appearance of such technological sociohumanistic sciences (TSHS) is connected with the fact that High-Hume technologies that had been exclusively technologies of social communication have become the methods of constructing information-communicative sociality itself.

Initially, High-Hume and High-Tech were considered to be elements of a strict dichotomy that removes any possibility of their synthesis. However, advances in computer science, cognitive science, bio-information, genetics, and nano-engineering dissolved the boundaries between those two types of technologies. As a result, instead of the High-Hume—High-Tech dichotomy, a mighty symbiosis occurred that incorporated almost all technologies. Despite the fact that practice in the sphere often goes ahead of its theory, High-Hume technologies are gradually leaving the objective-subjective fields of the existing disciplines of which they used to be a part, initiating the integration of objective-subjective fields of new scientific disciplines: "humanistic information science", "conflictology", "medialogy", "imagiology", "PRology", and other disciplines. The appearance of sciences that deal with the whole spectrum of the most complex problems that are connected with the production and realization of High-Hume technologies as communicative technologies should be considered as a trend that is responding to the character of the information-communication network society and its requirements and challenges.

The meta-object of such disciplines, being formed inside particular ontologies, is information-communicative sociality; the subject is an "interface" among science, technology, and society, which combines the processes of technologization and informatization of all social spheres in all forms of their premises, manifestations, and consequences. The major TSHS objective is to study the patterns of production, application, promotion, and social-humanistic expertise of various High-Hume as methods of solving current sociocultural problems and of constructing information-communicative sociality in general. The TSHS do not technologize social-humanistic phenomenology, but investigate the technologies, themselves, in sociocultural and humanistic context, referring to their anthropological senses, while avoiding the limits of gnoseological and purely technological aspects.

The problem areas of the TSHS include the variety of questions that are connected with High-Hume designing, ontologization, deontologization, functioning, and implementation as ambivalent sociocultural phenomena, as well as other questions. Moreover, the TSHS are not developed by the force of internal scientific problems, but rather those that are external sociocultural. Having being transformed by those sciences into cognitive problems, these issues may be short-term (that is, ad hoc), as well as long-term, or even preventative (that is, anticipatory). Therefore, the TSHS are not only limited by technology-focused knowledge, but the complex nature of these problems and their scales dictate the necessity of applying fundamental general scientific and social theories, representing a wide spectrum of specific scientific theories and methods from other scientific areas, their selection, adaptation, and further development regarding the sphere of particular technological sociohumanistic science. The TSHS are based on the pluralistic (that is, situational) methodology, which allows the use of "classical" and "nonclassical" methods in studying social reality, together with "post-nonclassical" ones (Styopin, 1999). These sciences often apply the modal methods (projective, script) as well as methods of analog modeling and "values expertise".

The TSHS have these specific characteristics: (1) "nontraditional" structure (for example, "contour", "network", "problem-oriented"); (2) an interdisciplinary (often transdisciplinary) nature; and (3) interaction with politics and business. In this case, interdisciplinarity is considered as the coordination among disciplines inside the SHSK (social and humanistic scientific knowledge); transdisciplinarity is considered as coordination between the SHSK, itself, and the natural-scientific and technical types of knowledge; and integrativity is considered as a combination of technological, applied, and fundamental types of scientific knowledge. I believe that the study of public relations, or PRology, belongs to such "technological sociohumanistic" sciences.

In addition to these common factors of the appearance of the TSHS, some other *specific* premises exist for the appearance of PRology:

- *Rapid development of public relations practice in the 20th Century and the risky (ambiguous, ambivalent, contradictory) character of public relations as High-Hume technology.* Unlike advertising technologies that never disguise their real goal, which is to develop consumer interest, public relations does not always openly announce its real goal, which is to develop some sort of public opinion. That is why the terms "public relations" and "PR" often have negative connotations in the public discourse. However, one cannot deny that, at the same time, public relations is one of the most effective means of social governance, because, unlike other technologies, it is implemented as a "strategy of trust" (Boiry, 1989) that provides a gloss of freedom and informed choice. Therefore, it appears to be necessary to systematically investigate the risks connected with the implementation of public relations as High-Hume technology.
- *Instantly growing need of the society for more ultimate PR-technologies, such as High-Hume, which can be established only on the scientific approach basis.* It contemplates a full understanding of all patterns of constructing and functioning of these technologies.
- *Urgent need for theoretical public relations knowledge of an appropriate level of generalization that is impossible to reach in the existing limits of the scientific disciplines such as sociology, political science, sociology, management theory, economic theory, philology, and some others.*

The integrative character of PRology, of its objective-subjective, methodological, and categorical spheres, is primarily reflected in their interdisciplinarity. For this chapter, I will focus only on the first sphere, that is, *objective-subjective.*

Thus, public relations, as a sociocultural phenomenon and as an object of cognition, has been of great interest for many scientific disciplines, which is proven by the numerous scientific publications and dissertations on the subject matter of public relations that attempt to define the term "public relations". As a result, there are more than 1,500 public relations definitions. This makes it difficult for representatives of different scientific thinking and special disciplines to come to a mutual understanding, which does not stimulate the development of an adequate social practice. It is time to convert these different separated subject patterns/schemes of public relations into a new integration, interdisciplinarity, and transdisciplinarity.

The methodology of the research on the problem of developing a model of the objective-subjective field of modern knowledge of public relations[1]

The space limitations of this chapter do not allow a complete description of each philosophical and conceptual approach. Therefore, these are short descriptions of the most essential approaches:

1) The *concept of sociotechnical objects*, by the Russian scientist and methodologist George Shedrovitsky
2) the *dimensional ontology*, by the Austrian philosopher, psychologist, and psychiatrist Viktor E. Frankl
3) *epistemological structuralism*, by the Italian culturologist and semiotician Umberto Eco
4) *the idea of the generalized codes*, by the German philosopher and sociologist Niklas Luhmann

According to Shedrovitsky (Shedrovitsky, 1984), the object of sociotechnical action (such as public relations and any other High-Hume) never coincides with the objects of particular sciences. That is why:

> it is necessary to talk about the "multilateral" and "complex" character of the socio-technical object, searching for practical ways to combine and to integrate separate knowledge from different disciplines that describe the object from different perspectives. As the result of this knowledge integration, the integral understanding of such complicated "multilateral" object must be formulated.
>
> (Shedrovitsky, 1984, pp. 68–69)

Frankl, an author of dimensional ontology, tried to explain the simultaneous existence of alternative projections of the same object of cognition (Frankl,

1990; Frankl, 2000). The first law of the dimensional ontology is that the same object of cognition that is projected out of its highest ("essential", "integral", "volumetric") dimension into the lowest ("plane") dimension is depicted in such a way that its different projections may contradict one another.

A cylinder, for example, is a single three-dimensional object, but, when it is projected onto a two-dimensional surface, it can appear either as a square/rectangle or as a circle. "Two-dimensional" people, living in a "two-dimensional" world, might argue whether the thing (cylinder) is actually a square/rectangle or a circle, when, in fact, it is neither. The process of projecting an object down onto lower dimensions causes the illusion of contradiction. The data from the lower dimensions remains relevant only in those dimensions. Frankl insists that researchers can, and even must, ignore the multidimensional essence of the reality, singling out only a certain dimension from the whole spectrum when it is necessary. This law may by applied in cases of analyzing simple "inanimate" objects, as well as in cases of complicated phenomena, such as the human mind and psychology (Frankl, 1990; 2000).

Frankl illustrates the latter statement with the example of Joan of Arc's personality. There is no doubt that, from the psychiatric point of view, Joan of Arc would have been diagnosed with schizophrenia, and, as long as we confine ourselves to the psychiatric frame of reference, Joan of Arc is "no one but a schizophrenic". Who she is beyond her schizophrenia is not perceptible within the psychiatric dimension. As soon as we follow her into the noological dimension, that is, from the systematic study and organization of thought, knowledge, and the mind, and observe her theological and historical importance, Joan of Arc is more than a schizophrenic. She being a schizophrenic in the dimension of psychiatry does not at all detract from her significance in other dimensions (Frankl, 1988).

Hypothetically, cognitive phenomena, including sociotechnical objects and scientific disciplines, obey this law of the dimensional ontology as well.

The essence of the epistemological structuralism by Eco involves the assumption of existence of "escaping" or "absent" structures (but still structures!), which are essential for "catching" the becoming reality in its "crosscuts". From this point, science is an open complex system at every moment of its formation. Its elements, interacting with each other as well as with elements outside, are generating new structures, making the system more complex and restructuring it. Eco gives several definitions of a structure that can be useful in solving particular problems. This definition may be of the most interest for us: "Structure is a model built with several simplifying actions that allow considering a phenomenon from one-and-only point of view..." (Eco, 2004, p. 80). Eco believes that consecutive reduction may lead to a *code* that represents a more generalized structure. At the end, a structure is comprehended as some sort of *transposition* as a basis for all possible *transformations*. But such structure can function only if it represents a code that can generate different messages. Eco said that structural (or "code") matrixes are especially essential in studying communicative models, including models of scientific knowledge. A codification as a semiotic method of structure analysis "not so much reveals a structure as constructs it, invents it as a hypothesis and theoretical model, and claims all investigated phenomena to be subordinated to the installing structural patterns" (Eco, 2004, p. 83).

The definition of a code by Luhmann does not contradict Eco's code concept and even supplements it. Luhmann said a code is "a structure that can find and regulate another additional element for every free element within its own relevance area" (Luhmann, 2001, p. 54). Symbolic generalized codes are mediators that provide successful communication. They are mechanisms of a self-organizing system. They have a selective and complementary character. Luhmann agrees with Eco that structures with code features play a significant role in constructing complex (that is, complicated) systems and to their obligatory maintenance.

The results of the research

All of these methodological approaches allow the assumption that PR, being a sociotechnical phenomenon (High-Hume technology) and a multidimensional object of cognition, may be reflected in various particular subject projections/ schemes, not only from the point of their ontological bases ("classical", "nonclassical", and "post-nonclassical"), but from the point of their special scientific and paradigmatic bases. Each of those projections has its own meaning that is limited by ontological, disciplinary, paradigmal frames and intervals. Compared to projections that are specific, there is an even more volumetric, integral "dimension" of public relations—a certain structure that functions as a *common subject scheme* toward the object under consideration. It represents some sort of a public relations "genotype" that consists of several key codes, that is, "genes". A code is: (1) a result and a mechanism of high entropy informational field-limiting; (2) a concentrated meaning that can expand into certain context, if necessary; and (3) a selective structure that chooses elements from outside the system that are correspondent to the elements inside it.

Several conditions are required for the common subject scheme to function, such as (1) the number of codes must be relatively small; (2) each code must be polysemantic (that is, also have a variety of definitions); and (3) the genotype must possess open system characteristics, that is, it must represent a complex of elements that create integral unity inside itself and with the system outside itself (supersystem). This complex must be capable of producing new elements and connections, as well as have features of a whole, which differs from a simple sum of properties of its separate elements.

Therefore, the problem of a definition of public relations as a multidimensional, polyontological, polysemantic, and ambivalent sociocultural phenomenon may be solved by finding the key codes that are highly generalized and, being integrated, construct an appropriate integral dimension of public relations (or of the public relations genotype). The genotype enables identification and construction of PR within any philosophic and scientific paradigm, sphere of social practice, special scientific field, and value-aimed orientation.

Five key concepts can be recognized as codes that construct the public relations genotype. They are *communication, technology, management, dialogue,* and *public opinion.* The basic codes are communication and technology. *Communication* allows identifying public relations as a communicative phenomenon that belongs to the general class of social communication. *Technology* affirms that public relations, unlike natural forms of communication (including those with a management background)[2] that are part of people's daily routine, is a purposely designed (that is, artificial) communication, maintained with a certain (strategic) goal. The *management* code points out the effecting, subordinating nature of public relations, which may occur directly or indirectly. The *dialogue* code features public relations as a bilateral communication process that allows distinguishing public relations from other types of communicative technologies, for example, propaganda and advertising, which are usually designed and carried out as one-way forms of communication. The *public opinion* code formulates the object of the public relations influence and its purpose.

The object of the public relations influence (as a High-Hume technology) is the public (internal and external), with its consciousness that is reflected in some sort of opinion. The goal, formulated as a "formation of public opinion", should be considered as a "meta-goal", taking into account that public relations also helps to solve particular problems that are framed, not only by similar, but also by alternative, value sets or some other kinds of sets by which public relations practitioners and researchers are guided when constructing various theoretical models. For example, public relations may appear as communicative technology that attempts to control public opinion in the form of a dialogue with the public. The goal of such dialog may be keeping someone's status quo (for example, that of authorities, social institutions, and corporate images) or deconstructing something that already exists, as well as legitimating something new.

Publicness (openness, transparency) is not one of the codes that construct the public relations genotype, even though some Russian researchers assume that public communication, in particular, is a public relations substance (Shishkina, 1999, p. 75). It is a priori impossible for the public opinion to be formed and to exist outside the public space (for example, Lippmann, 2004; Habermas, 1989). It means that the public opinion code is genetically connected with the concepts "publicity" and "public sphere"; thus, there is no need to put another code into the genotype, because a limited number of codes is one of the conditions of a genotype's universality and technological effectiveness. In addition, even though every public relations communication becomes public at the end, it does not mean that it is public in the beginning, for example, many Russian researchers relate so-called lobby technologies to the public relations sphere.

It must be emphasized that the elements of the public relations genotype must be polysemantic, as must the whole public relations genotype. In other words, in light of different scientific attitudes (such as sociological, political, philological, socio-psychological) and philosophical and scientific paradigms (including alternative), those elements possess different meanings. A genotype not only changes its semantics in every particular scientific sphere and paradigm, it also accumulates new additional (specific) codes. For example, when dealing with public relations in social and political research, the genotype often generates additional "power" and "influence" codes. The "influence" and "public consciousness" codes are generated in socio-psychological research, the "text" and "genre" codes are generated in philological research, and the "brand assets" and "reputation" codes are generated in economics research.

The hypotheses represented above make it possible to formulate this theoretical definition of public relations, which I consider to be operational:

> Public relations, being a type of socio-technical objects (High-Hume technologies), is a multidimensional, polyontological, polysemantic, ambivalent, and evolving anthropo-sociocultural phenomenon with a genotype that consists of five generalized interconnected key codes: communication, technology, management, dialogue, and public opinion.

Genotype is an invariant matrix. It constitutes a transposition for public relations transformations. It becomes a basis for constructing specific subject schemes, which appear as the result of selection. The genotype selects additional codes that place it inside a certain discipline, paradigm, or specific ontology. The genotype accumulates new codes, creating specific discipline patterns that constitute the crosscut of the PRology's object on every level of its establishment as an open self-organizing cognitive system (Kuzheleva-Sagan, 2008; 2009).

Table 6.1 is a "Mendeleev-like table"[3] that illustrates the changes of the objective-subjective field of scientific knowledge of public relations (PRology) in relation to its projections—classical, nonclassical, or post-nonclassical.

In this chapter, I have proposed a possible variant of defining the objective-subjective field of scientific knowledge of public relations (PRology) as one of the modern and continuously evolving technological sociohumanistic scientific disciplines. I hope this proposal will generate further discussion.

Table 6.1 Three projections of the objective–subjective field of PRology

	1. Classical projection	2. Nonclassical projection	3. Post-nonclassical projection
The metaphor that defines the essence of PRology in accordance with one of the three projections	"Social mechanics"	"Social cybernetics"	"Social synergetics"
The object of cognition	PR as an element of management of the social system, "the first (elementary) contour of a feedback" that functions as a simple regulator that responds to some instant impulses from the environment and is aimed at self-preservation of the social system and maintaining its integrity.	PR is either a "second contour of a feedback" that keeps the processes of self-regulation of the system (organization), its integrity, identity, and efficiency of both the internal and external communications (vertical and horizontal), or a means of control over the contours of management and self-management in an organization, a process of developing projects and strategic programmes that trigger the processes of self-regulation.	PR is a communicative technology or communicative and technological system (High-Hume technology) that creates crises as states of nonequilibrium and chaos in the social system. These crises are the starting points of the system's development and the resonant impulses that direct the system toward self-organization and self-development. They shape values and meanings as the most important parameters of order and set new goals for an organization.

The object of PRology

PR as a mechanism of a feedback control allows an organization to adjust to the external environment and control the internal social environment. Upon that, the internal communications are basically built as vertical.
PR is a means of the organization's *adjustment* to the external environment.

Organization is considered as an open social system, whose success is regarded relevant to how well it interacts with the external environment, e.g., economical, scientific and technical, and social and political. Such interaction leads to constant analysis and improvement of strategies of establishing organizational management systems, which involve PR.
PR is a way for social subjects *to interact* with the social environment, as well as a way they identify themselves and internalize.
Objectified social roles.
Patterns and principles of constructing and functioning of PR as a multidimensional, polyontological, and ambivalent sociocultural phenomenon that is an element of control over communications in any complex social system.

However, the dominant factor in the processes of self-organization and self-development is not a random coincidence but a necessity, opportunity, and practicability.
PR is a means of acceleration of the temporal structure of social activity and of *constructing* not only the "initial" environment, but also the external social system (supersystem) to which it is open.

Patterns and principles of analyzing, constructing, and functioning of PR as of a multidimensional, polyontological, ambivalent anthropo-sociocultural phenomenon that possesses characteristics of a complex self-organizing and self-developing system (technological, communicative, and management), which is a "man-sized object".

Patterns and principles of constructing and implying PR as a communicative technology for:
a) Managing the public opinion (target groups' opinion) in a linear dialogue-like subject-to-object communication;

(*continued*)

Table 6.1 Cont.

1. Classical projection	2. Nonclassical projection	3. Post-nonclassical projection
b) Strengthening the publicity capital of the basic subject of PR (a social structure or an individual); c) Adjusting the basic subject (a social structure or an individual) of PR to the external environment.	PR can be considered both as a separate communicative technology and as a complex communicative and (co–) management self-regulating technological system that establishes dialogue-like subject-to-subject communications that combine the characteristics of both linearity (on a system level) and non-linearity (on an individual level). The goals of such communications are: a) Management of public opinion of various scale; b) Intensive publicity capital strengthening; c) Basic subject's interacting with the external environment.	Therefore, in this case, PR is implemented: a) To form the public opinion of various scales, from the level of target audiences of large international corporations and state organizations to the level of transnational communities; b) To turn the publicity capital into informational capital (Castells); c) To construct the social environment.

| Existing and *potential* subject schemes (models) of PR | PR as a "social and goal-oriented rational action" (Conte, Spenser, Weber, Parsons, et al.); "structure and function" and "social institution" (Parsons, Merton, et al.); "ideal type of relations between social subjects" (Weber); "anti-crisis communication" (Coser, Dahrendorf, et al.); "pragmatic communication" (Pierce, James, Dewey, et al.); "social and behavioristic model" (Skinner); "social and psychological model" (Tarde) and other types of models, shaped inside various *classical* philosophical and special scientific disciplines. | PR as "understanding communication" (Schleiermacher, Dilthey, Gadamer); "Dialogue of values" (Jaspers); "institutionalization of other Selves" (Husserl); "speech act" and "language game" (Frege, Rassell, Wittgenstein, Ostin, Searle); "moral discourse", "strategic communication", and "symbolic interaction" (Habermas); "coordinated management of meanings" (Pierce); "discourse of authorities" (Foucault) and "power of discourse" (Bart, Greimas, Courtet); "individual's external extension" (McLuhan); "dramatic action" (Hoffman); "public performance" (Debord); "management of social contexts" (Kosheluk); and many other authors. | PR as a "self-organizing communicative-management system" (Budanov, Vasilkova); "man-sized object" (Styopin); "autopoietic" and "media-oriented communication" (Luhmann); "network communication" (Collirs); "trans-group communication" and "eastern model of communicative behavior" (Gundarin, Sitnikov); "symbolically generalized mediator" (Luhmann, Vasilkova), "design of the social environment" (Shedrovizkiy); element of the "informational network society" (Castells) and many other authors. |

Notes

1 General methodological complex of the research, *Onto-gnoseological and philosophical and methodological grounds for scientific knowledge of public relations* (2009), is a complicated structure that includes, among other theories, the *universal evolutionism* in its *system-wide* (L. von Bertalanffy, V.Vernadsky, N. Wiener, N. Luhmann, G. Malinetsky, T. Parsons, V. Styopin, and E. Jantch), *synergetic* (H. Haken, I. Prigogine, I. Stengers, and F. Varela et al.), *communicative* (K.-O. Apel, R. Collins, N. Luhmann, and J. Habermas et al.), and *constructivist* (T. Lukman, P. Berger, E. Knyaseva, and S. Kurdumov et al.) aspects; as well as the *transspective system analysis* (V. Klochko), and other methodological approaches (Kuzheleva-Sagan, 2011, 270–320).

2 Such as interactive "adult-child" and "superior-subordinate" types of interactive communication (Kuzheleva-Sagan, 2011).

3 My book, *Scientific knowledge of public relations (PR): A philosophical analysis*, has the full version of the transspective model of PRology that includes the representations of all its structural elements (for example, object and objective of scientific knowledge, cognitive ideal, prevailing type of system thinking, major methodology, definitions and dominating metaphors, and problem areas) (Kuzheleva-Sagan, 2011, pp. 425–433).

4 The reference section of my monograph, *Scientific knowledge of public relations (PR): A philosophical analysis*, includes over 550 scientific resources (Kuzheleva-Sagan, 2011, pp. 434–460). However, for this chapter, I have had to limit that number to the most relevant.

References[4]

Best book on communication studies of the 2013–2014 academic year. (n.d.). Retrieved from http://ifiyak.sfu-kras.ru/news/item/610-itogi-knizhnogo-konkursa-luchshaya-kniga-po-kommunikativnyim-naukam-i-obrazovaniyu-2013-2014-akademicheskiy-god.

Boiry, P.A. (1989). *Les relations publiques ou la stratégie de la confiance*. Paris: Eirolles.

Eco, U. (2004). *The absent structure. Introduction to semiology. (Translated from Italian)*. Saint Petersburg: Symposium.

Frankl, V. (1988). *The will to meaning: Foundations and applications of logotherapy*. New York: Meridian. Retrieved from www.amazon.com/Will-Meaning-Foundations-Applications-Logotherapy/dp/0142181269.

Frankl, V. (1990). *Man's search for meaning*. (Translated from English and German). Moscow: Progress.

Frankl, V. (2000). *The unheard cry for meaning*. (Translated from English). Moscow: April Press.

Habermas J. (1989) *The structural transformation of the public sphere: An inquiry into a category of bourgeois society*. Cambridge, MA: MIT Press.

Kuzheleva-Sagan, I. P. (2008). *Onto-gnoseological and philosophical methodological grounds for scientific knowledge of public relations* [Onto-gnoseologicheskie i filosofskie metodologicheskie osnovanija nauchnogo znanija o cvjazjah s obschestvennost'ju]. Doctoral dissertation, Tomsk State University, Tomsk, Russia. Retrieved from https://www.dissercat.com/content/gnoseologicheskie-i-filosofsko-metodologicheskie-osnovaniya-nauchnogo-znaniya-o-svyazyakh-s-.

Kuzheleva-Sagan, I. (2009). *Onto-gnoseological and philosophical methodological grounds for scientific knowledge of public relations: Post-nonklassicheskie praktiki I socio-kulturnye transformatsii* [Onto-gnoseologicheskie i filosofskie metodologicheskie osnovanija nauchnogo znanija o cvjazjah s obschestvennost'ju: Post-classical practices and socio-cultural transformations]. Moscow, Russia: MAKS Press.

Kuzheleva-Sagan, I. (2011). Nauchnoe znanie o svjazjah s obschestvennost'ju (PR): Filosofskij analiz. [Scientific knowledge of public relations (PR): A philosophical analysis]. Moscow, Russia: Book House Librokom. Retrieved from http://chamo.lib.tsu.ru/lib/item?id=chamo:421019&theme=system#.UpgxdOKirq8.

Lippmann, W. (2004) *Public opinion.* (Translated from English). Moscow: Institute of the Foundation for Public Opinion.

Luhmann, N. (2001). *The power.* (Translated from German). Moscow: Praksis.

Shedrovitsky, G. P. (1984). *Synthesis of knowledge: Problems and methods: Towards a theory of scientific knowledge.* Moscow: Nauka.

Shishkina, M. (1999). *Public relations in the system of social management.* Saint Petersburg: University of Saint Petersburg Press.

Styopin, V. (1999). *Theoretical knowledge: Structure, historical evolution.* Moscow: Progress.

7 Modern Russian legislation and regulation in advertising and advertising trends

Dmitrii Gavra, Elena Bykova, Andrei Dorskii, and Elena Kaverina

Introduction

This chapter describes the dynamics of the development and the current state of the advertising industry in the Russian Federation from 2000 to 2019. Using an historical and discursive approach that takes into account socioeconomic factors, the authors systematically consider the legislative regulation of advertising in the Russian Federation that represents the main state institutions that oversee compliance with advertising legislation. In addition to the description of control and supervision by state bodies, the chapter provides a brief description of self-regulatory institutions of the Russian advertising industry and shows the dynamics of their influence.

A trend has been identified of increasing the role of self-regulation, of moving from toughening government requirements for the placement and content of advertising to relaxing restrictions, of limiting regulatory impacts, and of strengthening the role of industry ethical regulators. The chapter gives a brief description of the key players in the Russian advertising market who represent Russian professional associations and associations of advertising producers. Based on industry analytics as well as state and departmental statistics, the structural parameters and dynamics of the Russian advertising market in cost and financial indicators are shown. It is noted that the advertising market in Russia is not sufficiently transparent; therefore, market capacity is determined by the expert assessment method.

In the period under review, the market showed consistently high growth rates (exception 2014–2015), significantly exceeding the growth rate of the economy as a whole. The main channels of distribution of advertising today are television and the Internet. A separate section of the chapter is devoted to the latest trends in the advertising market of the Russian Federation and the most striking projects of recent years. Technologically, the trends are in line with global trends—with a significant increase in online advertising and online video, the transition to mobile platforms, the use of gamification technologies when interacting with a consumer of advertising content, and the algorithm for targeting content on social networks. The authors emphasize the growth of consumer resistance to direct advertising and note the growing interest in native advertising. According to the researchers, a significant trend is the personalization of media consumption for the formation of new consumer loyalty.

Of interest is information on the successful participation of Russian manufacturers of promotional products in international festivals. Over the past years, Russian advertising agencies have collected an almost complete collection of awards from all the famous festivals—Cannes Lions, D&AD (London), One Show (New York), Webby Awards (New York, International Academy of Digital Arts and Sciences, IADAS), CLIO AWARDS (Miami), EUROBEST, RED DOT design award, EPIKA AWARDS, PIAF (Prague), KIAF (Kiev).

Thus, the authors demonstrate that, in spite of certain growth difficulties, advertising in Russia is developing dynamically and generally corresponds to global trends

Legal regulation and self-regulation of the advertising market

In the Russian Federation, creation and dissemination of advertising are regulated by a special law. The first law was adopted July 18, 1995, and became the third law on advertising in Europe, after the Spanish law (Ley, 34/1988)) and the Czech Republic law (Zákon, 1995). Today, the Federal Law of March 13, 2006 No. 38-FZ "On Advertising" is in force in Russia (Federal'nyj zakon, 2006). The Law includes six chapters:

1. General provisions (including general definitions, general requirements for advertising, requirements for social advertising)
2. Particular aspects of some advertising dissemination (advertisements on television and radio, in the movies, by telephone, outdoor, and mobile advertising)
3. Particular aspects of advertising of some goods (alcoholic products, medicines and medical services, dietary supplements, games based on risk, financial services, securities, annuity agreements, mediation activities)
4. Self-regulation in advertising
5. State supervision of advertising
6. Final provisions

According to the Act, advertising constitutes content that may be disseminated in any way, in any form, and using any means, which is addressed to an undefined number of persons to draw attention to the product or service being advertised, to form or support interest in that product or service, and to promote the marketing of that product or service (Federal'nyj zakon, 2006, Article 3). The Act also contains a list of phenomena to which it does not apply:

- Political advertising
- Information that the disclosure, dissemination, or communication to the consumer is mandatory in accordance with the Federal Act

- Reference and analytical materials
- Communications from public authorities
- Signs and markings
- Advertisements of persons or legal entities not related to conducting a business
- Information and any design elements that are placed on the product or its packaging
- References to a product or trademark that are organically integrated into the works of science, pieces of literary, or art

The evolving practice of advertising has raised additional questions for which the Act has not yet provided a direct answer. Specifically, these questions relate to advertising on the Internet. FAS (Federal Anti-Monopoly Service–Federal governmental agency) "On advertising on the Internet", dated August 28, 2015 No. AK/45828/15, establishes that Internet advertising is not:

1. Information on manufactured or sold goods that is posted on the website of the manufacturer or the seller of these goods or on their pages in social networks
2. Information on the company's economic operations, promotions (including information on discounts), and events (including stimulating purchases) held by the company
3. The list of hyperlinks that are provided by the search engine

Federal law also states that advertising may include materials that "are aimed not so much at informing the consumer of the range of goods or the company's activities, but to draw attention to a particular product and its highlighting among similar goods (for example, a pop-up banner)".

Thus, advertising in Russia is difficult to define and is not always resolved without special knowledge and additional investigation. According to Russian legislation, advertising shall be fair and reliable and must not mislead consumers by omitting important and sufficient information. Also, advertising should not incite illegal acts, encourage violence and cruelty, use foreign words and expressions without translation, show smoking and alcohol consumption, or contain abusive words and offensive images.

Monitoring of compliance with legislation on advertising is carried out by a special federal executive body, which is part of the Government—the Federal Anti-Monopoly Service (FAS). Figure 7.1 shows statistics of violations of the legislation on advertising is as follows, according to the 2017 FAS Report (Itogi, 2018).

To resolve issues of compliance with the Act, the FAS seeks advice from expert boards that are established at local offices of all constituent entities of the Russian Federation. Expert board members include well-known regional public figures, experienced employees in the advertising industry, and FAS

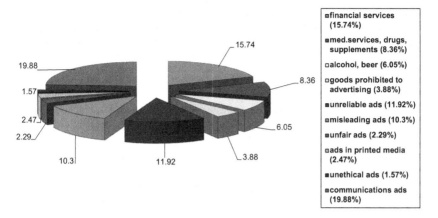

Figure 7.1 Violations of legislation on advertising.

employees. Board members begin their service at the request of the FAS, answering questions presented by the FAS officials. Board decisions are regarded as recommendations, but not as legal normative acts. During 2010 through 2018, FAS local offices regularly sought advice from the expert boards and usually followed these boards' recommendations. Most often, the boards consider issues related to the ethics of a particular advertisement. This system of industry regulation could be called the co-regulation (state bodies and non-governmental organizations) (Bykov. et al., 2015).

A fundamental distinction between the 2006 Advertising Law and the 1995 Law is the addition in 2006 of the chapter on self-regulation. The self-regulatory organization is a community of advertisers, advertising producers, advertising distributors, and other persons who are established as an association, union, or non-profit partnership to represent and protect the interests of its members, to develop requirements for ethical standards in advertising, and to ensure supervision over their compliance (Federal'nyj zakon, 2006, Article 31). The Federal Act of December 1, 2007, No. 315-FZ "On Self-Regulatory Organizations" adds the following requirements (Federal'nyj zakon, 2006, Part 3 of Article 3):

1) Association in a self-regulatory organization with members including at least 25 business entities or at least one hundred professional entities of a certain type, unless otherwise established by federal laws in respect to self-regulatory organizations that unite business or professional entities

2) Existence of standards and rules of business or professional activity that are mandatory for all members of this self-regulatory organization

3) The self-regulatory organization must provide each of its members with additional property liability for the consumers of manufactured goods (works performed, services rendered) and other persons...

Attempts to introduce self-regulation in advertising began long before the legislature provided a legal definition. In 1989, the Russian Association of Advertisers was established, which in 1996 was renamed the National Advertising Association. In 1991, the first document establishing the rules of the advertising community—"The Code of Advertising Practice" (Gribok, 2011)—was developed. Since then, several organizations that had united the advertising agencies, as well as the documents that had been adopted by them, have gone into oblivion (Yevstaf'ev & Pasyutina, 2017; Gribok, 2011; Denisova, Milovanova, & Hrapina, 2011). Today, the most authoritative is the Association of Communications Agencies of Russia (ACAR), which was established in 1993 as the Russian Association of Advertising Agencies (AKAR, 2019).

The ACAR includes an ethics committee. The Association took an active part in the development and adoption of the Russian Code of Advertising and Marketing Communications (Rossiyskiy Kodeks, 2012). The Code was signed by 15 representatives of these non-governmental organizations, including Association of Manufacturers of Rusbrand Trade Marks, Association of Communications Agencies of Russia, Association of Advertisers, National Association of Visual Communications, Association of Marketing Services, Russian Association "Advertising Federation of Regions", National Advertising Association, and the Russian branch of the International Advertising Association. The Consolidated International Chamber of Commerce Code on Advertising and Marketing Communication Practice of 2006 was adopted as a model for the Code (International Chamber of Commerce/World Business Organization Consolidated ICC Code of Advertising and Marketing Communication Practice). By the time the International Chamber of Commerce had adopted the Russian document, a new version of the Consolidated Code had already been drafted. As of 2019, the composition of ACAR Ethics Committee has not yet been approved (Sostav Komissii, 2019).

For many years, one of the best examples of this non-governmental organization resolving conflicts among the players of the advertising industry, and between them and advertising consumers, was the Regional Public Council for Advertising of St. Petersburg. It was established in 1995, with Sergey Pilatov as its founder and permanent president. In 2017, St. Petersburg became the first Russian region to have established an advertisers' non-government organization that complies with all of the legislative requirements on self-regulatory organizations and that is actually engaged in self-regulation of the industry (Kratkaya informaciya, 2017). On June 14, 2018, the Association of Marketing Industry "Advertising Council" was officially established, and Pilatov became its head.

In 2019 the Association of Marketing Industry "Advertising Council" consisted of 51 members, including advertising companies (for example, "Poster"), advertisers (for example, LLC Maksidom), and associations (for example, AKAR). The Association has concluded agreements with several state and public organizations, on the basis of which it exchanges information, organizes a series of joint actions, and conducts an examination of controversial advertising. When making its decisions, the Association is guided by both its own documents and ICC Advertising and Marketing Communications Code (2018). In April 2019, the "Association of the Marketing Industry Advertising Council" became an observer member of the European Alliance for Advertising Standards (Ob Assotsiatsii, 2019). Currently, the International Chamber of Commerce recognizes Russia as a country with developing self-regulation of advertising (ICC Advertising, 2019).

Economic indicators of the advertising market—the dynamics and structural parameters

The size of the market capacity and other indicators of Russian advertising are determined by experts as well as by market analytics, which suggests that the processes in the market are not completely transparent. Assessments are made by professional partnerships and associations, but not by official statistics. First of all, the analysis of the advertising market is made by ACAR (Ob"yomy rynka reklamy, 2018).

The advertising market's dependence on the current economic situation is a self-explanatory and consistent pattern. At the same time, the Russian market has demonstrated that, even amidst an economic slump, some segments are able to show a reasonable upward trend. For the beginning of the twenty-first century, this unique phenomenon is associated with completing the updating of the means of production and the dissemination of advertisements. We have summarized the data of ACAR by the volume of the advertising market in Russia for the years 2000–2018 (Ob"yem reklamy v sredstvakh yeye rasprostraneniya, 2018a). The result of the analysis is presented in Tables 7.1–7.4.

The last year within the framework of our analysis is 2018. Experts estimate the growth of the media advertising market in 2018 had ranged from 9 to 11%. Thus, according to ACAR (Association of Communication Agencies of Russia), the market volumes by the third quarter of 2018 were as follows (Table 7.4) (Ob"yem reklamy v sredstvakh yeye rasprostraneniya, 2018b).

Table 7.1 Russian advertising market 2000–2006: Financial performance and volume (billion rubles/billion USD)

Volume/year	2000	2001	2002	2003	2004	2005	2006
TV billion rubles	6.6	12.4	24.0	31.8	41.5	55.8	72.8
Radio billion rubles	1.4	2.5	3.8	5.0	6.3	8.0	10.2
Print media billion rubles	10.9	14.9	19.8	24.0	29.3	36.7	44.9
Out-of-Home billion rubles	3.9	6.5	10.2	13.4	17.4	26.1	32.9
Internet billion rubles	0.0	0.2	0.3	0.6	1.3	2.4	4.8
In general billion rubles	22.8	36.5	58.2	74.8	95.8	129.0	165.7
USD billion dollars	0.81	1.25	1.86	2.44	3.33	4.56	6.1

Table 7.2 Russian advertising market 2007–2013: Financial performance and volume (billion rubles/billion USD)

Volume/year	2007	2008	2009	2010	2011	2012	2013
TV billion rubles	95.9	117.7	96.4	110.8	131.5	143.4	156.2
Radio billion rubles	13.6	13.1	9.2	10.3	12.1	15.1	17.4
Print media billion rubles	55.9	63.8	35.6	38.0	40.4	41.2	37.7
Out-of-Home billion rubles	41.7	47.7	27.4	32.8	38.4	42.6	46.4
Internet billion rubles	10.2	14.9	17.8	27.0	42.2	59.0	77.0
In general billion rubles	217.3	257.2	186.4	218.9	264.6	301.3	334.6
USD billion dollars	8.5	10.33	5.88	7.21	9.0	9.69	10.48

Table 7.3 Russian advertising market 2014–2017: Financial performance and volume (billion rubles/billion USD)

Volume/year	2014	2015	2016	2017
TV billion rubles	159.8	136.7	150.8	170
Radio billion rubles	17.9	15.5	16.5	16.9
Print media billion rubles	34.3	25.3	22.3	20.5
Out-of-Home billion rubles	45.7	36.2	38.3	41.9
Internet billion rubles	97.0	112.3	136.0	166.3
In general billion rubles	354.7	326.0	364.0	416.5
USD billion dollars	9.23	5.34	5.43	7.13

Table 7.4 The advertising market of Russia in the first three quarters of 2018

Segment	January–September 2018, billion rubles	Dynamics, %
TV	130–131	12
Radio	11.5–11.7	1
Print media	12.8–13.0	-10
OOH	31.0–31.2	0
Internet	140.5–141.5	22
In general	326.0–328.0	13

In 2000–2018, the market grew unevenly, according to available ACAR data, but growth was evident both in quantitative indicators and in financial performance.

In the period under review, the most successful financial performance was in 2013—the last year before the instability in Ukraine and the introduction of anti-Russian sanctions by the United States and the European Union. That year, the volume of the advertising market in comparable prices amounted

Table 7.5 Annual dynamics of advertising volumes 2011–2017 (recalculation of ACAR data)

Segment	Annual dynamics, %						
TV	2011	2012	2013	2014	2015	2016	2017
Radio	+29	+8	+12	+4	−14	+10	+13
Print media	+18	+21	+14	+5	−16	+6	+3
OOH	+11	+3	−6	−10	− 29	−16	−8
Internet	+25	+10	+9	+2	−21	+6	+9
In general	+57	+45	+30	+20	+15	+21	+22

to about 10.5 billion dollars. With the exception of the press, all other media segments of the advertising market showed an upward trend compared to previous years. In 2013, the volume of the advertising market in the segment of BTL services was 13% more than the same segment in 2012. After the peak in the relatively stable 2011 (21%), the growth rate of the advertising market gradually reduced: in 2013, the growth rate was at 11%, and by the end of 2014 was only 6%. But, these were only the first stages of decline. Because of the sanctions of the European Union and of the United States, the economic crisis in 2015, the ruble collapse, and the steep drop in oil prices that had negatively affected the national economy, the volume of the Russian advertising market fell by another 8% compared to the previous period. Internet advertising was the only exception, which showed significant growth against the steep decline in other segments.

However, despite pessimistic macroeconomic indicators, the business has revived, major and medium-sized advertisers have taken the lead, and, in 2016 and 2017, the market started growing by 12% and 14%, respectively. During the past seven years (without taking as representative indicators due to the global economic crisis of 2015), absolute stability and an upward trend may be noted (Table 7.5). At the same time, the Internet segment shows growth, even against general stagnation in many segments, which makes Internet advertising most promising. Investing in the Internet continues, because the pattern of network behavior of a potential consumer does not depend on external circumstances: during an economic downturn, people spend even more time online. The Internet is the most accessible and popular entertainment, with endless potential for content delivery to any social group, regardless of age, level of intelligence, interests, and preferences.

In 2017–2018, the Russian advertising industry felt more free: the number of restrictions imposed by the authorities has decreased, and the quality of communications had increased dramatically. The volume of advertising market amounted to 417 billion rubles in 2017 (Ob"yem reklamy v sredstvakh yeye rasprostraneniya v 2017, 2017). The weighted average exchange rate of the U.S. dollar to the ruble was 58.298 in 2017 (Kurs dollara, 2017), and thus the volume of the Russian advertising market was 7.15 billion dollars in 2017. The Russian Association of Marketing Services (RAMS) reported that the volume of marketing services amounted to almost 103 billion rubles ($1.77 bln.), which is 9% more than in 2016 (Marketingovyye uslugi, 2018). Russian marketing communications, that is, advertising budgets spent on the creative solutions, the production of advertisements, and the payment for services of advertising agencies, amounted to about 730–750 billion rubles ($12.5—12.9 bln.)

This Russian record indicates that the advertising segment is moving in the right direction. While the economy in 2017 increased at a very moderate pace (1.5%, according to the official data of Rosstat) (ROSSIYA V TSIFRAKH, 2018), the growth of the advertising market amounted to 14%. This reflects the growing activity of entrepreneurs (Kateneva, 2018; Veselov, 2018a). The active-market players were not large international companies, but domestic advertisers—the representatives of medium-sized businesses. This is confirmed by the report of the Publicis Media advertising agency. The company's analysts found that most of the G20 major advertisers in 2017 reduced the purchases of advertising space on the Russian federal TV channels due to rising prices in this segment. (Krupneyshiye reklamodateli, 2018). However, small- and medium-sized companies have increased these costs. Sergey Veselov, co-chairman of the ACAR Research, Audit and Advertising Technologies Committee, said significant market growth in 2017 is mainly due to the increased activity of advertisers of second to third levels (2018b).

In 2017, TV was still the largest platform for advertising, collecting 170.9 billion rubles ($2.9 bln.), which is 13% more than in 2016. The volume of advertising on the Internet increased by 22% to 166.3 billion rubles ($2.85 bln.). Outdoor advertising increased by 9% to 41.9 billion rubles ($0.72 bln.), including mobile advertising 28% to 4.6 billion rubles. Advertising on the radio gained 3% (up to 16.9 billion rubles/$0.29 bln.), and print media lost 8% of the market (20.5 billion rubles/$0.35 bln).

Thus, the concentration of advertising budgets in the two leading segments is increasing.

> The television and the Internet accumulate together more than 80% of all advertising budgets, while in the world this figure is near 70–72% in 2017–2018. There is an increase in the volume of mobile advertising. This is facilitated by reorganization of the urban environment in the largest million-cities and the optimization of stationary advertising structures.
>
> (Komissiya ekspertov AKAR, 2018)

The general trend is the reduction of the number of prohibitions and restrictions in Russian advertising (Komissiya ekspertov AKAR, 2018). While in 2013–2014, 10 amendments to the Act "On Advertising" were adopted annually, only four amendments were adopted in 2017. This improves advertisers' confidence in market stability and increases the possibilities of long-range planning for communication agencies. However, the Internet has been the key factor and growth driver of the advertising market during the past 5 years (Ob"yem reklamy v sredstvakh yeye rasprostraneniya, 2018a). In 2018, investments in digital advertising in Russia for the first time overtook TV advertising—43% compared to 41%. The shares of the press, outdoor, and radio advertising are steadily decreasing in the overall structure of the advertising media market, giving way to digital media. In addition, brisk growth of online video among all other segments of Internet media is not only due to audiences moving to Internet platforms, but also to the growing interest of advertisers for brands' active development of new formats of interaction with the audience.

The key players of the Russian advertising market

The advertising market unites two types of business actors: customers of advertising services, that is, the advertisers; and the providers of advertising services. The Russian advertising market has developed into a complex structure that integrates large- and medium-sized international advertisers and Russian advertisers that represent both global and small businesses. Advertisers represent various business segments (for example, production, politics, culture, and sports) and market segments, such as business-to-consumers, business-to-business, and business to government. The Russian advertising market has all the features of the modern international advertising market and is integrated into its global structure. Advertising services in Russia are provided both by the largest international network advertising and communication groups/holdings and by Russian advertising and communication agencies. Communication and advertising holdings provide full services and offer clients different forms of cooperation.

At the same time, advertising services in Russia today are quite diversified. Specific niches have been developed, which are occupied by agencies for the development of creative solutions, design, digital communications, event communications, souvenirs, and promotional products. Media-selling and media-buying agencies are a separate segment of the market.

Analytical information about the market structure and dynamics has been provided since 1993 by the Association of Communications Agencies of Russia (www.akarussia.ru). Also, the professional portal sostav.ru (www.sostav.ru) offers analytical information about the activity of the advertising market and its core players and monitors the dynamics of the Russian advertising market. Also, that portal gives detailed information about areas of cooperation between leading advertisers and advertising producers (advertising agencies).

Research companies are engaged in the study and analysis of specialized markets in the Russian communications market. Mediascope (https://mediascope.net, n.d.), a marketing and media research company, is the leader in Russian media research and monitoring of advertising and media. The company's activities are based on international research standards. The company is a member of industry associations, such as European Media Research Organizations, European Society for Opinion and Marketing Research, and

Russian Association for Market and Opinion Research. Mediascope clients are the majority of media and advertising market participants: advertising agencies and groups, publishing houses, TV channels, radio stations, Internet sites, and advertising companies. Mediascope information serves as the basis for strategic marketing and promotional solutions. The ESPAR research company (www.espar.ru, n.d.) monitors outdoor advertising, and the Analytical Center of NSC (http://nsc.media) monitors Russian TV.

According to the data of marketing research agencies, major advertisers in Russia are traditionally the companies representing pharmaceuticals (OTCPharm, Berlin-Chemie Menari AG, GSK Consumer Healthcare, Sanofi-Aventis, Sandoz Pharma, Teva Pharma, Bayer AG); mobile operators (MegaFon, MTS, Beeline, Tele2); retail companies (M.video, X5 Retail Group, Metro Group); automotive industry (Volkswagen); consumer goods (Reckitt Benckiser, Unilever, Procter & Gamble, Johnson & Johnson, Henkel Group); cosmetics and perfumes (L'Oreal); food (PepsiCo, Nestle, Mars Russia, McDonald's, Coca-Cola, Ferrero, Danone, Essen Production) (Top-30, 2018).

Pepsi Co took the lead among the TOP-30 advertisers in 2017, with an advertising budget of 6.5 billion rubles. The top-five also included Reckitt Benckiser (5.8 billion rubles), OTCPharm (5.3 billion), Procter & Gamble (5.2 billion), and Nestle (5.1 billion). Top-30 major advertisers in Russia are presented in detail on www.sostav.ru (Top 30 largest advertisers in Russia). This list included the companies having the largest advertising budgets spent on promotion in 2017—108.6 billion rubles, which is 26% of the national advertising market that ACAR estimated at 417 billion rubles.

Major advertisers choose advertising agencies that, in their opinion, are the most authoritative in certain areas of advertising or those having a similar understanding of style. Information at www.sostav.ru represents advertising agencies and their work in some advertising segments for large business customers (Karta krupneyshikh reklamodateley, 2018). The leading players offering a full package of advertising services are traditionally the Russian representative offices of global network advertising groups, for example, BBDO (https://bbdogroup.ru, n.d.), TBWA (www.tbwa.ru, n.d.), Saatchi & Saatchi (http://saatchi.ru, n.d.), Leo Burnett (www.leoburnett.ru, n.d.), and these groups' affiliate agencies. The number of clients maintained by these holdings, and the scope of tasks with which they can cope, are too much for smaller domestic advertising agencies. Thus, these branches of global advertising holdings are the leaders in their scope of services and advertising budgets.

However, it is worth noting that domestic advertising agencies enjoy a great market share, especially in the regions. They have good reputations and enjoy relationships with domestic and international customers, especially among middle-sized businesses, providing these agencies the opportunity to successfully operate in the market. Russian advertising agencies have great creative potential, as is demonstrated by their frequent awards at international contests. Today, small advertising groups, independent agencies, and creative boutiques work actively and successfully in Russia. They have become the spearhead and set the targets for benchmarking. Only seven years ago, the customers wanted service that a "Leo Burnett" provided; now, everyone wants Russian "Friends" (http.//friends.moscow, n.d.) or "Voskhod" AD Company (https://voskhod. agency, n.d.). Actually, these two key players have set the trend of Russian advertising the past few years. Also, a high professional standard is set by advertising agencies such as these: Good Moscow (https://goodsupport.moscow, n.d.), TutkovBudkov (https://tutkovbudkov.ru, n.d.), SLAVA (http://slava.co.uk, n.d.), Possible Moscow (www.possiblegroup.ru, n.d.), Marvelous (https://marvelous.ru, n.d.), GREAT (https://great.ru, n.d.), and Red Pepper Film (http://redpepperfilm.com) the last of which is actively developing the "branded content" segment in Russia. A detailed map of the advertising market with existing advertising holdings and agencies is presented on the industry portal sostav.ru (www.sostav.ru/advmap, n.d.)

Contemporary trends in Russian advertising

The most notable trends in the Russian advertising market are determined by the change in the global content: consumers dip into the Internet and more often are interacting only with mobile formats. Hence the trends: making the nature of communications faster and sharper, increasing the personalization of messages, and growth in the popularity of branded content. This is the competition for attention that is already a feature of Russian marketing communications.

In general, experts highlight these trends in Russian advertising the last two to three years.

Taking the lead by online channels: Convergence of offline and online technologies

Today:

> the audience of the Runet is 90 million people; it has increased by 3% compared to 2017. The mobile audience has overtaken the desktop one and continues to grow: 24.3 million people—mobile only and 13.9 million people—desktop only. Mobile is ahead of desktop also by an exclusive audience: 61% of users, which is 9% higher than in 2016, while the desktop audience decreased by 2% to 51% of all Internet users who go online monthly. Mobile is far ahead of desktop in small settlements, while in large cities the distribution of mobile and desktop are almost identical. The time spent by users on the Internet is increasing. The average user spends online about 3 hours a day (mobile + desktop). The audience of Smart TV is 12% − + 20% for the year. Social networks are the leader in terms of the time spent on the Internet. But they are overtaken by video.
>
> (Runet podvel itogi goda, 2017)

Due to the onrush of new technologies, the Internet has been the key aspect and growth driver of the advertising market during the past five years. In 2017, the amounts invested in Internet advertising rose for the first time with investments in TV advertising: "116–117 billion rubles on TV and 115–116 billion rubles on the Internet and social networks" (Milosh, 2018). In Russia in 2018, digital advertising for the first time overtook investments in TV advertising—43% vs 41%. The shares of the press, outdoor, and radio advertising are steadily decreasing in the overall structure of the advertising media market, giving way to digital media. The best that "traditional media" may expect is to maintain the "status quo", but mostly they are surrendering their positions. In addition, attention should be paid to the brisk growth of online video, among all other segments of Internet media. And this is due, not only to the new features of the audience moving to the Internet platforms, but also to the growing interest of advertisers in such an advertising product. Online video in 2017–2018 has become booming, and ACAR experts foresee its active development by the leading brands.

The growth of consumer resistance to direct advertising: The growing demand for native advertising and its increasing distribution

According to Sales Generator, 91% of email users unsubscribe from corporate mailings, 86% of buyers ignore TV advertising, and 44% of buyers ignore direct mail (Nativnaya reklama pochemu ona vytesnyaet drugie formaty, 2018). At first, especially in the first decade of the 2000s, "advertising in Russia replaced journalism" (Novikov, 1999), and then native advertising absorbed the features of journalistic and public relations texts: "The materials of native format on the one hand are similar to journalistic articles or personal blogs, on the other hand—to PR-articles" (Nativnaya reklama v media obzor formatov i perspektivy razvitiya, 2016). Interviews with public relations professionals from major St. Petersburg companies noted that their publications on social networks serve as native advertising, written in a journalistic manner—"briefly, succinctly, without many words and addressable" (Bykova, 2018, June 18).

In 2019, the request for native content has the potential for sustained growth (Nativnaya reklama polnyj obzor i horoshie primery, 2018). "While in 2014 native advertising had only 20% of those in the media, then in 2015 the ratio increased to 30%, and by 2018 the native and direct media advertising were equal in terms of budgets" (Trendy nativnoj reklamy v 2015 godu, 2015). "In 2015, the share of native advertising amounted to 14% (of all advertising on similar platforms). By 2018, the figure can reach 28%" (NAI, 2016). "In many publications native advertising gives from 50 to 80% of revenue" (Krasilshchik, 2019). The native content helps the print media to earn money, "on premium (paid) editorial sites the audience is 50% higher than in usual free viewing" (Nativnaya reklama trendy 2019, 2019).

The contextual orientation increases

In 2018–2019, advertisers were increasingly focusing on information with care for a person: the reader *interacts* with the content, not just looking at advertising banners (NAI, 2016). The advertiser employed bloggers, whose network resources allowed the advertisements to look natural. The account of the blogger, who has a mass subscription to update the publications, is sometimes commensurate with the federal media, both pragmatically—in terms of impact, and legally—in terms of responsibility for the published content (Federal'niy Zakon, 2014).

> In the Russian realities, one of the main events for business is the launch of native advertising posts in the VKontakte user feed. Since July 1, 2015, the format is available to all interested communities of more than 10,000 subscribers and a minimum budget of 10 thousand rubles.
>
> (Trendy nativnoj reklamy v 2015 godu, 2015)

Change of the media consumption type: Sustained growth of advertising in online video and on mobile platforms, in applications, games

"There is a vigorous growth of advertising on mobile devices (19.2%), and video formats have especially large share (20%), due to the growing popularity of advertising views on smartphones … the focus shifts to digital" (Tempy rosta raskhodov na reklamu, 2019). Today, "the average Russian mobile user scrolls 178 meters of feed daily, while an experienced user—up to 277 meters (Nativnaya reklama trendy 2019, 2019). 3D banners, geolocation, messengers, and voice assistants are increasingly being used. The transition from clicks to dialogue is progressing, where chatbots and voice assistants take their place", says Inna Koryagina, the head of advertising and brand promotion department of "Russian Agricultural Bank" (Koryagina, 2019).

Personalization as the basis for the formation of new loyalty

Promotional content for the target audience is distributed by opinion leaders (popular bloggers). Svetlana Zeldina, P&G Marketing Director for Eastern Europe and Central Asia, believes that,

> The consumer becomes an agent of influence: it not only purchases the product, it sells the product when it puts ratings and leaves feedback. The people now trust the Internet ratings and feedback 12 times more than the advertising. Every brand buyer in the online shop becomes a brand lawyer, forming public opinion.
>
> (Zeldina, 2019)

Targeting algorithms

Targeting in Russian advertising is in line with global trends and is based, not on traditional socio-demographic characteristics, but on behavioral characteristics and customized behaviors and interests. "Algorithmically customizable segmentation should lead to the creation of personalized content and its personalized delivery at the right time", said Yuriy Samoilenko, Volkswagen Russia Marketing Director (Samojlenko, 2019). Eugene Kapustin, Director of Mondelez International Chocolate category in Eastern Europe, authoritatively observes that, "Programmatic is a trend that gives the opportunity to personalize an advertising message, thereby significantly improving the efficiency of investment" (Kapustin 2019).

The increased introduction of big data tools

This increase has allowed synchronization of the impressions of commercials for effective content targeting. Advertising campaigns are simultaneously launched on TV, YouTube, and Smart TV with pass-through links to the advertiser's website. Irina Kotik, Director of Media and Marketing Communications in "Unilever Rus", emphasizes the importance of big data influence: "forming segments for better targeting, adapting messages, navigating the user to a specific salespoint; ... to have full transparency how the communication affects the real business-result" (Kotik, 2019).

The most remarkable and vivid advertising campaigns and projects of the 2010s

Russian advertising agencies have been participating in the largest international advertising contests for more than 20 years. In recent years, Russian advertising agencies have gained an almost complete collection of awards at all of the famous festivals: Cannes Lions, D&AD (London), One Show (New York), Webby Awards (New York, International Academy of Digital Arts and Sciences), Clio Awards (Miami), Eurobest, Red Dot Design Award, Epika Awards, Piaf Awards (Prague), KIAF (Kiev), and even Grammy Awards (as nominees).

Below are landmark projects that have had a powerful impact on the Russian advertising industry, setting a new vector of professional development for representatives of the "old school" and inspiring the generation of young creators.

The project "Make the Politicians Work" of Voskhold Agency (Make the Politicians Work, 2012) is at the intersection of advertising and social commentary for online media URA.RU (URA.RU, 2012). This is a street art action, the essence of which is the caricatures of city and regional politicians that had appeared on the roads of Yekaterinburg. Pits and ditches were organically inscribed in the portraits, and, in speech bubbles, the politician promised to solve the problem. The project got into the news stories of the world's largest media and deservedly gained a collection of awards, including several Cannes Lions. Video about the project in English is at www.youtube.com/watch?v=48WoNWYUy7g.

"Car Curling" project[1] is another work of Voskhold Agency to promote the SmartPolis insurance agency (Avtokyerling, 2017). The agency held the world's first car curling competitions, but, rather than curling stones, the participants crashed real cars, a paradoxical way to promote car insurance services. The world's leading media told about "car curling", and SmartPolis became the leading player in the insurance market of the region. The project also has earned awards at the major festivals D&AD (London) and One Show (New York), including the Cannes Festival of Creativity. The agency is included in the Top Russian Agencies list and is an annual participant of the world's leading advertising festivals. Two projects of the agency were included in the Top 10 advertising campaigns that had change the world for the better.

Upside Down & Inside Out[2] by Tutkovbudkov Agency for S7 Airlines—one of the brightest representatives of the "branded content" category and the winner of all possible awards in the advertising industry (Cannes Lions, KIAF-2016—five Golden Awards)—created a clip for indie group "OK Go", which was recored in simulated weightlessness and was directed so that all key moments and tricks were performed within the free fall of the airplane. The S7 Airlines had developed a project that was unprecedented in its scope and implementation, for which the Russian air carrier became known throughout the world. The Agency has gained for its projects more than 100 awards at various international festivals.

"Sberbank Neighborhoods" (Sberbank. Neighborhoods, 2017) by Good Moscow Agency is a large-scale multi-stage campaign for the largest Russian bank. During the campaign, the bank created a diverse system of collecting information on the shops and other facilities that are required in certain districts of the city. Online tools and banners were used on empty trading areas. The collected information was used to generate advertising banners making credit offers for small businesses, with specific data on the actual needs of the citizens of a particular district. Sberbank said requests for loans to small businesses were three times more than from usual advertising. The project rightly became an event for the Russian advertising market. It also reached the international level and received awards in Europe, including at the Cannes Lions Festival of Creativity.

The Auktyon on the Sun project (Auktyon On The Sun, 2017) was created by Great—the leading advertising agency of North-West Russia for the Auktyon avant-garde musical group. On the eve of the release of a new album of cult avant-garde musicians called "On the Sun", a nonstandard promo was launched: the album with this name can only be seen and heard "on the Sun". The agency created the world's first music album, which begins to sound only if the listener focuses the phone's camera on the sun. Especially for this project, a unique application was developed that launches tracks from a new album when sunlight hits the phone's camera. A special photochrome pigment was used for the circulation of discs: the album design appeared only when the sunlight hit it and disappeared in the shadows. "On the Sun" has brought the agency more than two dozen prestigious awards, including the Cannes Lions.

In Russia, there are also advertising contests and festivals that are considered to be prestigious, both among domestic players of the advertising market and among foreign colleagues. The most authoritative contest since 1990 has been the Red Apple International Advertising Festival. This event gathers on one platform the leading creative specialists of the major international and Russian communications agencies as well as the heads of advertising and marketing departments of the largest advertising companies. The event includes competitive, educational, and entertainment programs. The festival is designed to bring together the creative cultures of Europe and Asia. The idea is that Russia can serve as a creative bridge, which is the distinguishing feature of the festival. The festival jury is represented by those holding top positions in the advertising industry and included in the Gunn Report rating, representing such global agencies as: BBDO, Ogilvy, Leo Burnett, Dentsu, Havas (Red Apple, 2019). The festival brings together 200 agencies from more than 30 countries. Fifteen jury members evaluate about 1,000 works of 18 advertising categories. The event has 170 speakers and generally about 3,000 participants. Special prizes include "Agency of the Year", "Advertiser of the Year", "Best Production", as well as the "For Good", the last which is awarded for charitable actions.

Summarizing, we note that, by the beginning of the 20s of the 21st Century, advertising in Russia is an established independent sector of the economy with developed economic indicators. A complex of legislative acts and ethical norms that regulate advertising activity has been formed. In Russia, public professional organizations, such as AKAR (Association of Communication Agencies of Russia, n.d.) are engaged in self-regulation of advertising activities.

The development of advertising in Russia is based on the integration of the best world experience and domestic practice. Leading American and European network communication agencies work in Russia. Russian advertising agencies are also actively working in the communication market, carrying out projects for foreign and domestic companies. The high professional level of Russian advertising agencies is confirmed by awards at prestigious international advertising competitions.

The advertising market in Russia has potential, having demonstrated the possibilities for stability and growth even in a situation of economic crises, which is confirmed by the financial data that have been presented in this chapter. Digital communications and the latest technological advances are mainstream and provide a stable financial string in advertising budgets. In general, we can conclude that the dynamics of the Russian advertising market is in line with the leading global communication trends.

Notes

1 www.youtube.com/watch?v=LWGJA9i18Co.
2 www.youtube.com/watch?v=LWGJA9i18Co.

References

Analytical Center of NSC. (n.d.). Retrieved from http://nsc.media.

"Voskhod" AD Company. (n.d.). Retrieved from https://voskhod.agency.

AKAR. Associaciya kommunikacionnyh agentstv Rossii (2019). (ACAR. Association of Communications Agencies of Russia). Retrieved from www.akarussia.ru.

Auktyon On The Sun. (2017). Retrieved from www.youtube.com/watch?v=nlTr_ZGWrFI.

Avtokyerling (2017). www.voskhod.agency/portfolio/avtokyerling/.

English version "Make the Politicians Work" (2012). www.youtube.com/watch?v=LWGJA9i18Co.

BBDO. (n.d.). Retrieved from https://bbdogroup.ru.

Bykov I., Cherkashchenko T., Dorskii A., & Kaverina E. (2015). Government regulation of advertising in the Eurasian Economic Union: Contradictions of public policy and advertising ethics. *International Journal of Economics and Financial Issues, 2015, 5* (Special Issue), 116–120.

Bykova, E. (2018, June 18). Author's personal archive.

Car Curling. (n.d.). Retrieved from www.youtube.com/watch?v=LWGJA9i18Co.

Denisova, A. V., Milovanova, N.D., & Khrapina Ye., V. (2011). Samoregulirovaniye v sfere reklamy: razvitije instituta i pravovyye problemy realizatsii: Vestnik Khabarovskoy gosudarstvennoy akademii ekonomiki i prava. 2011. N° 3. S. 44–57. [Self-regulation in the field of advertising: The development of the institution and the legal problems of implementation. *Bulletin of the Khabarovsk State Academy of Economics and Law. 2011*, (3), 44–57.]

ESPAR research company. (n.d.). Retrieved from www.espar.ru.

Federal'niy Zakon No. 97-FZ. (2014, May 5). "O vnesenii izmenenij v federal'nyj zakon 'Ob informatsii.informatsionnykhtekhnologiyakhi o zashchiteinformatsii' i otdelnyye zakonodatelnyye akty Rossiyskoy Federatsii po voprosamuporyadocheniyaobme nainformatsiyey s ispolzovaniyeminformatsionno-telekommunikatsionnykhsetey" [Federal law dated 5 May 2014 No. 97-FZ "*On amendments to the Federal law 'On information, information technologies and about information protection' and certain legislative acts of the Russian Federation on streamlining the exchange of information using information and telecommunication networks*"]. Retrieved from https://rg.ru/2014/05/07/informtech-dok.html.

Federal'nyy zakon ot 13.03.2006 N 38-FZ "O reklame". (2018, October 30). red. ot 30.10.2018). [Federal law of 13.03.2006 N 38-ФЗ "On advertising" (as amended on 10.30.2018).] Retrieved from www.consultant.ru/cons/cgi/online.cgi?req=doc&base=LAW&n=301298&fld=134&dst=1000000001,0&rnd=0.39102107947911646#08320296225541994.

"Friends". (n.d.). Retrieved from http://friends.moscow.

Good Moscow. (n.d.). Retrieved from https://goodsupport.moscow.

GREAT. (n.d.). Retrieved from https://great.ru.

Gribok, N. N. (2011). Stanovleniye reklamnogo soobshchestva v sovremennoy Rossii // Vlast'. 2011. N° 7. S. 83–85. (Gribok N.N. (2011). [Formation of the advertising community in modern Russia. *// Power. 2011*, (7), 83–85.]

ICC Advertising and Marketing Communications Code (2019). Retrieved from https:// iccwbo.org/publication/icc-advertising-and-marketing-communications-code.

Itogi osushchestvleniya gosudarstvennogo kontrolya i nadzora za soblyudeniyem zakonodatel'stva Rossiyskoy Federatsii o reklame za 2017 g. (2018) // Federal'naya Antimonopol'naya Sluzhba. [Results of state monitoring and supervision over the compliance with the legislation of the Russian Federation on advertising from 2017 // Federal Antimonopoly Service]. Retrieved from https://fas.gov.ru/pages/ rezultati_raboti_v_reklame.

Kakie trendy v mire i v Rossii budut opredelyat razvitie reklamnogo rynka v budushchem godu. (2019). [What trends in the world and in Russia will determine the development of the advertising market next year]. AdIndex.ru. Retrieved from https://adindex.ru/specprojects/marketing-trends-2018/168332.phtm

Kapustin, E. (2019). Kakie trendy v mire i v Rossii budut opredelyat razvitie reklamnogo rynka v budushchem godu. Retrieved from https://adindex.ru/specprojects/ marketing-trends-2018/168332.phtml.

Karta krupneyshikh reklamodateley Rossii. (2018). Map of the largest advertisers of Russia. 2018. Retrieved from www.sostav.ru/advmap/advertizersmap.

Kateneva, Y.Y. (2018). Rossiyskiy rynok reklamy: analiz trendov i prognoz na 2018 god [Russian advertising market: Analysis of trends and forecast for 2018]. Retrieved from https://tsargrad.tv/articles/rossijskij-rynok-reklamy-analiz-trendov-i-prognoz-na-2018-god_119552.

Komissiya ekspertov AKAR. (2018). podvela Podvela itogi razvitiya reklamnogo rynka Rossii za 2017 god. [The ACAR Commission of Experts summed up the development of the Russian advertising market in 2017]. Retrieved from www.akarussia.ru/ press_centre/news/id8182.

Koryagina, I. (2019) Kakie trendy v mire i v Rossii budut opredelyat razvitie reklamnogo rynka v budushchem godu. Retrieved from https://adindex.ru/specprojects/ marketing-trends-2018/168332.phtml.

Kotik, I. (2019). Kakie trendy v mire i v Rossii budut opredelyat razvitie reklamnogo rynka v budushchem godu. Retrieved from https://adindex.ru/specprojects/ marketing-trends-2018/168332.phtml.

Krasilshchik, I. (2019). Delat nativnuyu reklamu bez zhurnalistskogo i redakcionnogo opyta ochen slozhno. [It is very difficult to make native advertising without journalistic and editorial experience]. Retrieved from https://mediajobs.ru/ career/iliya-krasilschik-meduza-delat-nativnuju-reklamu-bez-zhurnalistskogo-i-redakcionnogo-opyta-ochen-slozhno/.

Kratkaya informatsiya po situatsii s sozdaniyem v Rossii sistemy samoregulirovaniya v sfere marketingovykh kommunikatsiy. (2017). [Brief information on the situation with the creation in Russia of the system of self-regulation in the field of marketing communications]. Retrieved from http://sovetreklama.org/reklamnoe-pravo/ kratkaya-informaciya-po-situacii-s-sozdaniem-v-rossii-sistemy-samoregulirovaniya-v-sfere-marketingovyx-kommunikacij/ (appeal date: 28.01.2019).

Krupneyshiye reklamodateli sokrashchayut raskhody na telereklamu, 2018. (2018). [The largest advertisers reduce the cost of television advertising, 2018] Retrieved from https://wek.ru/krupnejshie-reklamodateli-sokrashhayut-rasxody-na-telereklamu.

Kurs dollara. (2017). SSHA v 2017 godu. (US dollar rate in 2017). Retrieved from https://ratestats.com/dollar/2017/.

Leo Burnett. (n.d.). Retrieved from www.leoburnett.ru.

Ley 34/1988, de 11 de noviembre, General de Publicidad. (Law 34/1988, 11 November, General about advertising). Retrieved from http://noticias.juridicas.com/base_datos/Admin/l34-1988.html.

Make the politicians work (2012). www.youtube.com/watch?v=48WoNWYUy7g.

Marketingovyye uslugi (2018). v 2017 godu. RAMU, 2018 (Marketing services in 2017.) RAMU, 2018.RAMU, 2018.) Retrieved from www.ramu.ru/upload/files/%D0%9E%D0%B1%D1%8A%D0%B5%D0%BC%D1%8B%20%D1%80%D1%8B%D0%BD%D0%BA%D0%B0%20%D0%9C%D0%A3%202017.png.

Marvelous. (n.d.). Retrieved from https://marvelous.ru.

Mediascope. (n.d.). Retrieved from https://mediascope.net.

Milosh, I. (2018). 8 globalnyh trendov marketinga v 2018 godu ot Zenith (2018) [Milos I. 8 global marketing trends in 2018 from Zenith]. Retrieved from www.sostav.ru/publication/8-globalnykh-trendov-marketinga-v-2018-godu-ot-zenith-30308.html.

NAI: Glavnye trendy nativnoj reklamy v 2016 godu. (2016). [NAI: The main trends of native advertising in 2016]. Retrieved from https://spark.ru/startup/buzzoola/blog/19208/nai-glavnie-trendi-nativnoj-reklami-v-2016-godu.

Nativnaya reklama pochemu ona vytesnyaet drugie formatyformat. (2018). [Native advertising: Why is it replacing other formats]. Retrieved from https://sales-generator.ru/blog/nativnaya-reklama/.

Nativnaya reklama polnyj obzor i horoshie primery. (2018). [Native advertising: full Full review and good examples]. Retrieved from https://1ps.ru/blog/promotion/2018/nativnaya-reklama-polnyj-obzor-i-xoroshie-primeryi/.

Nativnaya reklama trendy 2019. (2019). [Native advertising: Trends 2019]. Retrieved from https://evo.business/nativnaya-reklama-trendy-2019.

Nativnaya reklama v media obzor formatov i perspektivy razvitiya. (2016). [Native advertising in media: Overview of formats and prospects of development]. Retrieved from https://vc.ru/marketing/17537-media-native/.

Novikov, A. (1999). Prevrashcheniye slova v tekst. [Turning words into text.] *Zhurnalist [Journalist]*, 3, 30–40.

Ob Assotsiatsii. (2019). About the Association, 2019. Retrieved from http://sovetreklama.ru/index.html.

Ob"yem reklamy v sredstvakh yeye rasprostraneniya v 2017 godu.AKAR. (2018a). [The volume of advertising in the means of its distribution in 2017]. Retrieved from www.akarussia.ru/knowledge/market_size/id8180.

Ob"yem reklamy v sredstvakh yeye rasprostraneniya v yanvare-sentyabre 2018 goda. (2018b).AKAR. 2018. [The volume of advertising in the means of its distribution in January-September 2018 AKAR, 2018]. Retrieved from www.akarussia.ru/knowledge/market_size/id8566.

Ob"yomy rynka reklamy. (2018). (Advertising market volumes) Retrieved from www.akarussia.ru/knowledge/market_size.

Pochemu nativnaya reklama stala glavnym trendom media i kak realizovat ee na rossijskih ploshchadkah. (2015). [Why native advertising has become the main media trend and how to implement it on Russian platforms]. Retrieved from https://blog.relap.ru/2015/09/pochemu-nativnaya-reklama-stala-glavnyi-2/.

Possible Moscow. (n.d.). Retrieved from www.possiblegroup.ru.

Red Apple. (2019). Retrieved from https://festival.ru.

Red Pepper Film. (n.d.). Retrieved from http://redpepperfilm.com.

ROSSIYA V TSIFRAKH. (2018). Kratkiy statisticheskiy sbornik. FEDERAL'NAYA SLUZHBA GOSUDARSTVENNOY STATISTIKI (Rosstat). M. 2018. (RUSSIA IN FIGURES. 2018. A brief statistical compilation. FEDERAL STATE STATISTICS SERVICE (Rosstat). M. 2018.

Rossiyskiy Kodeks praktiki reklamy i marketingovykh kommunikatsiy. (2012). Russian Code of Practice for Advertising and marketing communications, Moscow, RU. 2012). Retrieved from www.akarussia.ru/download/rrk.pdf8279 (appeal date: 01/28/2019).

Runet podvel itogi goda. (2017). [Runet summed up the year]. Retrieved from www.advertology.ru/article146117.htm.

Saatchi & Saatchi. (n.d.). Retrieved from http://saatchi.ru.

Samojlenko, Y. (2019). Kakie trendy v mire i v Rossii budut opredelyat razvitie reklamnogo rynka v budushchem godu. Retrieved from https://adindex.ru/specprojects/marketing-trends-2018/168332.phtml.

SBERBANK. NEIGHBORHOODS. (2017). Retrieved from www.youtube.com/watch?v=YEcvUQG3EX8.

SLAVA. (n.d.). Retrieved from http://slava.co.uk.

Sostav. (n.d.). Retrieved from www.sostav.ru/advmap.

Sostav Komissii po etike AKAR. (2019). (Composition of the Ethics Commission ACAR). Retrieved from www.akarussia.ru/node/8279.

Tempy rosta raskhodov na reklamu v mire v 2019 godu uvelichatsya na 3.8%. (2019). [The growth rate of advertising costs in the world in 2019 will increase by 3.8%]. Retrieved from www.advertology.ru/article146265.htm.

Top-10 Effie Russia. (2018). Retrieved from www.voskhod.agency/blog/top-10-effie-russia/.

TOP-30 krupneyshikh reklamodateley Rossii. (2018). Top 30 largest advertisers in Russia, 2018. Retrieved from www.sostav.ru/publication/rejting-krupnejshikh-reklamodatelej-rossii-2018–31422.htm.

Trendy nativnoj reklamy v 2015 godu. (2015). [Trends of native advertising in 2015]. Retrieved from https://blog.relap.ru/2015/07/trendyi-nativnoy-reklamyi-v-2015-godu/.

TutkovBudkov. (n.d.). Retrieved from https://tutkovbudkov.ru.

Upside Down & Inside Out. (n.d.). Retrieved from www.youtube.com/watch?v=LWGJA9i18Co.

Ura.Ru. (2012). Make the politicians work. Retrieved from https://adage.com/creativity/work/make-politicians-work/29041.

Veselov S. (2018a). Reklamnyy rynok Rossii pokazyvayet khoroshuyu dinamiku. [The advertising market of Russia shows good dynamics]. Retrieved from https://ruvod.com/sergej-veselov-reklamnyj-rynok-rossii-pokazyvaet-horoshuyu-dinamiku.

Veselov S. (2018b). Rost TV reklamy obespechil segment srednikh i malykh reklamodateley. [The growth of TV advertising provided a segment of medium and small advertisers]. Retrieved from www.advertology.ru/article144347.htm.

Yevstaf'yev V. A., & Pasyutina, Ye. E. (2017). Istoriya rossiyskoy reklamy: Sovremennyy period, 2-ye izd., ispr. i dop. [The history of Russian advertising: The modern period, 2nd ed.]. Moskva: Dashkov i K°.

Zákon. (1995, February 9). O regulaci reklamy a o změně a doplnění zákona č. 468/ 1991 Sb., o provozování rozhlasového a televizního vysílání, ve znění pozdějších předpisů [Law (1995) of 9. February 1995 on advertising regulation and amending and supplementing Act No. 468/1991 Coll., on the operation of radio and television broadcasting, as amended]. Retrieved from www.zakonyprolidi.cz/cs/ 1995-40?text=o+regulaci+reklamy.

Zeldina, S. (2019). Kakie trendy v mire i v Rossii budut opredelyat razvitie reklamnogo rynka v budushchem godu. Retrieved from https://adindex.ru/specprojects/ marketing-trends-2018/168332.phtml.

8 Understanding advertising in modern Russia

Role, functions, and problems

Marina Shilina and Dmitry Fedyunin

Introduction

According to the Federal Law of the Russian Federation No. 38-FZ "On Advertising", adopted on March 13, 2006 (The Federal Law "On Advertising", 2006), advertising is information that is disseminated in any way, in any form, and using any means, that is addressed to an indefinite circle of persons and is aimed at drawing attention to the object of advertising, forming or maintaining interest and promotion in the market. Currently, in Russia, new realities of the industry and technology reveal paradoxes in the definition of advertising—and then it provokes specific industrial problems. First, the Internet makes the target advertising audience-specific, that is, targeted advertising appeals to a specific person. Direct marketing, contextual advertising, and classifieds on the Internet thus cannot be classified as advertising.

What is advertising in such a paradoxical environment in modern Russia? Modern advertising began to take shape with the collapse of the USSR and the development of a modern market economy in the 1990s, when a need to promote goods and services in a competitive environment was formed, and advertising became an indispensable part of business. In a short time, a small, but dynamically growing, Russian advertising market is being integrated into the global industry and is becoming global, since all of the leading global advertising agencies and global advertisers are present in Russia today, such as PepsiCo, Reckitt Benckiser, Nestlè, Procter & Gamble, and L'Oreal (Top-30, 2019).

According to Russian experts, the advertising market in Russia is less institutionalized than in developed economies (Evstafiev & Pasyutina, 2017; Veselov, 2019). According to the level of development, the market can be likened to moderately developed ones (based on the share in GDP and on advertising expenditures per capita). This level is comparable to the development of advertising markets in Eastern Europe or Latin America. The peculiarity of the Russian advertising market is its scale, which is largely due to the size of the territory.

The question of the impact of advertising on business remains controversial to this day. The substantiation of the positions of experts requires evidence that, in the conditions of an opaque market, advertising is impossible. However, the

Association of Communications Agencies of Russia (ACAR) has conducted market research since 1997, despite a number of limitations that affect the reliability of the results (in particular, lack of data transparency, correct industrial audit, and research methods). Studies of their segments are carried out by other industrial organizations, for example, the Guild of Periodical Press Publishers, the Russian Academy of Radio, the Association in the Field of Outdoor Advertising, and Interactive Buro Russia. From 2018, ACAR (2018) has carried out calculations using a new methodology that takes into account the maximum number of parameters of advertising activity.

Despite these differences in estimates, the market, in general, has emerged from the crisis of 2009. Since 2014, the situation of instability has led to increases and, in 2019, inhibitions. This is primarily due to the unfavorable external investment climate as well as because of domestic economic and political reasons. However, the majority of large foreign advertisers have remained in Russia, in particular because they have local production. For example, Nestlè produces confectionery products of the brand "Russia is a generous soul" in Samara (Nestlè Factories and Branches, 2019).

According to Sergey Veselov, one of the leading Russian researchers in the advertising market and the Vice President of ACAR, the general development of the market is not influenced by certainty. There are no long-term and medium-term strategies, and contracts are usually for one year, which leads to an increase in the cost of transactions. Veselov also notes a sharp differentiation in which the Internet is developing most rapidly, television is keeping its positions, and the segments of the print press, radio, and outdoor advertising are practically not growing (Veselov, 2019). Among new tools, mobile in Russia has become a standard instrument of advertising (Shchepilova & Kozhanova, 2016).

The structure of advertising markets in different countries is similar. In Russia, the main subjects of the advertising market are: advertisers as basic subjects, regulators as mediated basic subjects, creative subjects—agencies, organizations, and companies that produce a creative advertising product, technical subjects—advertising producers, and distributors of advertising, for example, agencies and owners of media channels. New actors are platforms on which advertising is placed and that act as intermediaries for advertising. Taking into account the activity of artificial intelligence programs and neural networks, advertising interactivity on platforms becomes hybrid. New actors are also bloggers who may have millions of subscribers and who target audiences that exceed the audience of official media.

Basic subjects—advertisers define strategic and tactical goals, as well as the functional and operational objectives of their promotional activities. The advertiser can develop advertising materials and technologies for their design and promotion, as well as buy advertising spaces, areas, media, modules, and time, by using their own resources and related services. The costs are much higher per unit cost of promotional products than those provided by professional advertising organizations.

Creative subjects—specialized advertising organizations (agencies) are sellers of advertising services and the main buyers of space and time for advertising messages or intermediaries in these processes. They explore the target audience of advertising: final consumers, determining their problems, needs, demands, motivations, and interests, as well as sellers of advertising space and time, the possibilities of which are constantly evaluated (by innovation, quality, efficiency, and cost). Agencies develop industry goals, strategy, and tactics for organizing promotional activities, advertising campaigns, and PR campaigns.

Advertising agencies as market entities can be divided into selling, creative, strategic, and media by means of advertising, non-media (production). Today in Russia, there are 25 large advertising agencies and hundreds of medium-sized and small ones. Agencies have the necessary resources: relevant information databases; professional staff, including scriptwriters, directors, artists and designers; technologists; special equipment and technologies; production facilities; as well as competence in designing, producing, and distributing advertising through various channels. The functions of agencies are changing rapidly: for example, buying agencies have lived on the difference in the price of buying and placing advertising, but increasing the transparency of the industry has made this area less attractive.

Mediated basic subjects—owners of platforms and channels for advertising in media and sellers of advertising time, space, structures (mobile and fixed objects, indoor and outdoor, television and radio broadcasting, print and Internet media, mobile operators). These entities may also be professional producers of promotional products. These actors develop strategies and tactics, that is, long-term and short-term plans for the development of the media environment and media culture, including advertising in these programs.

The specificity of the markets lies in the development of individual segments. For example, the advertising market in Russia has a rather high share of outdoor advertising. This is largely due to the prohibition of tobacco advertising on television and the transition of tobacco giants, such as Philip Morris and Japan Tobacco, to other formats. Also the world's largest outdoor advertising company, NewsOutdoor, operates in Russia.

Classical structures and classifications of advertising holdings and agencies are transformed, since the emergence of new directions and technologies specializations makes the involvement of specialized campaigns in projects more effective. Digitalization determines the emergence within structures of the advertising business of structures that are essentially not related to the advertising business, for example, digital platforms, but that determine the functions and effectiveness of advertising activities.

Platforms are new mediated subjects. A platform launches affiliate programs and is the so-called intermediary between advertisers and publishers that provides technical and organizational tools to run cost-per-action (CPA) advertising campaigns efficiently. (CPA means the amount of money that is charged to a company, for example, that advertises on a website each time someone buys a product, fills out a form, etc., after clicking on the advertisement on the website.) Typical cost-per-action arrangements include the advertiser paying per lead, per sale, or when a form is completely filled out. Today, the publishers are the thousands of Internet users and companies around the globe that earn money off the traffic of their projects, communities on social media, YouTube channels, messengers, email newsletters, and other traffic sources. Advertisers are the companies that launch and run affiliate programs to attract targeted traffic with CPA payments, therefore increasing the number of target actions. For example, in Russia, according to AdIndex ratings, Admitad (www.admitad. com/ru) became the leader of sales generation in e-commerce (Technology Index, 2019). It is a global CPA affiliate network, with the largest volumes coming from the United States, Europe, the United Kingdom, and India. The company runs regular campaigns with e-commerce, travel, finance, mobile, and online games, for example. It also delivers a diverse range of valuable perks, including weekly prepayment facilities for exclusive and top-rated publishers worldwide, a great number of internationally recognized brands, detailed and transparent reports, as well as a huge number of useful tools and advanced technologies, including anticookie technology, cross-device tracking, lost orders, and fingerprint tracking.

An important subject of the market is the regulator, first of all the state. The advertising industry creates self-regulatory tools, such as the Coordinating Council for Social Advertising and Social Communications at the Public Chamber of the Russian Federation (Self-Regulatory Council, 2019). Self-regulation was the main theme of the International Advertising Association World Communication Summit, which was held in St. Petersburg in 2017. Within the framework of the Summit, a memorandum on the road map for the development of self-regulation in Russia was adopted with the participation of authorized state bodies and industrial associations. The pilot project on self-regulation began with advertising agencies in St. Petersburg.

Other indicators of the institutionalization and regulation of the market are contests, festivals, and ratings. Ratings are important for an advertising agency as an indicator and the "entrance ticket" for participation in tenders. Most significant are the annual ratings of agencies, creative, managers, and universities, which are carried out by ACAR. However, in the field of creative, awards and high places in the rating in two thirds of the cases reflect the uniqueness of advertising, that is made specifically for the festival jury; however, it may be uninteresting for the audience and ineffective for the business. The platforms for discussing industrial problems are the resources of sostav.ru, adindex.ru, cableman.ru, and abrus.ru, which attract thousands of subscribers in Russia, the CIS, and from abroad, which testifies to the massive interest in advertising.

Actors of the advertising market are universities, which prepare future professionals. In Russia, there are 260 departments, the rating of which is conducted annually by ACAR. The latest trends in research and industry are discussed at the annual conference at the RANEPA (The Russian Presidential Academy of National Economy and Public Administration), as well as at many sectoral national and regional forums.

Thus, the advertising market in post-Soviet Russia is rather young, but dynamic, and becomes a larger half of the marketing mix. What is its role and functions? Would advertising become strategic communication in modern Russia?

Methodology. To answer these questions, it is proposed to identify the features of advertising in modern Russia based on the relevant literature analysis and expert assessments (interviews and foresight sessions with academic and industrial experts, n = 6, 2019). A foresight session with researchers and practitioners allows analysis, on the basis of compiled maps of perceptions by both groups of experts, the features of the development of modern advertising according to two main parameters—peculiarities and application of the modern industry and the level of its impact. Also, models of modern Russian advertising, as well as public relations and strategic communication, will be compared and discussed on a foresight session.

The structure of this chapter is as follows: first, we analyze the relevant literature to reflect the advertising industry evolution as a discipline and as a field of research. Then the genesis of advertising in Russia, especially of Soviet advertising, will be discussed. To map the industrial landscape, the chapter presents the main features of commercial, political, and social advertising. The peculiarities of the "national character" in classical and digital advertising will be described. Further, the chapter presents the problems of modern advertising in Russia in the strategic communication paradigm. The main features of legal regulation of advertising activity problems in Russia will also be given. Finally, advertising market results in 2017–2019 will be presented.

Advertising in Russia: A constantly evolving discipline

During the USSR period, there was no complex research on advertising, because marketing was considered a bourgeois science that was contrary to the socialist principles of building a planned national economy. After the restructuring in the early 1990s, advertising has become a dynamic business and social institution that influences the Russian economy and society.

The development of researchers' interest reflects the advertising industry evolution. The first studies of the advertising industry development in modern Russia appear in the mid-1990s (Rozhkov, 1997; Uchenova & Starykh, 1994; 1999). The first works devoted to advertising in Russia were descriptive and did not have a clear method. But, over time, two broad areas of research on advertising had been formed—practitioners' applied books and educational literature. Only in the early 2000s was accumulated experience summarized in academic works. These works were sponsored by practitioners who had come to universities from the advertising industry.

The realities of the new professional activity sphere, the industrial relations formation, and the features of the advertising agency work organization are described by Evstafiyev and Pasyutina (Evstafiyev & Pasyutina, 2017). Also, the first studies of the advertising industry of foreign countries appear (Chechetkina, 1995; Cheryachukin, 1998).

The authors trace the change in advertising activity under the influence of socio-economic factors and changes in the functions of the advertising agency as the advertising business' main participant. The agencies are becoming multidisciplinary, and standardization of services is intensifying. The first and latest practice systematization in the Muzykant (2002) and Shchepilova and Shchepilov (2019) textbooks are presented, in which the modern Russian advertising industry basic parameters are given. In this period, the first and only social advertising textbook in Russia by Nikolaishvili (2008) was published. The market structure, the market functioning mechanisms, the business participants, as well as advertising and media producers' interaction, are the subject of research of Nazaykin (2018), Romat (2004), Tulupov (2011), Veselov (2003), and the authors of the annual *Russian Advertising Yearbook* (1999–2019) issued by ACAR and last year's edited by Veselov; and also the "Theory and Practice of Media advertising Researches" Almanac, edited by Kolomiyets (2014).

Vartanova emphasizes the importance of cooperation between media companies and advertisers, noting that advertising, in addition to its economic role in media systems, is an essential part of media content. According to Vartanova, with the beginning of social transformations, a new challenge emerged from the global environment, characterized by the rapid progress of digital communication technologies and the expansion of media and advertising business searching for new markets (Vartanova, 2012, p. 11).

The interaction and mutual influence of advertising and media grow from the simple communication of the publisher and the advertiser to the creation of an industrial base with the participation of advertising agencies, media meters, sellers, production studios, and other market participants. Therefore, the "media advertising business" concept is used in scientific circulation (Shchepilova, 2019). According to Shchepilova and Shchepilov, there are several levels of influence of advertising and media. Except for the aforementioned communication and marketing level, there is an organizational and financial level. Currently, advertising has an impact on the editorial policy, the print media structure, on the programming system, and the genre component of radio and television. Besides, a media advertising classification model has been developed (Shchepilova & Shchepilov, 2019).

Advertising in the political sphere was analyzed by Yegorova-Gantman and Pleshakov (1999) and Grinberg (2018). Advertising activities management in market conditions is reflected in the works of Khapenkov, Ivanov, and Fedyunin (2013).

The expansion of advertising practices and the advertising entrepreneurial nature determine the need for its organization and regulation research. However, the dynamic expansion of practices provokes the problems of their correct legal regulation. Therefore, the study of the legal problems of the industry today represents one of the key areas of research papers on advertising (Dorskii, 2019; Dorskii et al., 2017).

With the development of the Internet, the question of information technologies application in Russian advertising arises. However, there are small amount of the systematic papers in this area and research of modern advertising in the datafied digital economy as a part of data-driven marketing (Skorobogatykh, Nevostruev, Musatova, & Ivashkova, 2018).

Advertising industry expansion and continuing professionalization raise the issue of education and training of specialists in this sphere. The current agenda includes studies devoted to the practical component in the students' preparation (Boroday, 2006), the creative thinking formation (Rep'yev, 2008).

The ethical norms and the quality of the self-regulation system determine the maturity level of the advertising community and the industry. The relevance of self-regulation increases with the civil society development (Borisov 2004; Erkenova, 2003). The role of public organizations as a guarantor of the observance of ethical norms and conducting advertising business rules and the socioeconomic effects of advertising in Russia are also becoming the subject of study (Boyko, 2002; Gribok, 2011; Grishina, 2003).

Despite the growing number of works on advertising, questions of research methods in all directions remain controversial. The historical experience of public policy in the field of advertising, interaction of the state, public organizations, and the advertising market subjects (advertising agencies and advertisers) remains poorly studied.

A systematic communication approach is promising for research. Advertising as a part of media communication could be studied as a phenomenon of the relationships building through the transmission of meanings. According to Prof. Kolomiyets, modern media communication is the formation of public relations in the context of the widespread dissemination of digital technologies, which have assumed the role of a social actor (Kolomiyets, 2019).

Thus, advertising and publics alongside digital technologies as a specific social actor have got "a meeting point" in the modern media communication concept. It means that modern advertising in Russia is supposed to be two-way, peer-to-peer, nonhierarchical, and interactive, which is rather unusual for "classical" hierarchical advertising.

Specifics of pre-, post-, and Soviet advertising

Russian advertising has its roots in old traditions. The formation of advertising in Russia differs from that of Europe due to differences in cultural and historical features. Orthodox Russia was influenced by the Byzantine traditions, while medieval Western European culture was based on the Greco-Roman antiquity.

The influence of economic and political processes on the development of advertising in Russia also has a pronounced national specificity. Oral advertising in folklore, "lubki prints" (a Russian popular prints, characterized by simple graphics and narratives derived from literature, religious stories, and popular tale) as visual media and product promotion at fairs is mentioned in official documents dating back to the 13th and 16th centuries (Rybakov, 1948).

At the end of the seventeenth century, the first attempts of modernization and Westernization under Peter I (the Great) laid the foundation for the formation of political advertising in the media and local markets. Picturesque signs and printed posters appeared. Catherine II (the Great) stressed the importance of advertising her reforms (Evstafiyev & Pasyutina, 1997). In the eighteenth century, media advertisement appears. Political advertising and commercial ads were placed in the first Russian newspaper, *Vedomosti*. There are brief advertisements on the packaging—first on the boxes of pharmaceutical products, and later on the expensive confectionery.

The evolution of advertising in the nineteenth century is determined by the development of market capitalist relations. Fairs became popular, and brands and trademarks began appearing. Trademarks were especially valued if there were medals and prints of the state emblem as evidence of received Russian and international approval. The block of advertising information, even in general political publications, went to the front pages, comprising half of the total volume of a single issue.

There is no complex research of advertising on the edge of the nineteenth century. But there are many descriptions of ads in prerevolutionary Russia, for example, the first advertising films about the production of soap in the Brokar factory, cigarette sleeves, and the highest quality of services in Gustav's barbershop showed the widespread use of new technological solutions in Russian advertising. Poster, photo, and film advertising appeared at the turn of the nineteenth and twentieth centuries, contributing to the aesthetics of advertising, not only in Russia, but worldwide.

After the October 1917 Revolution, one of the first decrees of the Soviet government was to monopolize advertisement by the state, that is, to derive advertisement from market relations. Publication of advertising was declared the exclusive right of the Soviet government and the local Councils of workers, soldiers, and peasants' deputies. In 1918, the Council of People's Commissars (CPC) of Russia, by its decree, provided a centralized reception of advertisements from all persons and institutions for placing them in Soviet print media and at any postal and telegraph institution.

The opinion that there was no advertising in the USSR, because there were no market relations, is denied by studies based on new materials and new concepts. Gritsuk and Kutyrkina, in their monograph "The history of advertising in Russia. The tasks of advertising communication and the forms of organization of advertising activity in the USSR" (2007), proposed a method for the study of advertising that was based on the analysis of the world practice of mixed state-market regulatory models, due to the historical features of the national economy, cultural, and political traditions.

According to Gritsuk and Kutyrkina, several historical models of coexistence of state and market regulation in the USSR affected advertising activities: for example, goals, subjects, services, and advertising media (Gritsuk & Kutyrkina, 2007). The authors identify seven periods of advertising activity in the Soviet Union.

Postrevolutionary period (1917–1921). Advertising activity was aimed at legitimating the new government and was predominantly political. The subject of advertising services, including commercial, is the state. The Soviet government exported publishing facilities, advertising media, and private advertising firms and received both political and economic dividends from advertising.

Advertising activities in the period of the New Economic Policy (NEP) (1921–1928). Despite the emergence of private enterprise advertisers, the main subject of advertising remains the state enterprise, government bodies, and departments. The goal of advertising was to promote their products and services. Planned management eliminated competition, but even commercial advertising performed political and ideological tasks. Almost every publication in Soviet Russia was owned by the state and its departments, which received commercial benefits from advertising, including private advertisers.

Advertising in the 1930s was carried out by advertising organizations that existed under government departments that were engaged in domestic and foreign trade. In foreign and domestic trade, there was a state monopoly on advertising. Planned production did not correspond to the real structure of consumer demand, so advertising had to remove this contradiction, explaining why and how it could be used. Foreign trade activity required more complex promotional activities.

In the years after World War II, the structure of advertising activity became more complex. In a planned economy, trade was interested in the sale of products. The management of advertising activity in domestic trade fell on the USSR Ministry of Trade and the departmental advertising organization Soyuztorgreklama and, in the sphere of foreign trade, on the USSR Ministry of Foreign Trade and Vneshtorgreklama. Since 1953, within the framework of attempts to decentralize the economy, the powers of the allied bodies have shifted to the republican ones. Advertising organizations received a certain percentage of the volume of work performed.

In the 1960s, media advertising developed. Advertisements were placed in literally all Soviet editions, usually on the last page. Restrictions exist only in the central party newspaper *Pravda* and *Izvestiya*. Television and radio received government funding, so they were not interested in advertising.

In the 1970s, the economic reforms led to the fact that the efficiency of an enterprise was no longer determined by indicators of gross production, but by its implementation. This led to significant changes in the structure of promotional activities. Thus, together with the trade departments, a new pool of advertisers was being formed—manufacturing enterprises of a single industry, which combined their advertising efforts to promote a common product category, which is impossible in the conditions of market competition. For such large-scale campaigns, special advertising publications were created, and industry advertising organizations conducted All-Soviet Union advertising campaigns.

In the Soviet Union, advertising was primarily included in the political context and never became commercial, which was impossible in a planned economy.

Nevertheless, in Soviet times, there were advertising media and advertising campaigns that were primarily aimed at foreign economic communications and foreign audiences. The most famous example of such advertising was the "Fly Aeroflot!" campaign. For citizens of the country, this advertisement was unnecessary, because the USSR had only one civil air carrier. For foreign citizens, such a message was just information that said nothing about the company and its services.

In the last decade of the existence of the USSR, there were radical changes in advertising activity due to the reforms carried out by the state. So, in 1988, after the law "On Cooperation" was issued (The Law "On Cooperation", 1988), new subjects of advertising activity appeared: advertisers-cooperatives, which were non-state advertising agencies. Due to imperfect legislation, new advertising agencies had to build informal relations with advertising participants to survive. It turned out to be especially profitable for new media-buying agencies: state-owned media were not interested in selling advertising space, so the agencies bribed employees. However, cuts in government funding soon forced media to establish formal interaction.

The reduction of the planned system of procurement and sales of products forced state-owned enterprises to intensify sales activities, primarily advertising, so the demand for direct mass advertising, which was not always needed, increased. In foreign economic activity, the state monopoly has ceased. New actors, primarily joint ventures, needed advertising. At the end of the 1980s, foreign companies and large multinational corporations came to Russia, changing the advertising landscape.

In general, despite the "black" illegal or "gray" semi-legal relationship schemes, the "old" and new participants in the advertising process are gradually establishing market relations. The authorities in this period legally restrict business, primarily foreign; solve the tasks of certain financial and political groups; and demonstrate the absence of social priorities, thereby creating a specific combination of state and market mechanisms.

Thus, despite the deep roots, during the Soviet era, classic advertising models were politicized and hierarchical and not so "communicative" and public and technology-driven.

Advertising in new Russia: Mapping the industrial landscape

The birth of advertising of the new Russia, as well as the new economy and politics of Russia, began with Perestroika and the restructuring of the only advertising format in the USSR for foreign audiences. The beginning of perestroika in modern Russian advertising is considered to be the decision of the Communist Party of the Soviet Union (CPSU), described in "On measures for a radical restructuring of foreign economic advertising" dated February 6, 1988 (O merakh, 1988). The document gave the official opportunity to organize nongovernmental advertising organizations.

Commercials

Thanks to this decision of the CPSU, in 1989, the first in the modern history of Russia, the commercial advertising professional project of the federal newspaper *Izvestia* and the German publishing house Burda was started (two pages of an advertising supplement to the newspaper).

In 1989, an order was issued by the USSR State Committee on Television and Radio Broadcasting on the development of promotional activities on television and radio, and, in September 1990, the first commercial Channel 2x2 was created.

In the late 1980s–early 1990s, the first private advertising agencies appeared alongside commercial outdoor and radio advertising. The professional advertising production market was just beginning to take shape, and the authors of the commercials were comedians, cartoon artists, and film makers. The essence of advertising was interpreted widely, the public attitude toward it was not formed, and the videos often looked naive or ineffective. The first advertising campaigns fully reflected the chaos of economic restructuring: on television next to the advertisement of private bank Menatep, the audience saw a dog named Alice, whose owner called one of the first private Russian stock exchanges after it.

The legendary and the most ambitious advertising campaign of the mid-1990s was the promotion of the MMM (a Russian company that perpetrated one of the world's largest Ponzi schemes of all time in the 1990s) financial pyramid. In addition to regular television, newspaper, and magazine advertisements, sponsoring free trips of Muscovites in the subway, celebrating the capital's day, MMM President Sergey Mavrodi in 1993 made the following New Year's speech on the RTR state channel almost simultaneously with the traditional New Year greeting of the President of Russia, Boris Yeltsin, on the channel "Ostankino". For MMM, feature films were shot, an advertising series in which the main character was Leonid "Lenya" Golubkov, his family, and the family of his brother, Ivan, a miner. The large-scale campaign of MMM for the first time told not about the product and service, but propagandized Western, or rather American, values, since Lenya Golubkov became a millionaire and left for the United States. Lenya talked about the fact that investing is not fraud, capitalism opens up a fast path to enrichment, and in America they live happily.

Such simple stories and messages were new for the Russian audience. The advertising campaign was an incredible success, and up to 15 million people suffered as a result of the actions of MMM scammers. Since then, the Russian economy and the audience of advertising have evolved, so the return of MMM under a different name did not succeed in the 2010s. However, advertising promotion in this period was also less creative. During Perestroika, an advertising market begins to take shape. There weren't many foreign advertisers in this period (Veselov, 2017).

The commercial advertising market in its modern sense was formed by the beginning of the 2000s, and, today, in terms of institutionalization and structure, it is at the level of advertising markets of Eastern European countries (Veselov, 2019).

In the 2010s, the Internet became an advertising tool. Budgets for advertising on the Internet are growing. The Internet has been growing steadily throughout the years to about 20%, which is three times higher than the growth of offline advertising (although there is still no consensus among experts on the very essence of the online advertising concept).

According to the IAB Russia study (Digital advertisers barometer, 2018), the main drivers of budget growth are dynamic targeting, accurate measurement of investments, and a wide choice of a target audience, including the mobile Internet. The range of tools is expanding: companies use five to seven tools in a marketing mix, and more than a quarter of companies use up to ten tools.

According to 48% of experts, the fastest-growing format is targeted advertising on social networks, which share will increase. Mobile and video advertising and native advertising on the Internet are also becoming significant segments of the advertising market, and more than half of the experts believe that its share will increase.

However, Internet tools cannot solve all the problems, for example, to provide and ensure the audience awareness of the brand. Companies use bloggers for their campaigns. Besides, many companies cannot cut other media budgets for the Internet.

According to the IAB experts, the most used parameter for assessing the effectiveness of advertising campaigns is website traffic; it is used by 80% of the experts to evaluate it (digital advertisers barometer, 2018). It intermediately reflects the initial level of the Internet advertising market in Russia. Also, it means that digital communication is strictly "official". In other words, even the digital advertising model is rather hierarchical.

Political advertising

Political advertising is a paid, nonpersonal appeal to the target audience carried by various communication channels, for example, encouraging choosing a candidate or political ideas. In the post-perestroika period in Russia, the political advertising formation was largely determined by the features of election campaigns, each of which was determined by the use of certain technologies and tools. According to Grinberg, one of the leading political advertising researchers in Russia, political advertising started with the first alternative elections of delegates to the USSR Congress of People's Deputies (1989), which was carried out with a low professional supporting level (Grinberg, 2018). The elections were characterized by the lack of original ideas, the use of a party propaganda communication, and discounting foreign experience. Leaflets and a mailing list were the main political advertising tools.

Manipulative technologies in advertising were clearly manifested in the campaign strategy in support of Boris Yeltsin in a referendum on a vote of no confidence in the President and the Supreme Council (1993). The essence of the concept was to impose a slogan to the mass audience without explaining its content, and the message was radically reduced to the "necessary" questionnaire answers: "Yes—yes—no—yes".

In the 1990s, the political advertising products were not high quality. However, the range of genres, channels, and tools had expanded: advertising slots, videos, video films, and series of appeals appeared on television; and radio advertising, outdoor advertising, and direct mail had spread. The President of Russia election in 1996 strengthened the state-corporate specifics of political advertising. Eleven candidates ran for the post, but the most ambitious and original were the election campaigns of Alexander Lebed, the incumbent President Boris Yeltsin, and the "Vote or Lose" movement. The Lebed campaign was based on the strong-man image and was mainly implemented in TV advertising, in the series "There is such a person, and you know him" (Rostova, 2018). The frequency of this series increased a month before the elections. As a result, Lebed got 15% of the vote. The Yeltsin campaign consisted of the official election campaign (addressed primarily to young people) and the mass movement of support for the "Vote or lose" movement.

The vertical of power further strengthening led to the absence of the necessity to fight for the electorate. This situation declines the interest in political advertising. This happened due to the fact that, since the presidential campaign of 2000, PR had become the mainstream political technology. Prior to the campaign, the electoral headquarters of Vladimir Putin announced that the candidate would be engaged, not in electoral promises, but in concrete actions. In this regard, news programs and the media events, which were widely covered on leading TV channels, have become main advancement instruments.

The parliamentary campaign of 2003 and the presidential election of 2004 set the trend of monocentric elections system and the transition from direct advertising to PR.

In all subsequent elections, experts in the Committee on Political Technologies of the Russian Association for Public Relations named the most effective tools in their report (Doklad, 2016): elite agreements, a door-to-door field campaign, and advertising in traditional media. Fundamental differences in the toolkit were not revealed, which is explained by the lack of vivid political preferences among Russian political technologists. Despite the fact that digital technologies, due to the specifics of the Russian Internet, are not widely used, target audiences' databases and technology based on big data and its control systems are increasingly in demand.

The social network VKontakte has become the most popular social service among political technologists. Facebook is the second, Odnoklassniki is the third. YouTube and Twitter are used to a lesser extent—they were given fourth and fifth places, followed by Instagram, LiveJournal, and My World. Also, Telegram, WhatsApp, Viber, Periscope, and blogs of candidates, as well as local forums, were called instant messengers (Doklad, 2016).

The report compiled by the Gurov and Partners agency provides the rating of the Russian parties' presence on Internet effectiveness in terms of openness, interactivity, and technology. According to the report, most parties' websites did not meet modern requirements, and 20 parties did not have websites at all. At the same time, the United Russia party was the most active in mastering new communication tools. The Communist Party of the Russian Federation was technologically the best, and the "Fair Russia" site was the most informationally open (the only site with a working version for the visually impaired) (SMI, 2015).

According to the report "Election campaign tools: Has a new political reality come?" by the Committee on Political Technologies of the Russian Association for Public Relations (Doklad, 2018), similarly as in the 2016 survey, elite agreements remain the main election campaigns instrument. However, the media consumption structure has changed: in 2016, the use of social networks was recognized as the last important tool in the elections; on the eve of 2019, social networks outstripped traditional technologies: a door-to-door field campaign, a media campaign, outdoor advertising, and direct media advertising.

In election campaigns, the role of social platforms is growing, and Telegram is becoming the main platform for campaigning. The majority of respondents (83%) agreed with the thesis of the "new political reality" onset and an increase of antiestablishment attitude in Russia, which could become a driver for a new stage in the political advertising development (Doklad, 2018).

Social advertising

The social advertising definition in the legislation of the Russian Federation is not clearly presented, even in the 2006 edition. In general, according to the definition of Gyuzella Nikolaishvili, one of the leading Russian experts on social advertising and the founder of the advertising agency "Laboratory of Social Advertising", social advertising is a type of public communication aimed at attracting the audience attention to the society problems (Nikolaishvili, 2019).

The Russian social advertising market was formed in stages. In developed economies, social problems appeared in advertising in the 1970s–1980s; in Russia, only in 1990s. The first domestic social advertising campaign appeared in 1992 (Nikolaishvili, 2008). The starting point for the creative team was the data of sociological polls of that period. The polls named the gap between generations in the context of political and economic restructuring as the most significant problem. The "Call Your Parents!" campaign was for the first time aimed at solving a social problem—establishing family ties. (It needs to be mentioned that the creator of the idea of the campaign refused all mobile operators' offers aimed at making this advertisement commercial.) This creative team, for the first time in Russia, attempted to self-regulate the industry by creating an independent Public Council for social advertising, which was in operation from 1992 to 1999.

In 1993–1994, ecology appeared in the advertising agenda (Greenpeace, WWF). Attention to the importance of advertising in almost all social processes appeared after the mass creation of NGOs in Russia. Numerous advertising campaigns, which were made by organizations' participants, were not quite as high quality or effective. Professional advertising, for example, Perspective on AIDS, from the Focus Media Foundation, stood out especially (Nikolaishili, 2019).

In 2002, a new stage in market development began, with the need to announce the results of large international corporations in their corporate social responsibility performance. The first were the tobacco giants British American Tobacco and Phillip Morris, followed by the metallurgical companies. Social reporting was the positive factor in market development. Today, CSR is becoming an essential topic for social advertising, not only for large companies, but also for medium and small Russian businesses.

Russian political parties and other actors use mainly manipulative social advertising. Most vivid thus far was the social advertising campaign for the election of Russian Federation President Boris Yeltsin in 1996. Thus, when trust in Yeltsin fell, national TV Channel 1 began to include the social advertising campaign, "Russian project", Yeltsin's election campaign clips.

Since the beginning of this century, the state has been actively entering the advertising sphere as a customer. It is difficult to determine this direction of advertising as an independent type, but the differences in state advertising are obvious, for example, the use of simpler images and slogans ("Pay taxes and sleep well"). Social advertising in the branding of territories, which helps shape the image of cities, is becoming an extensive area (Kiselev, Fedyunin, & Kutyrkina, 2017).

In general, the social advertising market was formed by the 2010s. Structurally, it is similar to the Russian market for commercial advertising, with its typology determined by the industry-specific and specific features of the customers. The market maintains a balance of different areas of social advertising by subjects and topics. An indicator of the institutionalization of this segment is a unique festival of social advertising, which since 2009 has evolved from a student's educational project into a large-scale industry-wide international professional platform for the development and examination of social advertising, its organizer Guzella Nikolaishvili said (Nikolaishvili, 2019). Traditionally, nominations define competition in genres and technologies. Their number has grown from, and includes, such new areas as data visualization and street art. The awards are not only the "Person of the Year", but also the "Blogger of the Year". Every year, hundreds of people from many countries participate in the competition.

The best Russian social advertising in recent years has become laureates of prestigious international awards. For example, the project "Make an official work" (2016) won the Cannes Lioness Award. On the roadway of the streets of Yekaterinburg, portraits of officials appeared with their quotes about road repair obligations that had not been fulfilled for a long time. Portraits were drawn in such a way that the pits on the roadway represented their open mouths. As a result, most of the roads having these portraits were urgently repaired. It is noteworthy that the author of the project was the local advertising agency Voskhod, which heads the list of the best creative agencies in Russia.

In 2019, almost all young creators who will represent Russia at the Cannes Lioness competition reached the final of the national selection with social advertising campaigns (for example, Anastasia Sharykina and Natalia Grishina, RODNYA creative studio; Ivan Vlasov, Leo Burnett Moscow, and Sergey Pleshkov, BBDO Moscow) (Young Lions Russia, 2019).

Today, the state of the social advertising market (the share of social advertising in the media and, accordingly, the social responsibility of the media) is explored by the National Advertising Alliance (http://nra.media/en/, n.d.). This alliance examines social advertising, in particular, providing an opinion on the content of advertising and recommendations on its placement or refusal.

On February 8, 2018, the Coordination Council for Social Advertising and Social Communications was established in the Public Chamber of the Russian Federation. It includes five commissions. Working groups make proposals on the optimization of legislation in social advertising, monitor the media, and contribute to the emergence of social advertising on television, among other responsibilities.

Currently, the worldwide concept of social advertising is changing. Its task is not just to pay attention to the problem, but also to include social problems in the personal agenda to motivate people to make changes. Attitude toward the very term of social advertising has changed. Today, the public service announcement (PSA) concept is used. PSAs include an extremely full variety of messages—from a simple announcement to a federal advertising campaign.

According to Sergey Dolgov, creator of the Melnitsa Space art space and strategic communications Melnitsa Agency, this determines the relevance of online promotion tools. The requirements for social advertising on the Internet have become more complex: in the information flow of vibrant entertainment offers, it is necessary to achieve instant reaction and quick action. Moreover, the social advertising subject is not entertainment or consumption, but the solution to a social problem (Dolgov, 2019).

Thus, according to Dolgov, immersive technologies are especially important because they allow participants to immerse themselves into the problem and to feel its solution. For example, domestic developers from Luden.io created a ReWire VR game for educating children with autism, which can be used to study working and communicating with these "special" kids. The "Plant a Forest" project proposes to transfer a donation, after which a tree with a donor's name will be planted with this money. "Plant a Forest" is a regular online store, but it offers a new approach to social communication—when a donor becomes an integral part of it, both offline and online. Also, a well-known singer from St. Petersburg, Manizha, composed the dramatic song "Mom" about domestic violence, shot a video, and held a concert in support to the Silsila application she had made, which allows victims of aggression to seek help from relatives and friends (Dolgov, 2019).

In other words, the concept of "social advertising" is replaced by the concept of "social communications". In this combination, in addition to advertising itself, marketing, PR, and other technologies can be used. Communications become immersive, multichannel, and even omnichannel. Omnichannel is a cross-channel content strategy that brands use to improve their user experience and to make it efficient and pleasant. All these technologies are available not only to large companies but also to an ordinary prosumer, that is, those Internet users who are involved in native advertising and video content production.

Thus, the various areas of advertising digital tools have become more communicative, but political areas of advertising have become more "hierarchical". Commercial and social advertising are going to be more person-oriented, immersive, and omnichannel.

National features of advertising in Russia: The Russian character

The characteristics of different cultures must be considered when planning advertising campaigns in the era of global openness of communication. In advertising, attention is paid to the main manifestations of culture and values. Application of the results of the study of national cultural characteristics in advertising allows the creation of relevant positioning and promotion. Relying on the values of the national character gives the communication and the brand necessary differentiation and memorability, making it closer to the relevance to the target audience.

Based on the analysis of the basic needs of the audience in relation to different brands, these significant parameters of the "Russian character" have to be identified from the point of view of the brand's emotional benefits.

What features of Russian "national character" are important for advertising in Russia? According to Khapenkov, Ivanov, and Fedyunin, the characteristic feature of the behavior of Russians (Russian men) is based on the maximalism and idealism of the Russians, who take everything to the extreme, wanting everything at once. Therefore, the pleasure of consuming a product (brand benefit) must be real and "over the edge" (it is possible to designate this characteristic as "All or Nothing") (Khapenkov, Ivanov, & Fedyunin, 2013).

Ability to perform unbelievable acts, often hoping for "may be", can be defined as "hardness and craziness". Therefore, the pleasure should be special and memorable, despite the consequences. "The breadth of the Russian soul" is expressed in the fact that human relations are considered as the most important value in life, that is, you should not restrain impulses, including emotional ones; however, for the sake of pleasure, you can sacrifice essential things. The "freedom-lovingness" of Russians is well-known, who cannot be constrained or prevented from achieving the goal and receiving pleasure, the research mentions.

For Russians, it is also characteristic to see and think of oneself apart, in the context of "Russian civilization". The pleasure "in Russian" is not clear to others, especially to foreigners ("We have our own way").

According to Khapenkov, Ivanov, and Fedyunin, based on the peculiarities of the Russian character, it's possible to formulate these insights:

1) There is a lot of routine in my life; if the opportunity arises to have fun, I want it to be as bright as possible.
2) I usually live by established rules. But there are times when the "soul asks" for something, and then I can follow my impulses and break the rules. Otherwise, you will regret that you did not do what you really wanted and did not get that pleasure (Khapenkov, Ivanov, & Fedyunin, 2013).

According to Khapenkov, Ivanov, and Fedyunin, a classical example of taking into account the national characteristics of the target audience is the promotion of Baltika's Nevskoe Beer brand in the face of falling sales and deteriorating brand image indicators (for example, consumers did not remember the brand's advertising and could not explain what its features were). The objectives were to clarify positioning and launch an advertising campaign with a renewed strategy, idea, and creative, taking into account the peculiarities of the "national character". The main benefits of the brand (rational, emotional, consumer) should have remained on the "territory" of self-expression, status, and enjoyment.

The analysis revealed a fairly strong position of the brand compared to its competitors. "Nevskoe" was perceived as a "traditional", "authentic", "original" brand. In the minds of consumer, the position of the brand was strong enough, which is explained by positive personal experience. Nevskoye ranks with the brands that are characterized by associations with Russia, traditions, and authenticity. The common attributes of Russia and Nevskoe as brands are traditionality, friendliness, and authenticity. These "Russian" features added brand differentiation on the "territory of pleasure". The level of differentiation of the brand has grown due to the relevantly defined historical territory of the brand and its emotional drivers.

The study of the target audience revealed the peculiarities of the "Russian character", which were further used. The audience were men 30–35 years old, married, with children and with above-average incomes. They have good educations. The declared behavioral peculiarities are: rules and respect for other people, valuing stability, and preferring to act rather than to reason. They are specific and pragmatic and are focused on conservative values (home and family). The values of change (career and freedom) are secondary, but nonetheless are important, because they help to ensure a decent quality of life for themselves and their loved ones. First of all, they pay attention to the quality of the product, carefully approaching the choice of their favorite brands and retaining loyalty to them. They are committed to a small number of brands. The choice is influenced by the approval of the group: it is important to Russians that they have everything not worse than the others. Standing out is not accepted. The tendency toward conservatism and conformism leads Russians to choose "approved" brands for which they are ready to overpay. Beer consumers appreciate quality and taste. The history and traditions of the brand can serve as a guarantee for the quality of the beer.

As a result, two variants of the emotional benefit were identified:

1) Maximum pleasure: bright, full, not limited to the framework.
2) Giving in to the impulse to get what you really want, despite circumstances.

A description of the product was created, taking into account "character" and historical specificity: in the imperial era, beer was brewed from selected malt of the highest quality "Imperial" variety, which gave the beer great taste and an expressive, bright shade. And today, they use this sort of malt to make Nevskoe Imperial beer, as in the old days, achieving consistently high quality and great taste.

As a result, the description confirms the quality and taste without additional explanations, showing the connection with the empire and the historical epoch by focusing on the variety. The updated character of the brand made it possible to formulate the characteristics of the image of the hero, related to the brand's insight and the peculiarities of the Russian character, for use in advertising: the hero is bright (having caught the "courage", the consumer can do something and is capable of taking risks); and self-confident (independent, courageous). With the insight of the brand, the peculiarities of the Russian character and traditions of the quality of the brand is connected to the charisma of the hero: he attracts attention, and everyone wants him. As a result, taking into account the "Russian character", the Baltika campaign brought the Nevskoye Beer brand out of a difficult situation.

Inattention to the national and cultural characteristics of the consumption of advertising in Russia, that is, to the "Russian character" and national gender specifics, can cause a crisis in the communication of even a popular global brand. For example, the Russian office of the manufacturer of sports goods Reebok on February 7, 2019 launched an advertising campaign #NIVKAKIERAMKI (#GettingOutOfHand), the local adaptation of the international campaign #BeMoreHuman, which is obviously emotionally positive. The campaign carried a certain charge of feminism. The heroes of the #BeMoreHuman international campaign were Hollywood stars, top models, activists, and sportswomen. Controversial women and activists participated in the Russian campaign. (In the previous Russian advertising campaign, Reebok featured women having an ideal appearance—models and actresses—causing a largely negative reaction in social networks.)

In Russia, the brand used the visual concept and style of the global campaign in its advertising. However, the content of the campaign was radically different. The destructive slogan for Russia "Getting out of hand" was supplemented with rather shocking texts for advertising banners that were written by one of the heroines of the project, the creator of the feminist telegram channel Women's Power and Breaking Mad website Zalina Marshenkulova. As one example, the slogan read, "When they say 'to carry in his arms' I imagine carrying me in a coffin". In the video of this campaign, the heroines told how they are fighting against stereotypes about "female destiny" and have learned not to be afraid of all sides of their character. At the same time, in the campaign and banner advertising in particular, stereotypes about "female destinations" were not even shown.

The campaign instantly caused a huge resonance in social networks: from the photos, the image attracting the most attention was a picture of Zalina Marshenkulova with the slogan about the need for male approval. According to estimates of the Ashmanov and Partners agency based on the Kribrum monitoring system, in less than one day, the hashtag of the Reebok campaign had been used more than 2,500 times in social networks and continued to be actively used, with mentions about 300 times per hour. In general, the mentioning of the Reebok brand in social networks in two days, February 7–8, was 193% higher than in the previous two days. According to experts, after some time, it will be possible to evaluate and draw conclusions from the ratio of negative to positive. This video for a few days collected 2,300 dislikes against 355 likes (Igla, 2019).

Reebok decided to remove the banners and replace them with more neutral ones. Problems in the localization of the campaign began with goal-setting: if the global campaign "Be More Human" was associated with human values and called for being more human, then its translation into Russian as "Become a human being" can be described as Darwinist. Thus, the essence of the campaign was lost initially.

The slogan "Getting out of hand" may seem to correspond to the features of the "Russian character", but these characteristics apply to male heroes and traditionally have little relevance for women. Instead of confident, energetic, talented, and, at the same time especially feminine, heroines of the global campaign, heroines who cannot even be called truly shocking were offered (for example, in the proposed advertising version, the girl does not call for a new level of women's freedom, but only suggests changing her position). No feminist ideas of the heroine were promoted. The desire to give the campaign a pronounced feminist character was unsuccessful from the point of view of ideas: the range of emotions and meanings and emotional benefits has been minimized.

It should be noted that the director of the Glavpiar resource, Oleg Voronin, sued Reebok because of the advertising campaign # NIVKAKIERAMKI, stating in the lawsuit that he had suffered moral suffering. Voronin was sure that the actions of Reebok were illegal and wanted to hear a public apology and intended to receive compensation in the amount of 200,000 rubles. At the same time, active participants in the advertising market began to use this loud advertising campaign for newsjacking at lightning speed. There were advertisements of this nature: "Move from the needle of male approval to the flight to Vienna! Tickets are cheaper than a pair of sneakers" (Igla, 2019).

Thus, despite the global openness of the new Russia, these cases show the target audiences and public adherence to rather traditional values, and, in particular, gender values. Even young netizens are ready to defend the "classical" authenticity of the "Russian character" but specifically male and female. Also, these cases show the growing impact of the audiences on offline and online brand communication, even critical and crucial in the latter case.

Russian advertising in the digital era: A strategic paradigm

According to McKinsey experts, Russia is a digital country in which a data-based ecosystem is being built (McKinsey Global Institute, 2017), mainly due to paternalistic support of the digital economy by the state. The digital economy model (the so-called quadro helix of the digital economy) includes the state, business, science and the academic community, and the public (Fedyunin & Shilina, 2019; Shilina, 2012). In the digital economy modern model, it is necessary to ensure free direct public access to digital processes and to gain new personal experience (Deloitte, 2019). That is, professional communication—public relations and advertising, strategic communication—should be in demand; their models should be nonhierarchical/two-way symmetrical and interactive.

So, what is the strategic role and model of advertising in the digital paradigm? In Russia, both advertising and PR are parts of the marketing mix (Shilina, 2016). According to Buman Media, in 2019, PR specialists still called marketing (and digital marketing) tools one of the most popular (Buman & HeadHunter, 2019).

A digital marketing model, such as 4S Internet marketing model, and data-driven marketing model have characteristics such as personalization, as well as privacy, security, and communication with consumers and communities, especially with digital consumers in 4.0 marketing system (Skorobogatykh & Musatova, 2018; Skorobogatykh, Nevostruev, Musatova, & Ivashkova, 2018).

In 2019, digital technologies (for example, programmatic) are being actively implemented in advertising, and the quality of targeting is high. However, in Russia, for all communication channels, the main performance indicators, such as coverage and frequency, are still quantitative (Get Media Right, 2019).

Russian industry experts have confirmed the trends of digitalization and datification, when targeting is based on people, and not on advertising IDs or cookies (Vladimirova, 2019). According to Mikhail Voshchinsky, CEO of Dentsu Aegis Network Russia, there are a lot of data on the market, and it is not clear how to work with these data, but everything is ready for the future construction of data-driven communication and business results evaluation (Vladimirova, 2019).

In 2019, Russian public relations continued to operate in the digital marketing paradigm: according to Buman Media's research, Internet tools are expanding, primarily through social networks (23%), corporate blogging (4%), online media (18%), email newsletters (6%), and instant messengers (5%) (Buman Media & Ileadhunter, 2019).

In other words, is there no tight boundary between digital marketing (and advertising) communication and PR when their goal is to improve the personal experience and when digital communication models are a priori personalized and interactive?

How does this relate to the characteristics of strategic communications in modern Russia? The concept was formed at the intersection of theories and practices of marketing and public relations in recent years due to digitalization, which provoked a permanent increase in the diversity, differentiation, and fragmentation of target audiences and communication channels.

Strategic communication as an actual concept is not so widespread in Russian academia and practice. Its understanding is extremely wide in the scope of activities related to achieving strategic goals, promoting or changing cultural (ideological) values in the minds of target audiences, as an example (Bogdanov, 2017).

The strategic communication concept states that all the areas of corporate communication—public relations, marketing, etc.—acquire common goals, and their strategies become similar (Hallahan, Holtzhausen, van Ruler, Vercic & Sriramesh, 2007). According to van Ruler, it is a strategic communication goal that determines whether the communication is strategic (van Ruler, 2018).

The essence of strategic communication, according to the classical definition, is to promote the organization's mission through communication (Hallahan, et al., 2007). The characteristics of strategic communications are generally defined and largely coincide with the characteristics of actual person-centered marketing and public relations. In particular, all communication formats are focused on the interests and needs of the audience; communications, decisions, actions, and key messages are orchestrated to achieve strategic goals; key messages are adapted to many diverse audiences and channels; and communications are implemented continuously and continuously.

So, the basic models of Russian marketing and advertising, and, in particular, public relations and strategic communications, are characterized by interactive digital (and future datafied) subject-to-object personalized communication and joint values (and values of the "Russian national character" and gender in particular). In other words, the essence of advertising in modern Russia is rather strategic.

According to the results of our survey and the foresight session, as well as to the perception maps of both groups (researchers and practitioners), the state of modern advertising in Russia is defined as transitional. More than 50% of respondents rate the penetration of the datification into the industry as quite high. Peculiarities of datified digital communication and application of data-driven technologies in the industry are perceived by practitioners more positively than by theorists. The transition of advertising to strategic role and functions is considered probable by about a third of respondents but in the long run.

Legal regulation of advertising activity problems in Russia

Russian advertising activity is regulated by the Federal Law No. 38-FL "On Advertising", adopted on March 13, 2006 (The Federal Law "On Advertising"), as well as by several regulatory acts, including: the Federal Law No. 135-FL "On Protection of Competition", adopted on June 8, 2006 (The Federal Law "On Protection of Competition", 2006); the Civil Code of the Russian Federation No. 51-FL, adopted on November, 30, 1994 (The Civil Code, 1994); the Code of the Russian Federation on Administrative Offenses No. 195-FL, adopted on December 30, 2001(The Code on Administrative Offenses, 2001; 2020); and the Law No. 2300-I "On Protection of Consumer Rights", adopted on February 7, 1992 (The Law "On Protection of Consumer Rights", 1992).

The Law "On Advertising" regulates legal relations that arise in the process of creating and distributing advertising and is intended to promote the development of markets for goods, works, and services on the basis of fair competition in the economic space unity of the Russian Federation principles. The law is aimed at ensuring the realization of consumer rights in receiving fair and reliable advertising, at preventing violations of Russian legislation on advertising, as well as at preventing inappropriate advertising.

Due to constant changes in the economy and in the advertising industry, the provisions of the legislation on advertising have partly lost their relevance and need to be revised and/or clarified. Thus, the previous Law "On Advertising" of 1995 and the current Law "On Advertising" of 2006 do not address the question, what should be used to distinguish advertising from notification? The current law defines advertising through information, although it should apply to individuals and legal entities related to property relations. Violations of consumers rights to information disseminated through such announcements are diverse and widespread. These include, in particular, a misrepresentation of the product and the distribution of announcements about so-called leisure, as well as the use of ads in the commission of fraudulent acts in relation to their consumers. The lack of legal regulation in this area makes the distribution of information by these individuals unregulated.

Thus, advertising as it is understood by the 2006 Law on Advertising can be posted under the guise of an article praising a particular product or its manufacturer. In this case, the advertiser may not put an "advertisement" mark next to similar text. If the competition authority suspects an offense, then, in researching the published article, the competition authority will need to analyze it to determine whether it is advertising or educational.

The solution to this problem is to understand advertising as a presentation. The Federal Antimonopoly Authority (FAS Russia) and its territorial bodies exercise state control over the legislation of advertising. Other state and municipal authorities, such as the Ministry of Communications, also control advertising. In addition to state bodies, control in the sphere of production and distribution is carried out by self-regulatory bodies: public organizations that are associations and unions of legal entities that are engaged in advertising activities (for example, the ACAR).

To protect their interests in Russia, the largest advertisers in 2002 created the Commonwealth of brand manufacturers, "RusBrand". Today, "RusBrand" is the largest Russian consumer goods manufacturers association that brings together more than 60 leading domestic and international companies. The total annual turnover of these companies exceeds 30 billion U.S. dollars; their section in the television advertising market of the country is approaching 60%; and, in the entire advertising market, these companies comprise about one third of all advertising budgets in Russia. At the same time, in the Law "On Advertising", an advertising agency as the subject of Russian advertising business is not mentioned. Rather, such agency is considered an "advertising producer" and "advertising distributor".

Because advertising is addressed to an indefinite group of people, it should be distributed on Russian Federation territory in the Russian Language. Advertising can be additionally distributed at the advertisers' discretion in the republics' state languages and in the native languages of the peoples of the Russian Federation. In accordance with the Law "On Advertising", improper advertising is not allowed, that is, an advertisement that violates the requirements for its content, time, and the place and method of distribution (in particular, unfair, unreliable, unethical, false, hidden advertising).

The Law "On Advertising" also establishes special requirements that may concern various aspects of the production and distribution of advertising and its content. Special requirements are made on advertising of certain types of goods due to the fact that their use may harm life and health and the property of consumers. Thus, advertising of alcoholic beverages and tobacco products is not allowed in TV programs. Advertising of these products should not directly address minors, discredit abstinence from alcohol or smoking, or contain information about their positive therapeutic characteristics (Clause 1, Article 16 of the Law "On Advertising"). The imperfection of legal regulation of advertising has led to distortions in the formation of consumer demand for certain foods, tobacco, and alcohol, dietary supplements, and ineffective drugs. The law does not adequately protect consumers from unfair advertising, nor does it establish responsibility for false food-and-drugs advertising. Responsibility for violation is provided in civil and administrative law (Article 38 of the Law "On Advertising"). Furthermore, responsibility for deliberate violation of the Russian Federation advertising legislation may be set by other federal laws.

For an advertisement to be legitimate, it is necessary for it to meet these requirements: the consumer must understand that the information is an advertisement, and, thus, the advertisement must be recognizable; the consumer must be familiar with the mark of mandatory certification of the goods, if those goods are subject to it; advertising of goods that are prohibited for production and release in the Russian Federation is not allowed; and advertising that in any way violates the interests of minors is not allowed.

The existing legal mechanism must be improved by bringing regional and local advertising legislation in compliance with federal and international advertising law requirements.

Thus, since 2006, the problems of legal regulation of advertising in Russia have been connected with basic industrial activities. Digital advertising (and data-driven in particular) brings even more major problems. For example, the law is aimed at ensuring the realization of consumer rights, but more and more Internet users are becoming prosumers, that is they are involved in native ads and video content production. The "digital essence" of the new digital formats of advertising communication (e.g., search) is unclear even for industry experts (ACAR, 2019; Veselov, 2019). In other words, due to growing advertising on the Internet, its legal regulation—and the legal regulation of advertising—has to be radically changed (and special academic and industrial studies in this area are needed).

Advertising market results: 2017–2019

A feature of the Russian advertising market is its opacity: no official data exist on indicators and conclusions that can be drawn from existing data, which will differ from the real state of affairs. However, several organizations regularly issue expert assessments of the advertising market based on their own research. Most authoritative are the data of the Association of Communication Agencies of Russia (ACAR) and the international network of advertising agencies Zenith.

By the end of 2017, television remained the most attractive medium for advertisers. The volume of television advertising grew by 13% (in 2016 by 10%) and amounted to 170.9 billion rubles. By the end of the year, regional television developed faster (increased by 14%—to 24.8 billion rubles) than did federal television. At the beginning of 2017, advertisers invested more money in television advertising than on the Internet, but, by the end of the year, the costs for both segments became approximately equal. The volume of advertising on the Internet almost caught up with television and amounted to 166.3 billion rubles (ACAR, 2017).

The Internet still shows the highest growth rate of 22% per year (in 2016, 21%). Russia is the only advertising market in which the share of television and the Internet is high at 80% (the world average is 70%). By the end of 2018, the Internet overtook television in terms of advertising costs, which corresponds to world trends, with the other segments recovering slightly after a while. Since 2016, the volume of advertising on radio has grown by 3%, mainly due to the federal segment of advertisers, reaching 16.9 billion rubles. When summarizing the results for 2017, ACAR clarified the volume of regional radio advertising by adding sponsorship advertising budgets in million-plus cities. The advertising markets in cities with a population of 0.5–1 million people and settlements where less than 100 thousand people live were re-evaluated. Experts gave positive forecasts and believe that the segment of radio advertising will continue to grow (ACAR, 2018).

The press market at the end of 2017 was the only one that showed a negative trend. The volume of advertising in print media decreased by 8% to 20.5 billion rubles. Advertising in the central press had decreased by only 2%, and in the regional press by 21%. In January 2018, ACAR changed the method of calculating advertising in the press at the request of the publishing community, because the existing system, according to industry participants, distorted the real picture and adversely affected the reputation of publishers. In particular, companies were asked to add to the calculations of the income of publishers from digital advertising.

Digital advertising carriers are replacing classic outdoor advertising. Their share in Russia was 15% and, in Moscow, almost 30%. Out-of-Home advertising indicators increased in 2017 by 9% to 41.9 billion rubles. The volume of outdoor advertising grew by 8% to 33.8 billion rubles. Transit advertising grew the most: by 28% to 4.6 billion rubles. The industry will need at least two years to return to the pre-crisis level. Experts note that outdoor advertising is decreasing, but the price for this segment is growing, with budgets for outdoor advertising of mobile operators and retail remaining virtually unchanged. The main trigger for the growth of outdoor advertising was the construction business. Almost 25% of the income came precisely from this area. This trend continues for the second year in a row, with income in the regions stagnating.

Regional advertising in the four main media (TV, outdoor advertising, press, radio), excluding Moscow and the Moscow region, grew by 4% over the year to 49.3 billion rubles. Television remained the largest segment of the regional market, with revenues of 24.8 billion rubles. This amounted to half (50.3%) of the volume of the entire regional market. TV advertising, compared with 2016, increased by 14%. Radio and outdoor advertising grew by 4% and 1% to 9.1 billion rubles and 10 billion rubles, respectively. Among the Russian Internet companies, Mail.RuGroup grew more actively by 28.9%, or up to 23.76 billion rubles; Yandex grew by 20%, to 87.4 billion rubles.

According to the IAB and PWC survey, the interactive advertising market (39.9% of the total Russian advertising market, as estimated by ACAR, 2017) will continue to grow, outperforming the average growth rate of the advertising market in general. Most of the factors stimulating market growth are associated with the use of new technological solutions, for example, the use of machine-learning algorithms cross-platform measurements and an audit of advertising campaigns. Personalization and access to the end consumer define the development trends of the Russian interactive advertising market (The Russian interactive advertising market, 2017, p. 7).

In 2018, the total volume of advertising in the means of its distribution (excluding VAT) exceeded 469 billion rubles, which is 12% more than in the corresponding period of the previous year. Advertising on television and outdoor advertising showed a positive trend (+9% and +3%), in the press, it is negative (−12%), and radio was close to zero. According to ACAR experts, the total volume of regional advertising in its distribution media in four media segments (television, radio, press, outdoor advertising) amounted to about 48.4 billion rubles (excluding VAT). This is 2% lower than in 2017 (ACAR, 2018).

According to the ACAR experts, the Russian advertising market development results for the first three quarters of 2019 are positive (ACAR, 2019). The total volume of advertising in its means of distribution (excluding VAT) exceeded 340 billion rubles, which is 5% more than in the corresponding period the previous year.

The different segments of the advertising market dynamics vary. The TV market is growing slightly: only −9–10% to −4–5%. The radio segment is quite stable at −4–5%. The growth of the newspaper and magazine advertising segment in the third quarter of the year turned out to be low (−18%). At the same time, the growth of the largest publishing houses shows higher scores.

The experts could not come to a common opinion on the dynamics of the OOH and outdoor advertising, mainly due to the digital-OOH sub-segment. It is actively developing, but not properly measured yet.

The difficult situation in the Russian economy is reflected in the advertising market. The overall dynamics in the Russian market (+ 5%) is a very modest indicator compared to + 13% in 2018, although it seems high for many foreign advertising markets (ACAR, 2019). The growing Internet in case of the lack of legislation, measurement tools, and data-specialists would bring not only fresh tools and strategic ideas, but challenges and problems as well.

Conclusion

In Russia, advertising strategies have historically been rooted more in politics than in economics (except for a short period of nascent capitalism on the edge of the nineteenth and twentieth centuries). After the October Revolution of 1917, the Soviet government monopolized advertisement by the state immediately to deprive it from market relations. Moreover, it never became commercial, which was impossible in a planned economy. Nevertheless, even in Soviet times, there were advertising media and advertising campaigns, primarily aimed at foreign economic communications and foreign audiences. In other words, Russian historical advertising models were included in the "political communications mix" and were more impersonal and hierarchical than "communicative".

In post-Soviet Russia, advertising began to take shape along with the new domestic economy and society. In fact, during the "perestroika" period there were no advertising strategies. In the early 1990s, the authorities legally restricted business, primarily foreign, to solve the problems of certain financial and political groups and to demonstrate the absence of social priorities, thereby creating a specific combination of state and market mechanisms Despite the "black" illegal or "gray" semi-legal patterns of relations, participants in the advertising process gradually established institutional and market relations.

After the restructuring period, the advertising market in its modern sense was formed by the beginning of the 2000s. Today, in terms of institutionalization and structure, it is at the level of advertising markets of Eastern European countries. The question of the impact of advertising on business remains controversial to this day. This is primarily due to the unfavorable external investment climate, as well as for domestic economic and political reasons. Despite differences in estimates, the market, in general, has emerged from the crisis 2009. Since 2014, the situation of instability has led to growth and, in 2019, inhibition. It certainty does not affect the overall development of the economy and the advertising market, so there are no long-term or medium-term strategies. So, advertising has no real strategic goals.

The difficult situation in the Russian economy is reflected in the advertising market. The overall dynamics in the Russian market for the first three quarters of 2019 (+5%) is a very modest indicator compared to + 13% in 2018, although it seems high for many foreign advertising markets. (The total volume of advertising in its means of distribution, excluding VAT, exceeded 340 billion rubles or 5,396 billion U.S. dollars.)

Advertising communication strategies in different areas vary. Traditionally hierarchical political advertising is being transformed due to digital technologies: if, in 2016, the use of social networks was recognized as the last important tool in the elections, then on the eve of 2019 social networks outstripped traditional advertising technologies (a door-to-door field campaign, a media campaign, outdoor advertising, and direct media advertising). In election campaigns, the role of social platforms is growing, and Telegram is becoming the main platform for campaigning. At the same time, not all parties' websites meet modern requirements. However, elite agreements remain the main election campaigns tool. The "newest political reality" is the straightening of the antiestablishment attitude in Russia, which could become a driver for a new stage in the political advertising aims and development.

Thanks to digital tools, other advertising areas have become more interactive and "communicative". Commercial and social advertising is going to be more person-centered. The concept of "social advertising" is even replaced by the concept of "social communications". In this mix, in addition to advertising itself, marketing, PR, and other technologies can be used. Communications become immersive, multichannel, and even omnichannel, and technologies are available not only to large companies but to ordinary prosumer.

Digital and data-driven technologies are rapidly changing the Russian advertising landscape. Classical structures and classifications of advertising holdings and agencies are transforming, since the emergence of new technologies makes campaigns more effective. Digitalization determines the emergence within structures of the advertising business and structures that are essentially not related to the advertising business, for example, digital platforms, but that determine the functions and effectiveness of advertising activities.

The Internet provokes a sharp differentiation in content distribution means: the Internet is developing most rapidly, television is keeping its positions, segments of the print press is falling, radio and outdoor advertising practically do not grow. Advertising budgets on the Internet are increasing. The main drivers of Internet budget growth are dynamic targeting, accurate measurement of investments, and a wide choice of a target audience, including the mobile Internet. The range of tools is expanding to ten tools in one campaign. Meanwhile, Internet advertising campaigns are at their initial stage. For example, the most frequently used parameter for evaluating the effectiveness of advertising campaigns is website traffic, which means that digital communication remains strictly "official". Also, the Internet is not the only tool in an effective marketing mix to reach brand goals and solve its problems. In any case, the peculiarities and problems of datafied digital advertising are perceived by practitioners positively.

Moreover, the growth of the Internet provokes legislation problems, in particular, extremely nondigital ones. Since 2006, the problems of legal regulation of advertising in Russia have been associated with the basic industrial activities and are only growing. Digital and data-driven realities a priori were not reflected in the Federal Law "On Advertising". The growing Internet, in case of the lack of relevant "offline" legislation and digital advertising legislation, would multiply challenges and problems. For example, the "legal essence" of many advertising communication digital formats is unclear even for industry experts. But perhaps due to the growing advertising on the Internet, its legal regulation—and the advertising legal regulation—would be changed not only radically, but also quickly.

Russian audiences and netizens are involved in Internet communication. According to the Russian Association of Electronic Communication (RAEC, 2019), there are 95.9 million users in Runet, Internet penetration is 78.1%, the mobile audience has grown to 85.2 million people, that is, the technological prerequisites for access and Internet interaction are fully formed. Despite Russia's global openness and the growth of the Internet, Russian netizens demonstrate adherence to rather traditional patriarchal values, and in particular gender-patriarchal values.

Due to unpredictable transformations in the economy and technology, advertising functions will change, but these changes are impossible to predict. The mainline of specialties in the Russian context of the uneven development of digitalization will remain. Promising are the directions of digital, data-driven technologies, programmatic real-time bidding, and interactive video content.

Limitations of the study. Despite the digital technologies growth, experts cannot designate their parameters as advertising formats and accurately define measurement tools; there is a lack of industrial research practices and theoretical research concepts. So, the impact of the Internet on advertising in Russia as a strategic communication requires a special large-scale study.

References

ACAR. (2017). Ob"yem reklamy v sredstvakh yeye rasprostraneniya v 2017 godu [The volume of advertising in its distribution means in 2017]. Retrieved from www.akarussia.ru/knowledge/market_size/id8180.

ACAR. (2018). Ob"yem reklamy v sredstvakh yeye rasprostraneniya v 2018 godu [The volume of advertising in its distribution means in 2018]. Retrieved from www. akarussia.ru/knowledge/market_size/id8690.

ACAR. (2019). Ob"yem reklamy v sredstvakh yeye rasprostraneniya v 2019 godu [The volume of advertising in its distribution means in 2019]. Retrieved from www. akarussia.ru/knowledge/market_size/id9034.

Bogdanov, S. (2017). Strategicheskiye kommunikatsii: kontseptual'nyye podkhody I modeli dlya gosudarstvennogo upravleniya [Strategic communications: conceptual approaches and models for public administration]. *Public administration*, 61, 132–152. Retrieved from http://e-journal.spa.msu.ru/uploads/vestnik/2017/ vipusk__61._aprel_2017_g./kommunikazionnii_menedjment_i_strategitcheskaja_ kommunikazija_v_gosudarstvennom_upravlenii/bogdanov.pdf.

Borisov, V. (2004). Regulirovaniye reklamnoy deyatel'nosti: Pravovyye i eticheskiye aspekty [Regulation of promotional activities: Legal and ethical aspects]. *Bulletin of Moscow University. Series 21. Management (State and Society)*, 4, 18–24.

Boroday, A. (2006). *Kachestvo podgotovki spetsialistov po reklame: opyt, problemy i puti ikh resheniya* [The quality of training of advertising specialists: experience, problems and solutions. Quality management of the educational process]. Moscow: RSTEU.

Boyko, S. (2002). *Reklama v sotsial'no-ekonomicheskoy zhizni rossiyskogo obshchestva. Konets 1980-kh—nachalo 2000-kh godov* [Advertising in the socio-economic life of Russian society. The end of the 1980s—the beginning of the 2000s]. Moscow: Moscow Social Humanitarian Academy.

Buman Media and Headhunter. (2019). Buman Media i HeadHunter: chem zhivet rynok PR-kommunikatsiy Rossii v 2019 godu [Buman Media and HeadHunter: How the Russian PR communications market lives in 2019]. Retrieved from www.cossa.ru/ news/238217/.

Chechetkina, G. (1995). Osnovnyye tendentsii razvitiya mirovoy reklamnoy industrii v 90-ye gody [The main trends in the development of the global advertising industry in the 90s]. *Bulletin of Moscow University. Series 10. Journalism*, 6, 58–68.

Cheryachukin, Y. V. (1998). *Pravovoye regulirovaniye reklamnoy deyatel'nosti v Rossiyskoy Federatsii i zarubezhnykh gosudarstvakh (opyt sravnitel'nogo issledovaniya)* [Legal regulation of advertising in the Russian Federation and foreign countries (experience of a comparative study)]. Volgograd: Volgograd legal Institute of the Ministry of Internal Affairs of Russia. (Ph.D. dissertation.)

Deloitte (2019) *What is digital economy?* Retrieved from www2.deloitte.com/mt/en/ pages/technology/articles/mt-what-is-digital-economy.html.

Digital advertisers barometer (2018). IAB Russia. Retrieved from http://datainsight.ru/ en/iabbrometer2018_eng

Doklad komiteta po politicheskim tekhnologiyam Rossiyskoy Assotsiatsii po svyazyam s obshchestvennost'yu (2016). [Political technology committee of the Russian Public Relations Association Report]. Retrieved from https://politteh.ru/news/news_ 168.html

Doklad komiteta po politicheskim tekhnologiyam Rossiyskoy Assotsiatsii po svyazyam s obshchestvennost'yu. Instrumenty izbiratel'noy kampanii: nastupila li novaya politicheskaya real'nost'? (2018). [Campaign Tools: Has a new political reality come? Political Technology Committee of the Russian Public Relations Association Report]. Retrieved from https://politteh.ru/netcat_files/userfiles/1/ ISSLEDOVANIE_RASO_DINAMIKA_IZBIRATELNYH_TEHNOLOGIY_ 18.12.19_.pdf

Dolgov, S. (2019, May 19). Digital-trendy, kotoryye spasayut mir: Budushcheye sotsial'noy reklamy [Digital trends that save the world: The future of social advertising]. Retrieved from https://vc.ru/marketing/68009-digital-trendy-kotorye-spasayut-mir-budushchee-socialnoy-reklamy.

Dorskii, A. (2019). *Pravovoye regulirovaniye reklamnoy deyatel'nosti i svyazey s obshchestvennost'yu* [Legal regulation of advertising and public relations]. St. Petersburg: Publishing House of St. Petersburg University.

Dorskii, A., Pavlenko, M., Shutikova, N., Zubanova, S., & Pashentsev D. (2017). Advertisement in the EAEU Countries: Law Harmonisation Issues. *Journal of Advanced Research in Law and Economics, 8*(7), 2112–2120. doi: https://doi.org/10.14505/jarle.v8.7(29).07.

Erkenova, F. (2003). *Samoregulirovaniye v reklame* [Self-regulation in advertising]. Moscow: RIP Holding.

Evstafiyev V. A., & Pasyutina, Y. E. (2017). *Istoriya rossiyskoy reklamy: Sovremennyy period.* 2-ye izd., ispr. i dop … [The history of Russian advertising: The modern period, 2nd ed., corr. and added]. Moscow, Russia: Dashkov and Co.

Fedyunin D., & Shilina M. (2019). Tsifrovaya ekonomika i novyye paradigmy praktik i teorii PR [Digital economy and new paradigms of practices and PR theory]. *Russian School of Public Relations, 12*, 55–66.

Get Media Right (2019) Kantar Millward Brown's annual global Get Media Right survey. Retrieved from www.millwardbrown.com/gettingmediaright/2019/.

Gribok, N. (2011). *Deyatel'nost' gosudarstvennykh, obshchestvennykh organizatsiy i biznesa po razvitiyu reklamnoy industrii v Rossii: 1991–2006 gg.* [The activities of state, public organizations and businesses for the development of the advertising industry in Russia: 1991–2006]. Moscow: Moscow Humanitarian University. (Ph.D. dissertation.)

Grinberg, T. (2018). *Politicheskiye tekhnologii* [Political technologies]. Moscow: Aspect Press.

Grishina, I. (2003). *Reklamnyy rynok: Stanovleniye, osobennosti, mekhanizm funktsionirovaniya* [Advertising market: Formation, features, functioning mechanism]. Orel: Orlov State Agrarian University. (Ph.D. dissertation.)

Gritsuk, A., & Kutyrkina, L. (2007). *Istoriya reklamy v Rossii: Zadachi reklamnoy kommunikatsii i formy organizatsii reklamnoy deyatel'nosti v SSSR* [The history of advertising in Russia: The tasks of advertising communication and the forms of organization of advertising activity in the USSR]. Moscow: Moscow State Print University.

Hallahan K., Holtzhausen, D., Van Ruler B., Verčič D., & Sriramesh, K. (2007). Defining Strategic Communication. *International Journal of Strategic Communication, 1*, (1), 3–35.

Igla muzhskogo odobreniya: reklama Reebok vyzvala skandal v seti (2019, February 8). [Needle for male endorsement: Reebok ad triggered a scandal on the web] Sostav. Retrieved from www.sostav.ru/publication/feministskaya-reklama-reebok-vyzvala-burnyj-otklik-35603.html.

Khapenkov, V., Ivanov, G., & Fedyunin, D. (2013). *Reklamnaya deyatel'nost' v torgovle* [Trade Advertising]. Moscow: Forum.

Kiselev, V., Fedyunin, D., & Kutyrkina, L. (Eds.) (2017). *Brend-kommunikatsii* [Brand communications], (pp. 77–97). Moscow: Moscow Plekhanov Russian University of Economics.

Kolomiyets, V. (Ed.) (2014). *Teoriya i praktika mediareklamnykh issledovaniy* [Theory and practice of media advertising research]. Moscow: "Video International" Analytical Center.

Kolomiyets, V. (2019). *Kontseptualizatsiya mediakommunikatsii* [Conceptualization of media communication]. *Mediascope, 4.* Retrieved from www.mediascope.ru/2575.

McKinsey Global Institute (2017) Tsifrovaya Rossiya: Novaya real'nost' [Digital Russia: New Reality]. Retrieved from www.mckinsey.com/~/media/mckinsey/locations/europe%20and%20middle%20east/russia/our%20insights/digital%20russia/digital-russia-report.ashx.

Muzykant, V. (2002). *Reklama i PR-tekhnologii* [Advertising and PR-technologies]. Moscow: Armada-Press.

National Advertising Alliance (n.d.). Retrieved from http://nra.media/en/.

Nazaykin,A.(2018).*Illyustrirovaniye reklamy* [Illustrating advertising].Moscow:Solon-Press.

Nestlè: Factories and Branches. (2019). Retrieved from www.Nestlè.ru/aboutus/russuianNestlè/fabriki_i_filialy.

Nikolaishvili, G. (2008). *Sotsial'naya reklama: teoriya i praktika* [Social Advertising: Theory and Practice]. Moscow: Aspect Press.

Nikolaishvili, G. (2019). Expert Interview. Personal archive.

O merakh po padikal'noy restrurturizacii parubezhnoy ekonomicheskoy reklamy ot 6 fevralya 1988 goda (1988, February 6). [On measures for a radical restructuring of foreign economic advertising dated February 6, 1988] Retrieved from www.lawmix.ru/zakonodatelstvo/2578365.

Rep'yev,A. (2008). *Mudryy reklamodatel'* [Wise Advertiser]. Moscow: Eksmo.

Romat, E. (Ed.). (2004). *Istoriya otechestvennoy reklamy: Galereya reklamnoy klassiki* [The history of domestic advertising: A gallery of advertising classics] Kharkov, UA: StudCenter.

Rostova, N. (2018). Kak vzletal i padal general Lebed'. Rol' SMI v yego biografii [How General Swan soared and fell. The role of the media in his biography]. Retrieved from www.yeltsinmedia.com/articles/lebed/.

Rossiyskiy reklamnyy yezhegodnik (1999–2019). [Russian Advertising Yearbook] Retrieved from www.akarussia.ru/en/node/637.

Rozhkov, I. (1997). *Reklama: planka dlya "profi": Reklama v usloviyakh rynka 90-kh* [Advertising: the bar for the "pros": Advertising in the market conditions of the 90s]. Moscow: Yurayt.

Russian Association of Electronic Communication (RAEC) (2019). Aktual'nyye trendy i glavnyye tsifry Runeta na Rossiyskom Internet Forume [Actual trends and main figures of the Runet at the Russian Internet Forum] Retrieved from https://raec.ru/live/branch/10992/.

Rybakov, B. (1948). Torgovlya i torgovyye puti [Trade and trade routes]. In Grekov, B. Artamonov, M. (Eds.) *Istoria kultury v drevnej Rusi* [History of the culture of Ancient Russia]. (pp. 315–369). Moscow and St. Petersburg: Academy of Science of USSR Publishing House.

Self-Regulatory Council (2019). *Self-regulatory council at the Chamber of Commerce and Industry of the Russian Federation.* Retrieved from www.oprf.ru/about/structure/2608/.

Shchepilova, G. (2019). Expert Interview. Personal archive.

Shchepilova, G., & Shchepilov, K. (2019) *Osnovy reklamy* [Fundamentals of advertising]. Berlin: Direct Media.

Shchepilova, G., & Kozhanova, D. (2016) Mobil'naya reklama v Rossii: ekspertnyy analiz [Mobile advertising in Russia: expert analysis] *Media almanac,* 5, 22–28. Shilina M. (2012). *Tekstogennyye transformatsii infosfery. Metodologicheskiy eskiz stanovleniya Interneta* [Textogenic transformations of the infosphere. A methodological sketch of the formation of the Internet]. Moscow: "North-East", Higher School of Economics.

Shilina M. (2016). Rynok PR-uslug v Rossii v period krizisa: ob"yem, sub"yekty, spetsializatsii [The market of PR-services in Russia during the crisis: volume, subjects, specializations] *MediaScope, 2.* Retrieved from www.mediascope.ru/node/2119.

Skorobogatykh, I., & Musatova, Z. (2018). Osobennosti povedeniya "tsifrovykh" potrebiteley [Features of the behavior of digital consumers]. *Problems of the modern economy, 4*(68), 127–130. Skorobogatykh, I., Nevostruyev, P., Musatova, Z., & Ivashkova, N. (2018). Marketing v usloviyakh razvitiya tsifrovoy ekonomiki [Marketing in the digital economy development]. *Marketing and marketing research, 3,* 170–179.

SMI (2015) SMI: Sostavlen reyting effektivnosti prisutstviya partiy v internete [Media: Compiled a rating of the effectiveness of the presence of parties on the Internet]. December 3, 2015 Rambler: https://news.rambler.ru/politics/32117519/?utm_content=news_media&utm_medium=read_more&utm_source=copylink.

Technology Index (2019). Technology Index 2019: glavnyye instrumenty v digital-kommunikatsiyakh [Technology Index 2019: the main tools in digital communications]. Retrieved from https://adindex.ru/news/digital/2019/09/4/275172.phtml.

The Civil Code (1994). Grazhdanskyj kodeks Rossiyskoy Federacii N 51-FZ prinyat 30 noyabrya 1994 goda [the Civil Code of the Russian Federation N 51-FL adopted on November, 30, 1994]. Retrieved from www.consultant.ru/document/cons_doc_LAW_5142/.

The Code on Administrative Offenses (2001). Kodeks Rossiyskoy Federacii ob Administrativnyh Pravonarusheniyah N 195-FZ 2020, prinyat 30 dekabrya 2001 goda [The Code of the Russian Federation on Administrative Offenses, N 195-FL 2020 adopted on December, 30, 2001]. Retrieved from www.consultant.ru/document/cons_doc_LAW_34661/.

The Federal Law "On Advertising". (2006). Federal'nyy zakon Rossiyskoy Federacii No. 38-FZ O reklame [The Federal Law of the Russian Federation No. 38-FL "On Advertising"]. Retrieved from www.consultant.ru/document/cons_doc_LAW_58968/.

The Federal Law "On Protection of Competition". (2006). O zashchite konkurentsii Federal'nyy zakon, prinyat 8 iynya 2006 g. No. 135-FZ [The Federal Law "On Protection of Competition" No. 135-FL adopted on June 8, 2006]. Retrieved from www.consultant.ru/document/cons_doc_LAW_61763/.

The Law "On Protection of Consumer Rights" (1992, 2019) Zakon RF ot 07.02.1992 N 2300–1 (red. ot 18.07.2019) "O zashchite prav potrebiteley" prinyat 7 fevralya 1992goda [The Law of the Russian Federation of 07.02.1992 N 2300–1 (as amended on 07/18/2019) "On the Protection of Consumer Rights" adopted on February 7, 1992]. Retrieved from www.consultant.ru/document/cons_doc_LAW_305/.

The Russian interactive advertising market 2017–2020 (2017). *A survey by IAB Russia and PwC.* Retrieved from https://iabrus.ru/www/doc/research/DigitalAdspend_final_eng.pdf.

Top-30 (2019, April 17) *Top-30 krupneyshikh reklamodateley Rossii [TOP-30 largest advertisers of Russia] Sostav.* Retrieved from www.sostav.ru/publication/rejting-krupnejshikh-reklamodatelej-rossii-2018-31422.html.

Tulupov, V. (Ed.). (2011). *Teoriya i practika reklamy* [Advertising theory and practice]. Voronezh: Voronezh State University Publishing House.

Uchenova, V., & Starykh, N. (1994). *Istoriya reklamy detstvo, otrochestvo* [Advertising history childhood, adolescence]. Moscow: Smysl Publishing House.

Uchenova, V., & Starykh, N. (1999). *Istoriya reklamy, ili Metamorfozy reklamnogo obraza* [History of advertising, or Metamorphoses of an advertising image, place of publication]. Moscow: UNITY—DANA.

van Ruler, B. (2018) Communication theory: An underrated pillar on which strategic communication rests. *International Journal of Strategic Communication, 12*(4), 367–381.

Vartanova, E. (2012). Constructing Russian media system in the context of globalization. *World of media* (p. 9–36). Moscow: Lomonosov Moscow State University.

Veselov, S. (2003). *Marketing v reklame* [Marketing in advertising]. Moscow: MIR.

Veselov, S. (2017). *Sovremennyy reklamnyy rynok Rossii: kommunikatsionnyye trendy brendov* [The modern advertising market of Russia: Brand communication trends]. Moscow: Russian Economics University.

Veselov, S. (2019). Expert Interview. Personal archive.

Vladimirova, N. (2019). Marketing—2019: Ekspertnyy vzglyad na rynok, ili chto nuzhno derzhat' v fokuse v sleduyushchem godu vashemu direktoru po marketingu [Marketing—2019: An expert look at the market, or what should be kept in focus next year by your marketing director]. Retrieved from https://incrussia.ru/understand/marketing-2019-ekspertnyj-vzglyad-na-rynok-ili-chto-nuzhno-derzhat-v-fokuse-v-sleduyushhem-godu-vashemu-direktoru-po-marketingu.

Yegorova-Gantman, Y., & Pleshakov, K. (1999). *Politicheskaya reklama [Political advertising]*. Moscow: Center for Political Consulting "Niccolo M".

Young Lions Russia. (2019, February 5). Young Lions Russia 2019: Molodyye kreatory iz Rossii, kotoryye otpravyatsya v Kanny v etom godu [Young Lions Russia 2019: Young creators from Russia who will travel to Cannes this year]. Retrieved from www.sostav.ru/publication/young-lions-35716.html.

Part IV

Examples of current studies in Russian communication(s)

9 Media relations in contemporary Russia

Media catching

Taisiia Lagutenkova

Introduction

Today's media relations in Russia are developing toward a co-creation concept and an active public involvement in content creation. This chapter focuses on "media catching", a trend in relationships between journalists and newsmakers that had emerged in 2014. Media catching represents an alternative to traditional forms of media relations such as media pitching, which primarily serves the needs and interests of newsmakers—public relations (PR) practitioners or, less often, experts. Instead of being just recipients of content, reporters initiate communication with practitioners to obtain specific information to complete their stories. An increasing number of publications in the United Statesand in Europe signifies an expanded role of media catching. Although media catching as a trend in media relations seems to be gaining popularity in other countries, this term still is not widely used in Russia, and almost no research is being conducted despite this trend in Russian practice.

Media catching in the West

A wide range of studies can be found in the field of media relations. Macnamara (2014) reported that, since the early 1900s, more than 200 research studies were conducted. Most of them date back to the 1980s–2000s. At that time, Grunig et al. identified the first theoretical models of public relations. One of them, the two-way symmetrical model, is considered to be an ideal model, affecting in a way "that a neutral observer would describe as benefiting both organization and publics" (Grunig et al., 1995). This approach is close to the dialogic theory of public relations by Kent and Taylor. Those authors observed the key principles of the dialogue approach (mutuality, propinquity, empathy, risk, and commitment) and three ways of incorporating dialogue into the practice of public relations (Kent & Taylor, 2002). These theories do not lose their topicality today. Langett reviewed Kent and Taylor's dialogic principles, describing an interpersonal relationship theory between practitioners and journalists that was approached "through dialogic, social and behaviorist lens" (Langett, 2013).

This brings us back to the question of how a new concept of media catching emerged in everyday public relations. Despite mutuality and interdependence, relationships between journalists and newsmakers have always been characterized by a complicated, if not contradictory, character. Both groups have different interests, goals, and values. Zorin (2011) found that, while reporters intend to produce mass information, public relations departments strive to shape public opinions and attitudes. This resulted in different perceptions about each other. Shin and Cameron (2003) said that practitioners perceive informal media relations as ethical and influential more often than do reporters, what may be determined by "the practitioner's self-serving motive and journalist's fear of undue influence". Vercic and Colic's coorientational analysis (2016) showed that public relations specialists misestimated reporters' opinions in three out of four statements. Indeed, most journalists were not satisfied with the quality of services that practitioners provided as well as the personal characteristics of public relations specialists. Sallot and Johnson (2006b) emphasized that most journalists complain about practitioners' lack of news sense, ethics, self-serving motives, timeliness, and poor quality of writing. In 2006, these scholars also conducted another survey with an increased number of respondents. They noted that, despite that most journalists consider the relationships with practitioners as positive and valuable for agenda-setting, some "love-hate" sentiments and Jeffers's syndrome sentiments were expressed (Sallot & Johnson, 2006a). According to Jeffers' syndrome, journalists tend to evaluate public relations specialists with whom they have already worked more favorably than they did "the first time" contacts (Jeffers, 1977). Macnamara (2014) expanded the meaning of Jeffers' syndrome, noting that "journalists acculturate experienced PR practitioners who they know and deal with frequently into their circle of 'expert' contacts and trusted sources and no longer see them as PR" (Macnamara, 2014). Simultaneously, Macnamara (2014) maintains that journalists are not satisfied with practitioners' lack of social responsibility, ethical and moral qualities, and skills of speech.

All of these studies are focused on media relations that is approached through media "pitching", which means pushing public relations messages directly to journalists, regardless of these journalists' needs. The inefficiency of this approach was proven by Frac.tl, an American agency that measures the performance of media pitching. In 2015, the average American journalist received from several dozen to several hundred pitches per day, and only 11% of them were reflected in their articles (Kanevskaya, 2015). This low conversion of pitches into publications and the general disappointment of journalists required the appearance of another approach, media catching.

Although the media catching process was first described by Waters, Tindall, and Morton (2010), we can speak about the birth of this phenomenon when the first professional services were presented for journalists seeking sources of information. ProfNet was created in 1992 by *PRNewswire* in the USA to connect reporters with the sources wanted for their stories. There is no fee for journalists, but practitioners have to pay for membership. Another popular service in the USA called Help A Reporter Out (HARO) is completely free for both groups of users. Based on Facebook, it was launched in 2007 by Peter Shankman. Soon that community on social media was transformed to the website intended to serve journalists' requests.

Waters, Tindall, and Morton (2010) were the first to present this concept of media catching, described as: "using the e-mail mailing list, individual journalists ask for very specific content for stories they were working on while reaching large numbers of public relations practitioners". Through content analysis of HARO requests, Waters, Tindall, and Morton (2010) observed which typical media and journalists were using HARO services and for which types of information they asked. A year later, these authors conducted research that was focused on the role of deadlines in media catching. As a result, ten recommendations, called "best practices", were proposed for successful integration of media catching in everyday public relations (Waters, Tindall, & Morton, 2011). These "best practices" were checked and critically revised by Tallapragada et al., who noted that some of these recommendations did not properly correlate with successful media placements (Tallapragada et al., 2012).

Media catching in Russia

What can be said about media catching in Russia? It began in 2013 with a nonprofit community on Facebook called "Help the journalist" and functionally resembled an American analogue. In 2014, Konstantin Bocharsky, a former journalist, launched Pressfeed, the first Russian service connecting reporters and newsmakers. It offers a choice of accounts ranging in cost and available options from basic to agency profile. One year later, an international service, HackPack, appeared in Russia. It provides a trial configuration for free, and, after a test period, further subscription is paid. Finally, a free Russian service, Deadline.Media, was created in 2016 for effective communication between media professionals and experts. All services are organized in the same way: after signing up on the website as a journalist or a newsmaker, the user, depending on that individual's status, can request information and specify the deadline, or, respectively, view a requests list and respond to those relevant to the newsmaker's expertise.

To examine the process of media catching in Russia and to conceptualize this term, we conducted research, based on in-depth problem-centered interviews with Russian journalists and public relations practitioners. In the next stage, these interviews were analyzed with a method called grounded theory. The final step presented a comparative analysis of the American and Russian practices of media catching and developed recommendations for Russian public relations practitioners. The study confirmed that media pitching slightly decreased after the rise of media catching. Most respondents believe that pitching content through emails and phone calls is no longer enough to satisfy the needs of both public relations practitioners and journalists. Reporters request mainly comments, official opinions, or insights when they need new heroes for their stories, or, on the contrary, "known" newsmakers from their contact list

(Lagutenkova, 2017). The media catching recommendations appeared somewhat different from the best practices designed in the United States due to the national peculiarities of media and the sociocultural context.

Media catching and agenda-setting

One must ponder how media catching correlates with agenda-setting. The contemporary media environment is associated with strategic partnerships between the press and its audiences and the public's involvement in news production. This is what media catching services are expected to instigate and promote. By asking newsmakers for information, journalists can expand prospects of brands, organizations, and famous persons for contributions into the news agenda and influence the saliency of issues. On the other hand, topics of requests remain pre-set for newsmakers, and the selection of experts for publication still is not transparent. This raises into consideration whether media catching actually brings agenda-building to the public.

Since 1972, when McCombs and Shaw first revealed the media impact on audiences in Chapel Hill, North Carolina, during the 1968 presidential elections, agenda-setting theory has evolved within the framework of the constructionist approach (McCombs & Shaw, 1972). This approach supposes that every social institution shapes its own saliency of issues, taking part in the construction of media agenda as a set of stories covered by journalists of what is followed by creation of public awareness and concern of salient issues. In 2004, McCombs termed relationships between sources and media agenda as a "fourth stage" of agenda-building (Sweetser, Golan, & Wanta, 2008). The previous studies demonstrated strong positive correlations between traditional media relations and news coverage. Sigal (1974) said nearly 50% of stories in the *New York Times* and *Washington Post* across a 20-year period were influenced by information subsidies. Cameron, Sallot, and Curtin (1997) argued that 25–80% of news stories are based on press releases and other PR materials. Callison (2003) observed that online pressrooms positively meet the information needs of reporters.

Particular attention was paid to the setting saliency of political issues. During election campaigns, PR practitioners strive to affect candidate images in news outlets through candidate news releases, interviews, and press conferences. Kaid (1976) said that political information subsidies are often run in press exactly as PR practitioners distribute them. A dependence on sources, contribution was maintained by a wide range of researchers, for example, Boyle, Lopez-Escobar, Roberts, Anderson and McCombs, Walters, Walters and Gray, Tedesco, and Gans. Exploring the 2002 gubernatorial elections in Florida, Kiousis at al. (2006) investigated first- and second-level agenda-building and agenda-setting effects. In first-level agenda-shaping, when media emphasize certain candidates or issues, these objects are perceived as more important in public opinion. Second-level agenda-setting deals with the framing and emphasis on the attributes of the objects while ignoring others, influencing not only what people think about, but also how they do it. Kiousis et al. (2006) observed significant positive correlations between saliency of the issues in press releases, media coverage, and public opinion at both levels.

Integration of newsmakers and journalists' efforts was found beyond political communication as well. Curtin and Rhodenbaugh (2001) said that environmental issues in news outlets originate from press releases and other materials that were suggested by public relations practitioners. Carroll and McCombs (2003) examined agenda-building effects on business communication, proposing that "organized efforts to communicate a corporate agenda will result in a significant degree of correspondence between the attribute agenda of the firm and the news media".

New digital tools for interaction between journalists and newsmakers that are developed on the Internet are an object of the next generation of agenda-setting studies. Web-based media relations are operated through blogs, social media, and, from recent time, media catching services. They possess accessibility and interactivity that make possible a two-way transfer of information and, respectively, mutual influence. If media and sources are spreading the same news, the next question to be asked is who sets the agenda? Sweetser, Golan, and Wanta (2008) used cross-lag analyses for revealing strong correlations between candidate blogs and major television networks during the 2004 presidential election in the United States. They also noted that the media set the candidates' agendas and that blog discussions were simply reacting to news coverage (Sweetser, Golan, & Wanta, 2008). However, another study related to the same presidential election provided evidence of the existence of a bidirectional relationship between political blogs and mainstream media. Wallsten (2007) reported that 19 out of 35 issues in popular blogs and 21 out of 35 issues in less-popular blogs showed two-way correlations with media coverage. That study indicated that the blogosphere induces a significant impact on news outlets and vice versa. These findings were followed by studies exploring linkages between the press and social media. Kiousis et al. (2016) observed substantial correlations between news coverage and public relations subsidies delivered through social media such as Facebook, Twitter, and YouTube without clarifying the direction of the information flow. Sayre et al. (2010) found a bidirectional relationship by pointing out that posts on social media may influence news coverage as well as react in response to them. No attempt to research media catching had been made before we decided to investigate whether media catching reflects news coverage or precedes it.

A concent analysis of media catching in Russia

This study employed two content analyses with the same sets of categories. We analyzed Pressfeed requests (n = 181) to determine the media catching agenda. The second sample included 817 news stories from the TOP-5 most cited news outlets, according to the ratings by Medialogy, a leader in monitoring and analysis of media in Russia. In both samples, we concentrated only on one topic—financial and economic issues, during the period March 1–31, 2017. Categories coded in this study included basic demographics of the item (date, URL, media, headline, and source type from several sources) and issues mentioned (Russian budget, inflation, privatization, taxes, global economic issues (except trade), IMF/Western aid (for any country, including Russia), international trade, agriculture, corruption, strikes, economic crimes, energy, modernization/innovation, The Eurasian Economic Union/European Union, and economic crisis). We used a dichotomous variable, identifying if issues are present (1) or absent (0). After coding was completed, we computed Pearson correlations to compare the saliency of the issues. This is a common measure applied in the previous studies in agenda-setting theory. After that, the Pressfeed requests and news outlets were further explored through cross-lagged correlations to come up with the answer to the question—who sets the agenda. As a result, a tangible correlation between media coverage and Pressfeed agenda was found for a half of issues. Next, we observed that Pressfeed agenda turned out to be an independent variable and that the issues that first appeared in the media catching service exert an influence on news coverage. This means that newsmakers have an opportunity not only to respond to the journalist's request, but also to set media agenda.

In conclusion, a cursory review of media catching as a cooperative and dia- logic approach of media relations provides evidence of a shifting toward co- creation and co-production of news in practice. Despite controversial goals and self-serving motives, it seems that both groups finally realized the existence of the substantial role that each other play in agenda-setting and started a long way toward a mutually beneficial and convenient cooperation.

References

Callison, C. (2003). Media relations and the Internet: How Fortune 500 company websites assist journalists in news gathering. *Public Relations Review, 29*(1), 29–41.

Cameron, G. T., Sallot, L., & Curtin, P. A. (1997). Public relations and the production of news: A critical review and a theoretical framework. *Communication yearbook 20* (pp. 111–155). Newbury Park, CA: Sage.

Carroll, C. E., & McCombs, M. (2003). Agenda-setting effects of business news on the public's images and opinions about major corporations. *Corporate Reputation Review, 6*(1), 42–51.

Curtin, P. A., & Rhodenbaugh, E. (2001). Building the news media agenda on the environment: A comparison of public relations and journalistic sources. *Public Relations Review, 27*(2), 180–193.

Grunig, J. E., Grunig, L. A., Sriramesh, K., Huang, Y-H., & Lyra, A. (1995). Models of Public Relations in an International Setting. *Journal of Public Relations Research, 7*(3), 163–186.

Jeffers, D. W. (1977). Performance expectations as a measure of relative status of news and PR people. *Journalism Quarterly, 54*(2), 299–306.

Kaid, L. L. (1976). Newspaper treatment of a candidate's news releases. *Journalism Quarterly, 53*, 135–157.

Kanevskaya R. (2015). Chempioni piara-2 [PR Champions 2]. *Business-Journal, 12*, 60–66.

Kent M. L., & Taylor M. (2002). Toward a dialogic theory of public relations. *Public Relations Review*, *28*, 21–37.

Kiousis S., Mitrook, M., Wu, X., & Seltzer, T. (2006). First-and second-level agenda-building and agenda-setting effects: Exploring the linkages among candidate news releases, media coverage, and public opinion during the 2002 Florida gubernatorial election. *Journal of Public Relations Research*, *18*(3), 266–278.

Kiousis S., Kim, J. Y., Kochhar, S., Lim, H.-J., Park, J., & Im, J. S. (2016). Agenda-building linkages between public relations and state news media during the 2010 Florida Senate Election. *Public Relations Review*, *42*(1), 241–243.

Lagutenkova, T. I. (2017). Media catching v sovremennoi Rossii: Stanovlenie trenda I perspectivi razvitiya [Media Catching in contemporary Russia: Trend emergence and development prospects]. *Sovremennaya mediasreda: Traditsii, actual'nye praktiki i tendentsii. Vzglyad molodyh issledovatelei*, *17*, 136–141.

Langett, J. (2013). Meeting the media: Toward an interpersonal relationship theory between the public relations practitioner and the journalist. *Prism*, *10*(1), 1–12. Retrieved from www.prismjournal.org/homepage.html.

Macnamara, J. (2014). Journalism-PR relations revisited: The good news, the bad news, and insights into tomorrow's news. *Public Relations Review*, *40*(5), 739–750.

McCombs M. E., & Shaw, D. L. (1972). The agenda-setting function of mass media. *Public Opinion Quarterly*, *36*(2), 176–187.

Sallot L. M., & Johnson, E. A. (2006a). Investigating relationships between journalists and public relations practitioners: Working together to set, frame and build the public agenda, 1991–2004. *Public Relations Review*, *32*(2), 151–159.

Sallot, L. M., & Johnson, E. A. (2006b). To contact … or not? Investigating journalists' assessments of public relations subsidies and contact preferences. *Public Relations Review*, *32*(1), 83–86.

Sayre, B., Bode, L., Shah, D., Wilcox, D., & Shah C. (2010). Agenda setting in a digital age: Tracking attention to California Proposition 8 in social media, online news and conventional news. *Policy & Internet*, *2*(2), 22–29.

Shin, J.-H., & Cameron, G. T. (2003). Informal relations: A look at personal influence in media relations. *Journal of Communication Management*, *7*(3), 239–253.

Sigal, L. V. (1974). Reporters and Officials: The Organization and Politics of Newsmaking. *Political Science Quarterly*, *89*(3), 672–67.

Sweetser, K. D., Golan, G. J., & Wanta W. (2008). Intermedia agenda setting in television, advertising, and blogs during the 2004 election. *Mass Communication & Society*, *11*(2), 198–208.

Tallapragada, M., Misara, I. C., Burke, K., & Waters, R. D. (2012). Identifying the best practices of media catching: A national survey of media relations practitioners. *Public Relations Review*, *38*(5), 926–931.

Vercic, A., & Colic, V. (2016). Journalists and public relations specialists: A coorientational analysis. *Public Relations Review*, *38*(5), 926–931. Retrieved from http://dx.doi.org/10.2016/j.pubrev.2016.03.007.

Wallsten, K. (2007). Agenda setting and the blogosphere: An analysis of the relationship between mainstream media and political blogs. *Review of Policy Research*, *24*(6), 567–578.

Waters, R. D., Tindall, N. T. J., & Morton, T. S. (2010). Media catching and the journalist—public relations practitioner relationship: How social media are changing the practice of media relations. *Journal of Public Relations Research*, *22*(3), 241–264.

Waters R. D., Tindall N. T. J., & Morton T. S. (2011). Dropping the ball on media inquiries: The role of deadlines in media catching. *Public Relations Review, 37*, 151–156.

Zorin K. A. (2011). Sravnitelny analiz tsennostnyh predstavlenii jurnalistov, reklamistov I spetsialistov po svyazyam s obschestvennost'yu [A comparative analysis of values among journalists, advertisers and public relations practitioners]. *Vestnik Krasnoyarskogo gosudarstvennogo pedagogicheskogo universiteta im. V.P. Astaf'eva, 2*, 178–179.

10 Social media and Russian society

Nikita Savin and Olga Solovyeva

Introduction

The emergence of social media in the 2000s has transformed Russian information dissemination and social relations. Brisk Internet penetration has set new platforms for civic and political discussions and has provided additional channels for newest communication strategies emergence over the next decades. A growing body of research is devoted to both consequences. This chapter outlines strengths and challenges of extant social media research, identifying key themes and problem issues in given areas. In the beginning, we provide a brief historical overview of existing social media platforms, communication patterns, and users' practices on social media. In the second section, we compare research agendas and current findings in applied social media inquiries and summarize social media's effect on politics, business, and society. In conclusion, we set an agenda for further research, focusing particularly on the growing role of social media in contentious politics in Russia.

Internet consumption has risen dramatically in Russia during the past two decades. Sociological polls indicate that only 4% of the population had Internet access in 2000, compared to 66% in 2014 (FOM, 2014, April 25). Today, about 80% of Russians are active Internet users, and the major trend is a growing social media audience with social media penetration standing at about 49%. Since its occurrence, the Internet in general and social media in particular have dramatically changed the Russian media environment, causing significant political and social effects.

Web 2.0 proliferation and the growing trend of digitalization are rapidly changing patterns of communication and information consumption among the Russian population as researchers underline the shift from desktop Internet consumption to mobile and traditional previous-decade sources of Internet media to social media, the former which has its own history in Russia that is outlined in the first part of this chapter. Despite cautious forecasts that social media will not find their usage after the peak activity in 2007 (Duzhnikova, 2010), the practices of Internet users on social media were relatively diverse: top involvement was of an audience age 18–35, and the overall active part of the social media community reached almost 30%, which contained categories such as content creators and critics reflecting on proposed agendas (Lebedev & Petukhova, 2010). The shift to online media and the shrinking audiences of traditional media are the major characteristics of the field in the first decade of the 2000s. News consumption patterns have changed due to the growing prominence of online media, bringing attention first to user-generated content and, distinctively, to social networks. Users' behavior in social media is described in the second part of this chapter.

An ongoing debate exists about the social and political consequences of the growing social media proliferation in authoritarian regimes. The "cyberoptimist" perspective connects social media penetration with information transparency and openness that causes democratization or, at the least, contributes to contentious politics. Russia provides relevant evidence for such debates since the mass protests of extensive electoral fraud during the 2011 State Duma elections through a series of local issues to 2019 mass protests that activated significant attention both online and on the streets. Scholarly attention was attracted by to what extent domestic and global social media had contributed to information spread and collective actions. Nevertheless, "cybersceptics" approached social media and the Internet in general as a tool for authoritarian control. Since 2011, continuing efforts to delimit the freedom of the Internet have been made through formal and informal restrictions. Moreover, privacy issues and data speculation appear to be in the forefront of the discussion of Russian Internet. These issues are examined in the chapter.

Brief history of Runet

On 7 April 1994, ru-domain, often addressed as Runet, was officially registered, manifesting a new era in the Russian Internet sphere and Russian business development. Despite the Soviet Union Internet domain that had already been registered, ru-domain became the main area of the growing Russian Internet sector. That emerging Russian Internet domain rapidly began to produce its own infrastructure. Consequently, in 1996 and 1997, two Russian search systems, Rambler and Yandex, were launched. Although Rambler was closed in 2011, Yandex became the most popular search system in Russia and in other post-Soviet countries. In addition to search service, Yandex also began to provide mail and news aggregation services, becoming the main hub in Runet.

Since its origin, Runet has become part of a fast-emerging news production industry as well. The second half of the 1990s saw growing political competition and economic growth, followed by extensive regression, that provided good conditions for its development. The first Russian online news media was Gazeta.ru, founded by Anton Nosik (collaborating with the pro-Kremlin Foundation for Effective Politics) (God bez Antona Nosika, 2018). Then, in 1999, the same team launched Lenta.ru that focused on breaking news, rapidly becoming one of the most important Russian news sources (Runet Ya Tvoi Otec, 2017).

The political bias in Runet strengthened in the 2000s, when the mass media public sphere was formally or informally captured by the state. While strengthening the authoritarian media system, Runet remained independent and did not feel the pressure of state control until the beginning of 2010s. There is the paradoxical phenomenon of LiveJournal—a system of creating and reading online blogs, which became an entertainment source for the young and, in the Russian context of the 2000s, became a platform for intellectuals that united writers, publishers, journalists, and politicians (Alexanyan & Koltsova, 2009). Serving as a substitute for free and transparent public debate, LiveJournal became a vehicle of public opinion for users of the Runet, substantially contributing to online political activism (Lonkila, 2008).

The new era of the Runet started in 2006 when VKontakte (VKontakte. com) and Odnoklassniki.ru (OK.ru) were launched. VKontakte ontake was originally intended as a Russian substitute for Facebook. VKontakte served as a network for university alumni and students, providing user opportunities to connect, message, like, and share. Another social network, Odnoklassniki, was launched to connect classmates, but became rapidly popular among adults. After more than 10 years, both of these social media platforms had become the most popular in the post-Soviet area.

Users' behavior

Distinct practices of Russian users on social media vary, and the maintenance of interpersonal communication and the support of existing social ties are only one dimension of social media potential (Rose Marketing Agency, 2010). Soon after their emergence, social media were actively used for information searches and exchanges, civic society activist coordination and mobilization, advertising, and small and online business development. Research (Rose Marketing Agency, 2010) revealed that more than one-third of their users approached social media to seek information about products prior to purchasing as well as to become involved in discussions about these products. Yet, we can formally divide the past 15 years of social media usage into two parts: first was the growing popularity of blogging, and the second came with widespread social media networks. During the 2010s, blogging remained the most influential social media practice, as it accumulated individuals who were overall empowered to maintain and to transform the public agenda online (Machleder & Asmolov, 2011). One of the first findings showed that LiveJournal users tend to concentrate around opinion leaders, rather than on the topic of the discussion (Alexeeva, Koltsova, & Koltcov, 2013). Therefore, social media a played crucial role in arranging public protests in 2011–2012. Koltsova and Shcherbak (2015) found a strong correlation between political activity in the blogosphere and the preelection ratings of candidates from the opposition, based on topic modelling in their quantitative research conducted on LiveJournal. The authors claim a reciprocal relationship of blogging and political activities, noting that we should not overestimate the role of blogging, which is overall connected with social media as a tool for information dissemination. Researchers further focused on public opinion, concluding that the content of opinion leaders does not differ much from the other users and that these opinion leaders do not focus more on social and political issues compared to others (Alexeeva, Koltsova, & Koltsov, 2014). Other research on a chosen sample of 2,000 top LiveJournal bloggers that applied the topic modelling method proved a correlation between the rise of users' activity online and the social issues discussed, with primary attention being given to the protests occurring at that time (Koltsova & Koltcov, 2013).

The early 2010s, following the presidency of Dmitry Medvedev, who was actively promoting social media usage and digitalization as a part of modernisation, can be considered the Golden Age of the Internet in Russia (Gorham, 2016). As an active social media user, Medvedev was using social media networks such as Twitter for public announcements and to comment on policy issues. During this period, a plethora of officials and politicians also began using Twitter for public communication. The Internet had quite ambiguous attitudes from the ruling party and the opposition that defined the usage practices for both. However, due to the remaining authoritarian conditions, officials' usage of Twitter produced a limited contribution to state-society dialogue. Officials' microblogs were predominantly depoliticized, supporting the dominant discourse with an absence of open and transparent public debate on domestic issues:

> The new technologies of immediate and interactive communication seem to yield more effective results for resistance to power than for its consolidation. For state servants the new media are more a part of their image-making strategies than an indispensable political tool.
>
> (Bode & Makarychev, 2013)

This trend was recently adapted by authorities, leading to the development of a few tools meant to organize and, thus, control public participation through the system of e-governance tools (for example, Bundin & Martynov, 2016; Vidiasova, Trutnev, & Vidiasov, 2017; Srednik & Cha, 2017). However, the overall approach to the public sphere is restricted to the terms of compliance or reporting, rather than on providing room for organized civic discussion. Moreover, political parties, officials, and politicians tend to maintain their presence on social media, ensuring coverage and broadcasting their agenda to publics (Smorgunov, 2014; Bode & Makarychev, 2013).

Addressing the most recent statistics on social media usage patterns, a few can be identified that will determine further research (Novruzova, 2017). First is the continuous shift to mobile, changing the lifestyle practices of individuals, ranging from news consumption to work issues and organizational communication. This is followed by the rapidly increasing amount of user-generated content that produces and changes the role of messengers. Today, messengers offer a new type of communication: the merger of mass media and discussion chat, compared to SNS messengers. Hence, statistics support the growing popularity of instant messengers: by January 2017, the Telegram audience had expanded to 6 million users, and it is growing continuously (Sergina, 2017). In particular, messenger becomes rapidly a social media niche: its interface provides users with opportunities to create mass channels that deliver content instantly, and it offers discussion groups as well as its initial function of sharing within contacts lists. Indeed, messenger is taking over the role of media; according to the most recent research, interest in information updates from public channels on Telegram is followed by the original function of message exchange among users (Rakhmanova, 2017). Therefore, users still endure major VKontakte presence and use it more actively because it has the largest audience and the highest amount of user-generated content.

According to one recent study conducted by IPSOS Connect and Google, the most active segment of social media users, that is, those ages 18–24, reflects on the changing nature of SNS usage patterns: these social media users check on updates more often, they prefer visual content for consumption and communication, and the adolescents rely on YouTube bloggers' opinions and show higher engagement in online activity compared to older users (Ipsos Connect & Google open report, 2016). Regarding the social media usage, 60% of Russians in 2018 use social media networking sites everyday. Moreover, users show the growing concern with their personal data usage by the third parties. WCIOM indicated that users are not satisfied with the idea of data being gathered and redirected further on, although the majority do not perceive it as any source of threat (WCIOM research, 2018). Such practice of data aggregation by mobile operators and Internet providers is now becoming a new norm for Russian society, being observed as an inevitable fact of the regulative and legislative system. Speculations with data, legal cases being open on the basis of inappropriate content consumption, or users publishing on their own social media pages appear through the news agenda and receive controversial responses.

Yet researchers tend to focus on Moscow and St. Petersburg, and only few focus on social media influence on information dissemination in the regions (Lankina & Skovoroda, 2017).

Social media and political engagement

While there was a growing restriction of freedom of speech and political expression in mass media (radio, press, TV) during the 2000s, the Internet remained unrestricted and provided spaces for online political talk. Kiriya (2014) maintains that the Russian public sphere was divided into the official public sphere and several information ghettos that were formed by political forces that were excluded from the former. Because mass media remained the main source of political information, the Internet did not produce any significant political effects. Nevertheless, in the 2010s, the situation had changed. Rapid Internet penetration resulted in the rise of the 2011–2012 protest movements and civic activism. Social media became a significant source of political information for urban people. According to the 2017 FOM survey, social media became the most commonly used source of political news for young people, who are moreover engaged in the discussion on political issues both on- and offline (FOM, 2017).

After the Arab Spring in 2011, the topic of social media as a tool for protest behavior in authoritarian regimes attracted extensive attention from scholars. The 2011 State Duma elections were marked by extensive electoral fraud, which was followed by mass protests with requests for democratization. Protesters actively used social media for disseminating information on electoral fraud and to coordinate protest activity. Greene (2013) concludes that Twitter was widely used during the 2011–2012 by the both sides—opposition and pro-governmental activists. However, there are substantial differences in the mode of communication: edges of the pro-Kremlin network were generally thicker, while the mode of communication was more routinized and formalized, than was the opposition one (Greene, 2013). Notably, that research shows that Facebook and Twitter were actively used by the opposition to disseminate information on electoral fraud, while VKontakte and Odnoklassniky were not politicized at all (Reuter & Szakonyi, 2015). Enikolopov et al. (2016) did not find any evidence of VKontakte impact on protest participation.

There is no consensus on the reasons why VKontakte and OK are less politicized than are Twitter and Facebook. First, VKontakte and OK are domestic social media with servers located in Russia. Second, opposition leaders traditionally use Western social media to promote their political messages. Third, VKontakte and OK contain entertaining content, which makes them less oriented toward communication among users and user-generated content. Combining all of these arguments enables us to conclude that social media loyalty in Russia produces a type of "media habitus", which is characterized by a common political agenda and similar perceptive patterns. White and McAllister (2014) showed that, in contrast to use of VKontakte, the use of Facebook is connected to the evaluation of 2011–2012 protest rallies.

Despite the restricted contribution of social media to protest behavior, Russian authorities began a campaign to delimit Internet freedom after the 2011–2012 protest rallies. Governmental regulation of the Internet began with the law on extrajudicial website blocking that was adopted in 2012, and soon after protests were held in the largest Russian cities. This legislative act formed the basis for prohibited web-sites registry, although it mainly focused on platforms that distributed movies and TV series as a violation of copyright. The law established the possibility of extrajudicial resolution of disputes between bona fide Internet sites and rights holders (V Rossii vstupil v sily, 2015).

During the next two years, several additional restrictions were applied. Federal law No. 398, known in the Runet as the "political censorship act", led to legal prosecution for online activity that had unclear requirements for texts and opinion expression, referring mostly to extremism, which has no clear definition in current legislation. Thus, the law becomes a well-operating tool to restrict the agenda and basic freedom of expression. Continuing with the law on "bloggers and information dissemination organization", online opinion leaders were equated with media and were expected to follow the major restrictions applicable for official media resources. The resonant legislative act known as "the right of oblivion" provided an opportunity to legally extract unfavorable information from Internet search.

All of these laws unfavorably influenced the freedom of expression on the Russian Internet. Along with the vague extremism laws, they enable political repressions toward oppositional activists and protest leaders. As Freedom House reports, "while most citizens are not subject to regular state supervision, authorities are thought to monitor the activities and personal communications of activists" (Freedom in the World 2019: Russia, 2019). All the facts that Freedom House and Agora report confirm that authoritarian governments have extensive opportunities to undermine civic activism and denigrate political opposition using new communication technologies.

Conclusion

In this chapter, we have outlined Russian social media, with an emphasis on users' behavior and political engagement. Despite no consensus on whether social media significantly contribute to political protests and civic mobilization, Russian authorities since 2012 have successfully attempted to restrict freedom on the Internet, undermining its plausible political effects.

Despite growing attention to social media's political effects in Russia, exhaustive gaps of knowledge exist on its role in political life. First, there is no knowledge on the differences in online political talk. Empirical turns in the research agenda on deliberative democracy place the issue in online discussions in social media (Graham, 2010). Although current research does not show evidence of the role of VKontakte and OK in protest rallies, these social media provide spaces for discursive engagement (Alukov, 2015) and reduce costs for coordination to collective action (Enikolopov et al., 2016). Despite the absence of direct political effects, social media can produce counterpublic spheres that encourage information spread and that identify strengthening oppressed groups (Fraeser, 1990). Moreover, to reveal differences in users online behavior, it might be fruitful to compare political talk in politicized social media (FB and Twitter) and nonpoliticized social media (VKontakte and OK).

Second, there is a lack of studies that show the extent in which social media are used in pre-political protest mobilization. Dahlgren (2009) notes that, behind the spaces for political discussion, social media produce spaces for local problem resolution, spreading information and mobilizing citizens for collective actions. In the restriction of political talk online and offline, as well as regime strategy toward depoliticization of any grievances, this topic might illuminate plausible points of politicization in the future.

Third, there is a lack of studies on authoritarian strategies toward Internet restriction and its impact on users' behavior. An extensive literature on authoritarian strategies in various authoritarian contexts is predominantly restricted to particular cases. Despite the huge variation of authoritarian regimes, studying common means of restriction in the Internet seems important to recognize the further development of contemporary authoritarianism. Comparative studies of Russia and China cases might be a good agenda for further research in this direction.

References

Alexanyan, K., & Koltsova, O. (2009). Blogging in Russia is not Russian blogging. In A. Russel & N. Echchaibi (Eds.), *International blogging: Identity, politics and networked publics* (pp. 65–84). New York: Peter Lang.

Alexeeva, S., Koltsova, O., & Koltsov, S. (2014). Obschestvennoe mnenie online: sravnenie struktury i tematiki postov "obichnich" i "popularnyckh" bloggerov Zhivogo Zhurnala [The public opinion online: Comparison of the structure and topics of "average" and "popular" LiveJournal bloggers' posts]. *Supplementary Proceedings of the 3rd International Conference on Analysis of Images, Social Networks and Texts (AIST 2014)*, 177–181. Retrieved from http://ceur-ws.org/Vol-1197/paper27.pdf.

Alukov, M. (2015). *Ot public k dvizheniyu: Kontrpublichnyje sfery v rossihskom Internet-prostranstve pered protestom* [From publics to movements: Counter-public spheres on the Internet upon the protest]. In C. V. Erpyleva & A. V. Magun (Eds.), *Politika apolitihnykh: Grazhdanskie dvizhenija v Rossii 2011-2013 godov.* [Politics of apolitical: Civil movements in Russia in 2011-2013]. Moscow: Novoe Literaturnoe Obozrenie [New literature review] Publisher.

Bode, N., & Makarychev, A. (2013). The new social media in Russia: Political blogging by the government and the opposition. *Problems of Post-Communism, 60*(2), 53–62. doi:10.2753/PPC1075-8216600205.

Bundin, M., & Martynov, A. (2016). Use of social media and blogs by Federal Authorities in Russia: Regulation and policy. *Proceedings of the 17th International Digital Government Research Conference on Digital Government Research* (pp. 8–11), Shanghai, China. doi.: 10.1145/2912160.2912211.

Dahlgren, P. (2009). *Media and political engagement.* Cambridge: Cambridge University Press.

Duzhnikova, A. (2010). Social'nye Sety: SovremennyeTtendencee i Tipy Polzovanya (Social media: Modern tendencies and types of usage). *Monitoring of Public Opinion, 5*(99), 238–251.

Enikolopov, R., Makarin, A., & Petrova, M. (2016). Social media and protest participation: Evidence from Russia. CEPR Discussion Paper No. DP11254.

FOM Official statistics (2014, April 25). Polzovaniye Internetom: vchera i segodnya [The Internet usage: Yesterday and today]. Retrieved from http://fom.ru/SMI-i-internet/11481 (in Russian).

FOM Official statistics (2017, April 17). Interes molodezhy k politike (Young people interest to politics). Retrieved from http://fom.ru/Politika/13285 (in Russian).

Fraeser, N. (1990). Rethinking the public sphere: A contribution to a critique of actually existing democracies. *Social Text, 25/26*, 56–80.

Freedom in the World (2019): Russia. Retrieved from https://freedomhouse.org/report/freedom-world/2019/russia.

God bez Antona Nosika (2018, July 9). Post. Gazeta.ru. Retrieved from https://www.gazeta.ru/tech/2018/07/09/11831041/nosik_year.shtml

Gorham, M. S. (2016). *Digital Russia: The language, culture and politics of new media commu-nication*. London: Routledge.

Graham, T. (2010). Talking politics online within spaces of popular culture: The case of the Big Brother forum. *Javnost – The Public, 17*(4), 25–42.

Greene, S. A. (2013) Beyond Bolotnaia: Bridging old and new in Russia's election pro-test movement. *Problems of Post-Communism, 60*(2), 40–52.

Ipsos Connect & Google, open report. (2016). Chem zhivet novoe pokoleniye: Statistika o rossijiskoiy molodezhi (What are the interests of new generation: Statistics on Russian youth). Retrieved from: https://storage.googleapis.com/think-v2-emea/v2/00404_Google%20Youth%20Study%20RU.pdf (in Russian).

Kiriya, I. (2014). Social media as a tool of political isolation in the Russian public sphere. *Journal of Print and Media Technology Research, 3*(2), 131–138.

Koltsova, O., & Koltsov, S. (2013). Mapping the public agenda with topic modeling: The case of the Russian livejournal. *Policy & Internet, 5*(2), 207–227. doi:10.1002/1944-2866.POI331.

Koltsova, O., & Koltsov, S., & Nikolenko, S. (2016). Communities of co-commenting in the Russian LiveJournal and their topical coherence. *Internet Research, 26*(3), 710–732. doi:10.1108/IntR-03-2014-0079.

Koltsova, O., & Shcherbak, A. (2015). "LiveJournal Libra!": The political blogosphere and voting preferences in Russia in 2011–2012. *New Media & Society, 17*(10), 1715–1732. doi:10.1177/1461444814531875.

Lankina T., & Skovoroda, R. (2017). Regional protest and electoral fraud: Evidence from analysis of new data on Russian protest. *East European Politics, 33*(2), 253–274, doi: 10.1080/21599165.2016.1261018.

Lebedev, P., & Petukhova, S. (2010). Sotstoyaniye media: Pokezatel razvitia sovremennogo obschestva (Social media: Markers of modern society development). *Monitoring, 5*(99), 16–25 (in Russian).

Lonkila, M. (2008). The Internet and anti-military activism in Russia. *Europe-Asia Studies, 60*(7), 1125–1149.

Machleder, J., & Asmolov, G. (2011). Social change and the Russian network society. *Internews*. Retrieved from www.internews.org/resource/social-change-and-russian-network-society.

Novruzova, E. (2017, June 29). Sotsialnie seti v Rossii, leto 2017: Tsifry i trendy [Social networks in Russia, summer 2017: numbers and trends]. Retrieved from http://www.cossa.ru/289/166387/.

Rakhmanova, V. (2017). Issledovanie: Portret naibolee aktivnoiy auditoriji Telegram v Rossiji. [The research: Portrait of the most active Telegram audience in Russia]. Retrieved from https://vc.ru/25614-audience-of-telegram (in Russian).

Reuter, O. J., & Szakonyi, D. (2015). Online social media and political awareness in authoritarian regimes. *British Journal of Political Science, 45*(1), 29–51.

Rose Marketing Agency. (2010). Issledovanie sotsialnyx media v Rossii [Research on social media in Russia]. Retrieved from www.cossa.ru/149/2467/.

Runet Ya Tvoi Otec. (2017). Lenta.ru. Retrieved from https://lenta.ru/articles/2017/07/09/nosikdead/.

Rykov Y., Nagornyy O., & Koltsova O. (2017). Digital inequality in Russia through the use of a social network site: A cross-regional comparison. In *Communications in Computer and Information Science, Vol. 745* (pp. 70–83). Berlin: Springer.

Sergina, E. (2017, February 7). Baza aktivnykh pol'zovateley Telegram vyrosla v 3 raza i dostigla 6 millionov. [The base of active users Telegram in Russia for the year grew

3 times and reached 6 million]. Retrieved from www.vedomosti.ru/technology/articles/2017/02/08/676588-telegram-rossii.

Smorgunov, L. (2014). Setevye politicheskie partii [Networked political parties]. *Polis. Political Research,* (4), 21–37

Srednik, E., & Cha, J. K. (2017). Assessing e-government adoption in Russia: Impacts of Service Delivery Attributes. *Journal of International Trade & Commerce, 12*(2), 15–26.

V Rossii vstupil в silu novyi antipiratskyi zakon. (2015). Retrieved from https://ria.ru/society/20150501/1062033269.html

Vidiasova L., Trutnev D., & Vidiasov, E. (2017). Revealing the factors influencing E-participation development in Russia. *Electronic Participation. ePart 2017. Lecture Notes in Computer Science*, vol 10429, 65-74. Retrieved from https://link.springer.com/chapter/10.1007/978-3-319-64322-9_6.

WCIOM Research. (2018). Personalnye dannye v internete: vozmozhnosty i riski. Research by WCIOM. Retrieved from: https://wciom.ru/index.php?id=236&uid=9401 (in Russian).

White, S., & McAllister, I. (2014). Did Russia (nearly) have a Facebook revolution in 2011? Social media's challenge to authoritarianism. *Politics, 34*(1), 72-84.

11 How advertising agencies are transforming

View from Russia

Alexander Mozhaev and Lyudmila Kryuchkovskaya

Introduction

In 2009, U.S.-based Ignition Consulting Group's Tim Williams presented his view on how communication agencies should transform for the future (Williams, 2009). He said their inflection point could be explained by fundamental global changes: fragmentation of media and audiences, democratization of creativity, online interconnectedness, digitalization of everything, and brand advocacy in place of brand management. The Russian communication industry seemingly began to meet these changes, both at the structural and product levels, embracing an Integrated Marketing Communications strategy.

The Russian communication industry seemingly began to adapt to fundamental changes, both at the structural and product levels, over the past several decades. This chapter provides an overview of Williams' propositions and discusses them in relation to the Russian market. Then, the chapter analyzes interviews of top industry managers to learn how Russian communicators are answering global challenges. Particular attention is given to evaluating the implementation model of IMC, which remains a big challenge for the communication industry. IMC combines all of the above-mentioned transformations: Media, consumer, product, and structural. The problem lies mainly in the economics and organizational structures of communication holdings. Back in the late 1990s, advertising in Russia started booming. This coincided with the entrance to the market of the big international companies and their network agencies. They brought initial marketing and communication expertise. Initially, all of the developments were introduced here with some time-lag versus Western markets. However, very soon Russia began to rapidly close this gap in volume, scale, and practitioners' expertise. Therefore, the agency and market in Russia today arequite similar to the Western approach to the agencies of the future. They are discussed in detail in this chapter.

It's time to move

For decades, the structure of the communication industry, the interconnectedness of its segments, and the nature of relationships between clients and their agencies have remained relatively stable. Although this sector of the economy is probably among the most turbulent (because it deals with the social sphere, that is, with media), changes in recent years are occurring with such speed that we begin facing their consequences, not within decades or years as in the past, but sometimes within months. And these changes significantly influence the communication industry.

In 2009, U.S.-based Ignition Consulting Group's Tim Williams presented his view on how communication agencies should transform for the future (Williams, 2009). Because Williams is an author, teacher, consultant, and a recognized practitioner and thought leader in the advertising and marketing industries, his ideas immediately attracted attention from top managers in these industries. In June 2009 in Kansas City, Williams conducted a professional development seminar with the American Association of Advertising Agencies (4A's) (Agency 2.5). During that seminar, he had explored what agency professionals must do to deliver the solutions and services that clients need to compete in the new digitally enabled, economically challenged marketing environment. It was clear that the agency business model had been under assault for the past decade, and the economic crisis only underscored the critical changes that agencies had to make in the way in which they're structured, the way in which they provide service, and the way in which they make money. Williams urged marketing communications firms to come face-to-face with what he saw as the realities facing communication businesses. Among the most important challenges for agencies were less demand for their traditional product and more for online marketing, particularly social media, differences with clients in focus: ATL (Anove The Line) vs BTL (Below The Line), advertising ideas versus business-building ideas; and pressure on price speed for work and accountability that agencies are not prepared to address(Agency 2.5).

That workshop examined traditional agency functions and discussed what to relinquish, what to rework, and what to reinvent. Agencies' top people discussed the emerging functions that were reframing the agency skill set, including social media, analytics, user experience, and reputation management. Later, other industry events also examined this topic (CEOs Give a Thumbs-up to Agency 2.5, 2011). And Williams' book, *Take a Stand for Your Brand: Building a Great Agency Brand from the Inside Out* (2012), immediately became the standard for agency brand development, ranking among the top ten books on branding on Amazon. The book told agency owners that this "need for transformation" extended to the level of practical agency brand-building.

Other articles and documents were later issued on marketing transformation under these new challenges (Technology and the Evolution of the Marketing Agency, 2013), but nothing had had such an impact on the industry as has the Agency 2.5 concept. This was probably because Williams, although addressing all of the marketing communication industry, had in mind creative businesses and creative agencies, which are most prominent in the marketing communication industry, but also are the most difficult and vulnerable to run. As Williams (2012) wrote in his book:

Advertising agencies are also among the toughest companies to manage. If you can learn to successfully lead and manage an advertising agency (which is not unlike herding cats), you can certainly do the same with a gentler, saner kind of company.

(p. 29)

Why agencies need transformation

Williams' "Agency 2.5" concept touched upon focal points of the communication industry today, all of which are critical to agencies' future, and some of which are quite painful. The author of this chapter shares a belief in Williams' concept in principle, which is supported by his observations and experience as an advertising industry practitioner (including in managing creative agencies—network and independent, large-sized and boutique type). Communication agencies are at the inflection point, facing full-scale changes in the way in which they do business, due to fundamental changes globally as well as competition from these agencies' former suppliers, customers, or even partners. These global changes identified by Tim Williams (2012) include: (1) fragmentation and addressability of media and audiences, (2) democratization of creativity, (3) inexpensive and instantaneous production, (4) online interconnectedness, (5) digitalization of everything, (6) brand advocacy in place of brand management, and (6) pricing pressure due to an oversupply of providers.

Williams (2012) also indicated that agencies' new competitors emerge from "'upstream' of the industry business process flow," including management consultantices, brand consultancies, and marketing research, and from "downstream," which includes media (its biggest competition, in which media act as their own agencies in dealing with companies), production houses (in which small experienced filming crews and production teams can offer full-scale high-quality advertising production), client in-house resources (as every company becomes increasingly capable of its own production and invests in publishing on owned platforms), and crowdsourcing by clients (an inexpensive way to interact with audiences by encouraging them to be brand advocates) (Williams, 2012).

Changing paradigms

These challenges are also pushing the communication industry to change traditional paradigms to view the media, consumers, approaches to planning, and evaluation of communication (Williams, 2012). These paradigms, according to Williams (2012), include: (1) from interruption to engagement, (2) from mass media as channel to everything as a channel, and (3) paid-earned-owned media. Below we discuss in more detail each of these paradigms.

From interruption to engagement—the main method of brand message delivery has been interruption: Advertising, public relations messages, and even promotional contacts were mainly imposed upon the audience, interrupting their media consumption, entertainment, or even purchasing process. This was possible because audiences were not fully in command of their media and, therefore, their consumption was of built-in communication messages. When it became feasible for media consumers, not only to passively ignore advertising (TV ad avoidance) or to switch this advertising off (that is, in a search engine), but also in principle not to allow advertising in their personal social network, a dramatic transformation in the attitude of brands finally took place. Today, brands have to have "permission" to be in consumers' private worlds. To obtain this permission, brands must be more than just interesting; rather, they also must be engaging, valuable to consumers, and involved in constant dialogue as equals that sincerely share the same values of their consumers. This could be called nothing other than a real partnership model. Obviously, not every brand can succeed in this revolutionary transformation, but each brand must try, because there is no acceptable alternative.

From mass media as channel to everything as a channel—The changing media landscape has brought an unprecedented fragmentation of mass media and a multiplication of media channels. At the same time, many other realities have begun to emerge as media and, thus, channels for communication with the audience (These channels may be less "mass" than traditional, group, or even individual, media). What are these new channels? Brands' online properties such as media (e.g., content platforms and YouTube channels), content as media (branded content in various forms, ranging from literature to fiction films and music videos), product-as-media (communication may appear on a physical product label or, more often, in intellectual products that are delivered via RSS, subscriptions, and mobile applications), and even personal views and attitudes as media (e.g., blogging, twitting, and posting in social media). These new types of "communication channels" constantly appear, develop, transform, and sometimes morph into something else before we manage to fully appreciate their merits.

Paid-earned-owned media—These three classes of media have only recently been a real target for brands to plan and to craft the media environment. Although the first two have always been in the communication language and in the practice of advertising (paid media) and public relations (earned media), "owned media" is quite a new term in communication—meaning brands' owned media platforms or properties that they create and use, not only to deliver their brand messages to consumers anytime and in any volume that they believe to be appropriate (basically using "owned media" in the old meaning of media as broadcasting channels), but also to interact with their consumers in a new way—deeply and on a prolonged basis engaging these consumers with ad hoc created content. This content can help consumers, not only with information and advice on these brands' products, but also with professional or marketing reviews and other useful information and expertise that educate consumers, who pay back with a partnership attitude toward the brands. The sequence of using these media is also changing from a traditional "paid-earned-owned" model to a reversed order, that is, sometimes paid media are used to promote already-established and well-functioning owned media platforms or are adding to them.

Future role for agencies

All the above-mentioned fundamental challenges, that is, changing communication paradigms and especially competitive pressures on agencies' traditional approach to business, raise another important question: What is the future role of agencies?

In "Agency 2.5", Tim Williams has made some assumptions about how agencies should transform for the future (Williams, 2012). First of all, how should these agencies behave with their clients? Should they be "doctor", "craftsman", or "advisor"? Or should they be a certain combination of these professions? And, probably even more importantly, in what areas of particular expertise should agencies try to positions themselves, developing necessary skills to firmly and convincingly establish themselves with clients? Clearly, those areas should be responsive to the above-mentioned challenges and become new versus offering the traditional range of communication agencies' services, according to Williams:

1. An area that appears important, but remains more of an extension of existing expertise, is "brand guardian". It comes from existing relations in which agencies place emphasis on strategic planning for brands, reflecting a real and frequent situation in which there is more consistency in working on the brand on the agency side than within the client's organization. However, it's quite unlikely that clients may decide to hand over such responsibility (for their most important asset—their brands!) onto their suppliers, even with those having high track records of partnership.
2. Roles that deal with the most important vehicle for brand communication—content, that is, "content collaborators", "content curators", "program producers", and "rights managers". This area is potentially of interest for agencies because it is building on their traditionally strong creative and copywriting skills. It is also a quite important and one of the most difficult and resource-consuming areas for clients.
3. Another important area in marketing and communication today is data. Agencies could act as "data providers" or "data aggregators" for their clients. This is already happening with customer-relationship management agencies.
4. Agencies may focus on creating their own media and, therefore, act as "media brand owners" for their clients (even if they will also maintain their traditional agency services). If the media increasingly enter agency business, why not vice versa?

Integrated marketing communications

Message consistency over time and across communication channels has always been the main focus of communication. "Brand should speak one voice everywhere", a "360 degree" approach, and similar statements have been a motto of the industry in the early 2000

Gradually, all these ideas and approaches have been aggregated into the concept of integrated marketing communications (IMC). IMC became the theoretical platform for the industry and a "should be" approach for successful implementation of communication efforts. However, theory does not always go hand-in-hand with practice. To create a working implementation model of IMC remains a big challenge for the communication industry. And the problem lies mainly in the economics and organizational structures of communication holdings.

If we look at the past couple of decades of the 20th century, we will see that the most significant industry transformation—dividing the full-service advertising business into media and creative (and later BTL, that is, below-the-line marketing)—paved the way to great specialization in the industry. In place of full-service agencies were flourishing agencies that specialized in various areas of communication services and in various communication channels. A "full-service approach" remained as the predecessor of IMC theory on the level of communication groups, which was pronounced by everybody, but which was hardly ever realized by anyone in practice. Sporadic attempts to unite efforts and resources to create IMC campaigns on the level of a communication holding generally stumbled over "conflict of profit and loss" or different economic interests of so-called "disciplines" or "corridors", that is, agencies specializing in their specific communication channels.

Clients, who should have been the main promoters of an IMC approach, didn't help much either. Their policy was: "not to put all eggs in one basket", that is, not to give the whole communication budget to one communication holding as their partner (splitting media, creative, BTL, and, later, digital assignments among competing agencies/groups). By doing this, clients formally kept the responsibility for the integration process for themselves. In reality, this rarely happened. The reasons were basically the same: Suppliers' different economic interests (everyone "pulling a blanket onto oneself"), rather than integration priorities with the client organization (such as choosing "the best supplier" in every discipline, which they claimed was difficult in one main partnering group; achieving cost efficiency by pitching every project aspect; and keeping control over relationships with suppliers who were in fierce competition among one another).

Finding the right IMC model is, therefore, another challenge for the communication industry that remains unresolved and is probably among the central issues since IMC combines all the above-mentioned transformations: Media, consumer, product, and structural. In the future, those agencies or communication holdings that will find the right IMC model and that will learn how to consistently and efficiently implement it will be in the pole position.

Implications and opportunities for marketers

Apart from his visionary thinking about the future role of the communication agency, Williams listed several practical "implications & opportunities for marketing organizations" (by this term, he addresses mainly agencies, but sometimes his message is relevant to both agencies and clients because they both face these global challenges and, therefore, must respond to them effectively and in partnership). This is how Williams' suggestions are seen in Russia.

1) Williams' Trend 1: "'Everything as channel': Plan touch points and communication channels, not media;start with owned, then earned, and then paid channels; help clients build marketing into their products".

"Touch points" have, for a long time, been in the language of strategic and media planners in Russia; now it is a standard practice, even in professional education, and the same is true with "paid-earned-owned", although not with the reversed-order imperative. Now it's time to put the reversed order into planning practice. "Building marketing into the product" requires deep agency-client collaboration and early involvement, that is always more in practice by big networks, but also in some independent Russian agencies and creative boutiques.

2) Williams' Trend 2: "'Brand experience': Help optimize experience of the brand, not just perception; help your clients move up the effectiveness hierarchy (to actual experience with the brand); become expert in brand interactions, not just brand messages".

"Brand experience" is already the focus of some communication disciplines in Russian communication groups, such as events, consumer promo and in-store; however, in the strategic planning process, we still plan at the level of brand perception, trying to change this perception mainly by brand messages. Nevertheless, experiential marketing, brand story living is already at the forefront of planners and creatives of more advanced Russian agencies (eg., BBDO group)

3) Williams' Trend 3: "'Consumer as media': Understand not just the demographics, but the technographics of your audience; ,ake it easy to share and distribute your content; proactively plan for consumers "as media"; realize that your brand will never have enough money to outspend consumers".

Here again, we in Russia are a bit behind of the trend, with little proactivity and focus on technographics of the audience; sometimes "digital channels" are still planned separately from "non-digital," and this should be changed:

a "consumers as media" approach must be incorporated in the communication strategic planning process.

4) Williams' Trend 4: "'Utility instead of persuasion': Put more effort into helping consumers instead of selling to them; look at "utility" as an opportunity to develop some of your own intellectual properties".

"Helping instead of. Selling" as the main differentiator behind the content marketing approach was adapted by several Russian marketors and their agencies in both B2B and B2C segments. In some areas (eg., banking) companies started developing their brand media.

Developing their own intellectual property is a trend that is clearly seen in the social media environment; many brands view this as an important aspect of their "social orientation" behavior toward their customers. Some interesting cases of building intellectual properties on this approach have begun to emerge (e.g., jointly with the high-level school educational platform for doctors in the professional social network "Evrika" within one of the biggest Russian independents, the TWIGA Communication group).

5) Williams' Trend 5: "'From one-to-many to one-to-one': Soon, all media will be both searchable and addressable; the new agency skill set is mass customization in place of mass messaging; agencies can package and sell data analytics as a service; precise addressability will allow more niche brands to advertise, creating more opportunities for agencies".

This is clearly an opportunity for the majority of Russian agencies, especially medium- and small-sized; this, however, requires work to adapt their product offers. Big communication groups are already well ahead of this trend. ADV group, for example, is providing their clients with services and communication product based on big data and AI.

6) Williams' Trend 6: "'From digital department to digital competency':Digital must be at the core of the agency business model, not an add-on; soon, no difference will exist between 'traditional' and 'digital' agencies; being digital means technologists must join creative and media teams".

"Digitalization of everything" is undisputable as an approach; however, it was difficult to efficiently implement, both on the agency and on the holding-group levels, at the beginning in Russia. Many holdings began from the easiest side, that is, to buy or to form a partnership with a digital agency; however, the problem was that "digitalization" would become stuck there—as a stage/aspect of the communication planning process or as a separate digital project\assignment, and it would not become an integral part, as an approach, of every project. However, it's not a problem anymore: digital expertise is now well incorporated into all Russian agencies' levels, both specialized and traditional.

7) Williams' Trend 7: "'From controlled communication to open conversation': Learn to market 'consumer to consumer', instead of just 'brand to consumer'; shift the egency's skill set beyond 'presentation' to 'participation'; erase artificial line between advertising and PR; make publicity a central goal of your marketing efforts, not just a hoped-for byproduct; experiment with ways to move what used to be offline online".

This fundamental change from one-way communication to dialogue/open conversation challenges a lot of disciplines in their attitudes and interactions; many traditional instruments become obsolete unless they're changed completely; agencies' skill sets must also change dramatically; public relations and advertising should not be divided by the client or by the organizational structure, since both are parts of one integrated communication process; rather than shifting their skill sets, they should focus more on "conversation with audiences (public relations)" and "creating content (advertising)". This is happening rapidly in Russia, mainly under the umbrella of the Integrated Marketing Communication approach.

8) Williams' Trend 8: "'From high volume/low margin to low volume/high margin': Realize that the traditional agency cost structure cannot support high value/high cost services and low value/low cost pricing approach from the client".

This is true in theory, but a tough economic situation (unfortunately, which is becoming a constant reality globally as well as in Russia) pushes the agencies to use both models (in most cases within a group and not a single agency); on the other hand, we still operate in a market in which clients are less willing to pay for ideas (intangible) than for executions/production (something they can touch and in which they know how much it costs). This is more and more reflected in remuneration schemes (payment by results, short-term projects committed "as we go"), both on international and local Russian agencies' level.

9) Williams' Trend 9: "'From full-scale to agile': An always-on marketing program requires agile teams and an agile approach; the agile approach requires fewer people, fewer layers, and more autonomy".

There are many examples in Russia of this trend as a "project team" approach in various disciplines, but few agencies are built on "agile" as an organizational approach to their business.

Russian holdings' view on "Agency 2.5"

To be more relevant and insightful, we verified various specific points of the "Agency 2.5" concept with the "chieftains" of the Russian communication industry. Ten in-depth interviews (about an hour each) were conducted in February 2014 in Moscow with top managers and owners of communication holdings, both Russian representation offices of global networks and independent Russian communication groups. All the experts are among the pioneers in Russian advertising in the 1990s and rapidly advanced to the top level of the agency's structure. Among them are two women business owners who are greatly respected, both for their professional skills and enterpreneral talents.

Changes in the communication industry

All experts agreed that we in the communication industry are living in times of dramatic changes, which is both challenging and interesting. One of the most impactful changes is technological breakthrough.

> As it is difficult for many people to see the difference between iOS and Android, it is the same difficulty for many agencies to adapt to these rapid and constant changes: since they used to produce one TV spot and one print per year for a brand.
> noted Vladimir Tkachev, Chairman of the Board and CEO of Leo Burnett Eastern Europe and Russia

He believes that the biggest transformation power in our industry is e-commerce. "E-commerce and mobile marketing have definitely 'killed' the traditional way of doing business of our clients, and we don't even have the option whether to adapt to this or not." With mobile marketing coming to retail, we have both a great challenge and the greatest opportunity. Those *who manage to craft their product in this digital-trade intersection will* be extremely valuable to clients and get outstanding business results (V. Tkachev, personal communication, February 6, 2014).

While observing the most important trends in the communication industry, Igor Kirikchi, Managing Director and Chief talent Officer (BBDO Russia), noted the following three processes (I. Kirikchi, personal communication, February 11, 2014):

1) *Integration*—everybody is talking now about Integrated Marketing Communications, "one window", people who can assemble the communication campaign, with one idea working in all communication channels with top budget-saving expectations; from an agency point of view (POV), however, integration means additional resources—time and cost for rare and expensive specialists. This all results in dissonance between the client's savings expectation and the practical cost of integration.

2) *Specialization*—especially in new areas: In digital, for example, we see narrow specialization, with agencies that do viral campaigns and those that do only distribution of the viral.

3) *Digitalization*—in the old days, everything was clear; now, everything is mixed—creative, mechanics, media; in terms of metrics—in old channels, everybody was clear and in agreement, but this does not work in digital, in which new ways to measure efficiency emerge constantly, but nobody really knows exactly how they are working, plus we have many new digital professions. Every agency tends to call them in new trendy ways (in reality, it turns out to be more or less the same).

Yaroslav Kucherov (CEO JWT Russia) nostalgically noted that the "golden era of advertising" with great movie spots in Cannes had come to an end. As had happened with classical Hollywood pictures, new realities in media, consumer behavior, and therefore communication resulted in democratization and commoditization of creativity. This predominance of commoditization and a savings approach doesn't do any good to the agency business and pushes forward an average creative product.

The emergence of new communication channels and the changes in consumer behavioral models bring forth changes in the communication paradigm: Maybe it will be more oriented toward direct contacts with the consumer, and more selling messages versus image. Because the model is not formed and set up yet, it's not clear how to work with this. What is clear, however, is that every brand still needs positioning and communication strategy. Therefore, it's too early to "throw away" the classical ad agency, the brand communication keeper (Y. Kucherov, personal communication, January 29, 2014).

Integrated marketing communications

What is the attitude of our industry "captains" to one of the central concepts of communication, which is both the reality and the driving force for the future of marketing and communication, integrated marketing communications (IMC). It is clear that practitioners' opinions are centered on the issue of how it should be efficiently implemented.

There is no dispute about whether communication should be integrated or not. "Communication holdings that do not implement IMC or that do it poorly will simply die," says Vladimir Tkachev (personal communication, February 6, 2014). Whatever you call it, an IMC approach or "cross-sell" of services to one client within the group doesn't change the substance. It is much easier to sell your additional services to an existing client than to pitch it in new business. This is, of course, how it is seen from the agency's side. Clients very often oscillate between extremes: Either putting everything in one place or splitting their budget with 12 small specialized agencies and then having to spend all their time to coordinate. "If you look at the strategy of every holding, you will see specialization and integration is our way forward", Vladimir Tkachev said. That is obvious from the business point of view. A creative (brand) agency often plays the role of coordinator of IMC efforts of sister-agencies within the group and of independent companies. Therefore, a creative agency needs to develop its integrator's skills (V. Tkachev, personal communication, February 6, 2014).

There is no single model for how to implement IMC within the holding company (even the global networks do not have one). However, it is easier to avoid famous "profit and loss conflict" for groups that belong to networks and don't have a franchisee local partner as an owner of the part of the group. "BBDO Group has this advantage, although even in our situation, agencies should find agreement, economic compromise", stresses Igor Kirikchi (personal communication, February 11, 2014). It is impossible to force the integration approach to the agency, that is to artificially create an integrated campaign without the willing interests of participating agencies. The attempts to create a special integration unit has stumbled over economic differences in ADV Group (in 2006–2007, when the author had headed one of the creative agencies as a participant in that painful process), and now same has happened in the BBDO Group. TWIGA CG is also trying to find the right model for integration, both on the agency level and in the group, leaning over TWIGA Total, its specially created business development unit. Attempts to create a special integration unit (although mainly unsuccessful up to now) do not substitute for other practical ways to promote the culture of integration.

BBDO Group, for example, conducts special training programs: TWIGA has a special "cross-sell" instrument-like "selling committee" and the already-mentioned business unit, Total, that are focused on integrated efforts. Almost all the communication groups with a separate function of business development expect from this function integrated or multi-channel business opportunities that will lead to bigger budgets and integrated assignments.

Separate mention should be given to the School of Integrated Communications, HSE, where "integrated communications" is not only the central theoretical concept (it couldn't be otherwise, since "the name on the door" calls for this), but its very practical approach to the basic set of skills and competencies that students develop during their studies at the University. Simulation, role-playing games (that is, pitches among student teams, imitating integrated agencies) is an integral part of the students' education and training. Therefore, the school's graduates enter their communication and marketing professions with the strong culture and practical tools of IMC. However, as Igor Kirikchi rightly stressed, whatever the culture, if there is no willingness and economic interest in participants of integrated efforts, there won't be an integrated campaign. So organizationally, integration stumbles over famously in the Theory of Games' prisoner's dilemma. Another practical and still not resolved issue is the "full-service agency vs. integration dilemma". Putting it in other words: What is better, adding competencies to an existing agency team "buying" new specialists or integrating them as functional parts of the partner agency within integrated efforts? (personal communication, February 11, 2014).

Yaroslav Kucherov (who was in charge of the earlier-mentioned ADV integration unit) believes that true integration is feasible only with very strong vertical control from one top integrating manager (personal communication, January 29, 2014), and this is very difficult to implement based on the different economic interest of business units).

Alexander Alexeev (Executive Creative Director of Publicis United) knows very well how to set up a capable creative team to cope with an integrated assignment, and his strong message is: Only a team approach (specialists working in a group) can give the result; any conveyor way of handing over pieces of work from one discipline to another will result in losing what happens to be in the end of the process (personal communication, February 1, 2014).

Challenges leading to Agency 2.5

It was interesting to learn how our top communication managers view various challenges that Tim Williams described as leading today's agencies to the inflection point.

> *Digitalization*—all of the experts agreed that digitalization was impacting everything from media to consumer behavior; at the same time, they paid attention to the deeper understanding of the term "digital": it is not just a channel, but first of all a set of technologies that transform everything (V. Tkachev, personal communication, February 6, 2014); in digital as in all other environments, form is important, but secondary to the content, especially it is valid for video images and the ways that they are decoded.
>
> (A. Alexeev, personal communication, February 1, 2014)

> *Owned media*—it is definitely the most controllable class of media, the most controllable way of delivering your message; but what was said before for digital as a whole is as important, if not more so, for "owned" media. You need *interesting content* to keep the dialogue.
>
> (V. Tkachev, personal communication, February 6, 2014)

> *Brand advocacy*—it is quite natural for people to be advocates of something, so why not be advocates of a brand? You just need to make them proud of being your consumers and to start sharing these feelings with their friends. In practical terms, brands start bringing up their advocates with the community of early adapters: launching the campaign, brand owners start monitoring whether the audience begins to pass over the brand message, whether this message touches them emotionally, and then correct and further build their communication strategy.
>
> (V. Tkachev, personal communication, February 6, 2014)

> *Agility*—Any big structure in any field of activity with time tends to become slow and inert and also self-protective from any changes from outside. At

the same time, a number of cheerful young fishes always emerge, but few of them survive and become big and famous (for example, Weiden+Kennedy, BBH in advertising). Advertising's competitive landscape, especially the creative segment, is interesting because numerous agile start-ups have a low cost of entry.

(V. Tkachev, personal communication, February 6, 2014)

And it is difficult not to agree with Yaroslav Kucherov, who believes that variety exists in the world. Since there is always a huge demand (for something), there will also be huge companies to meet this demand.

(personal communication, January 29, 2014)

Crowdsourcing—this trend was assessed by experts mainly from the product-quality point of view. They noted that crowdsourcing might be an interesting way of audience involvement, but always bear in mind professional standards.

(Kucherov, personal communication, January 29, 2014)

A similar view was expressed by Alexander Alexeev: "It's just another instrument and should be used for its purpose. You will not hammer nails with a screwdriver! On the other hand, the lack of a screwdriver in your toolbox is limiting you". As democratization of creativity, user-generated content (UGC) has two sides: Positive—it produces proximity with your consumer; and negative—because it significantly lowers the quality level (personal communication, February 1, 2014).

Future agency

To be able to stand up to these challenges, the agency of the future should find its new role. Tim Williams marked the options as "doctor", "craftsman", and "consultant". Top managers gave us their understanding of this role and of how today's agency professions might evolve.

Role of the agency

Kucherov combined the proposed three options into the very ambitious role— "crafted doctor who gives professional advice". Indeed, agencies that focus on strategic solutions for their clients are like doctors who carefully examine and make a diagnosis and only then advise on how to cure the disease. At the same time, they are like local physicians who know their patients and their families and who are constantly working with their patients to keep them healthy. He also noted a convergence of the skills set of the strategic brand agency (traditionally, more positioning/image-oriented, but gradually moving through the whole consumer journey, including purchase and after-purchase) and that of the specialized agency (that tries to add strategy and creative in its set of brand skills) (personal communication, January 29, 2014).

Tkachev believes that the future advertising agency will still be driven by artists and writers. People talent is a quite rare quality and as long as the talented people will create cool ideas for the agency, the clients will come here (personal communication, February 6, 2014).

Future agency professions

If we look into the future, we will see somewhat changed traditional agency professionals. BBDO Group also thought of the future agency and came up with a concept BBDO NEXT, which they imagined as a combination of the following professionals:

1. *Business Commander*—this is the future account executive, an intelligent manager who is capable of strategic thinking, plus is a bit of a consultant. He is capable of understanding the client, putting together an agenda for him and selling the agency product.
2. *Operation Wizard*—this is a mixture of account executive, traffic manager, and producer. This professional is a guru in logistics, that is, on top of all the processes, capable of finding necessary resources, and coordinating everything. If Business Commander is more of a strategic job, this one is tactical.
3. *Brand Pilot*—this is actually the current strategic planner, but without stressing his belonging to creative or media disciplines—just a communication planner.
4. *Communication Architect*—this is today's creative professional. Because he is creating, he is therefore responsible for the overall architecture of communication

Although this is the vision of the future from today (and it may be changed at some point), Igor Kirikchi stressed that the reality is still far away from this organizational model (personal communication, February 11, 2014).

Conclusion

In 2009, Tim Williams came up with a timely and valid appeal for communication agencies to start transformation for the future. His "Agency 2.5" concept was well-grounded by global changes and challenges in media, technology, and consumer behavior and therefore required certain actions from the industry. This appeal, and especially his suggested practical "implications and opportunities" for marketers and communication agencies, were heard by the industry and received full support during a series of seminars and workshops.

To learn the attitude toward this concept of the Russian communication industry, we conducted a series of one-on-one interviews with top managers and owners of Russian communication holdings. The research showed that the Russian communication industry understands the global challenges that Williams had highlighted in his concept, observing evidence of the majority of these changes in local market realities. We also noticed that our industry seems to have begun moving gradually to meet these changes, both at the structural and the product levels. The process of fully embracing IMC strategy and re-thinking its implementation models are underway, with some interesting options and organizational instruments.

References

Agency 2.5 (n.d.). How agencies are transforming for the future. Retrieved from https://ams.aaaa.org//eweb/upload/events/061809_agency25kc.pdf.

Alexeev, A. (2014, February 1). Personal communication.

CEOs Give a Thumbs-up to Agency 2.5. (2011). Retrieved from www.aaaa.org.my/activities/_pdf/Astro_4As_Scholarship_2011.pdf.

Kirikchi, I. (2014, February 11). Personal communication.

Kucherov, Y. (2014, January 29). Personal communication.

Tkachev, V. (2014, February 6). Personal communication

Technology and the Evolution of the Marketing Agency. (2013). Retrieved from www.marketo.com/_assets/uploads/Technology-and-the-Evolution-of-the-Marketing-Agency.pdf.

Williams, T. (2009). Agency 2.5. How Agencies Are Transforming for the Future. Retrieved from www.slideshare.net/ignitiongroup/agency-25-selection-of-key-slides.

Williams, T. (2012). *Take a stand for your brand: Building a great agency brand from the inside out.* [Kindle DX version]. doi: ISBN 978-1-887229-91-3.

12 Hybridity of crisis communication professional discourse in Russia

Elena Gryzunova

Introduction

This chapter addresses hybridity of Russian crisis communication professional rhetoric, primarily focusing on a combination of two types of discourses: Black public relations defense and crisis communication. The study contains a qualitative pilot analysis of texts that are related to crisis communication that illustrates the influence of black public relations frames on communication with stakeholders. The finding has practical applications for foreign communication industry specialists entering the Russian market.

Although Russian corporate and governmental organizations face several crises, issues, and reputational challenges, crisis communication as a field of practice and academic research is still in the process of institutionalization. Lack of integration into the world's crisis communication professional and academic discourse is dramatically illustrated by the absence of essential expert guidelines and milestone scientific works that are translated into Russian. Few publications by Russian crisis communication specialists exist on the subject as well. Russian crisis communication is more institutionalized as a practice than as an academic field of research.

To understand the characteristics of Russian crisis communication, it is important to explore the semantics of professional discourse on the subject. According to Fairclough (1996), "linguistic phenomena are social phenomena" (p. 23). Discourse both reflects and constructs social identities, social relations, and knowledge and belief systems (Fairclough, 1992). Crisis communication professional discourse in Russia is characterized by hybridity, which is the mixing of different discourses, genres, and styles (Fairclough, 2011). It absorbs, not only vocabulary, but also mental representations that belong to other discourses and meaning systems: From geopolitics ("information war") to criminal slang ("railroading"). Linguistic specifics with the basic crisis-related terminology should also be noted: For example, Russian public relations specialists mostly add the prefix "anti" to emphasize that communication is aimed, not to provoke, but to resolve a crisis ("anti-crisis communication" or "anti-crisis PR"). A critical discourse analysis (CDA) method applied to professional crisis communication discourse can provide insight into culture-related specifics of this field in Russia.

The emergence and development of crisis communication professional discourse

Crisis communication has developed during the past three decades as an essential element of crisis management practice and as a subfield of communication research. From the standpoint of cognitive psychology, crisis communication serves as a mental model for reasoning and decision making in an abnormal situation. The label "crisis" provides executives with a structured representation of reality and possible keys to problem-solving based on available discourse, including expert recommendations, research, and success stories. Crisis communication discourse may also form expectations of stakeholders who have perceptions of organizations' proper conduct, especially when it comes to conventional recommendations such as responding quickly, providing accurate information, and showing compassion for the victims. However, the discourse is deeply rooted in cultural frameworks: Both "conceptions of what occasions are designated as disasters and crises" and "norms indicating what course of action should be followed in different situations can vary tremendously" in different parts of the world (Quarantelli, Lagadec, & Boin, 2007, p. 31). Crisis communication discourse reflects the level of crisis communication development and institutionalization that "has not taken place at the same time or in the same manner in all countries" (Frandsen & Johansen, 2010, p. 543).

Conceptual and theoretical frameworks for crisis communication research and their practical implementation primarily emerged and evolved in the United States. Pioneer authors in in the field formed the narrative for crisis and crisis communication.

Fink (1986), in the first business book on crisis management, developed a model of a crisis life cycle that consists of several stages (prodromal crisis, acute crisis, chronic crisis, and crisis resolution), which was later developed by Sturges (1994), who proposed specific types of crisis communication required at each stage. The model of an ongoing crisis process that differs from laymen's perception of a crisis as a single breaking point is widely used among crisis communication scholars and professionals. A prominent crisis communication expert and researcher, Coombs (2007) uses a three-staged approach: Precrisis, crisis event, and postcrisis. The importance of the precrisis stage in the crisis cycle model extends the concept of crisis communication and integrates it with related fields such as issues management, risk communication, reputation management, and, in fact, any other forms of external or internal communication that contribute to crisis prevention.

Another pioneer book on crisis management by Meyers and Holusha mentioned that crises provide opportunities for transformation (1986, p. 46). The vision of a crisis as an opportunity influenced further crisis communication rhetoric and formed the basis of "discourse of renewal", which is a positive theoretical and practical crisis communication approach that emphasizes an optimistic vision of moving forward and organizational learning, with the main focus on change communication (Ulmer, Sellnow, & Seeger, 2007).

Crisis communication follows the stakeholder-oriented approach to the definition of a crisis as "the perception of an unpredictable event that threatens important expectancies of stakeholders and can seriously impact an organization's performance and generate negative outcomes" (Coombs, 2007). Therefore, existing classifications cover a huge number of situations that can be potentially perceived as crises, including emerging social media crises such as challenges, organizational misuse, and dissatisfied customers (Coombs, 2014). Most crisis communication frameworks are focused on reputation management and repair: Corporate apologia (Hearit, 2006), image restoration theory (Benoit, 2005), and situational crisis communication theory (Coombs, 2007).

Crisis communication and crisis management are closely interconnected fields in the United States: The experts share the same conceptual ground and usually mention both crisis management and crisis communication in their work (Coombs, 2012; Lerbinger, 2012).

The cross-cultural dimension of crisis communication

Cross-cultural research in crisis communication emerged due to the globalization of crises and the rise of transnational business. Scholars are focused on the influence of the stakeholders' national culture on their perceptions of a particular crisis communication strategy (Frandsen & Johansen, 2010; Claeys & Schwarz, 2016). Such research is based on experiments using hypothetical scenarios (Lee, 2004) and case studies of transnational companies (Ogrizek & Guillery, 1997) aimed at tracking cultural differences in stakeholders' reaction to crisis response. A vast interest exists in exploring approaches to crisis communication research in different parts of the world, including cultural and historical influences on the development of the field. The state of crisis communication research throughout the globe was portrayed in *The handbook of international crisis communication research* (Schwarz, Seeger, & Auer, 2016).

As far as Russian crisis communication is concerned, many cultural aspects are not yet explored. It's curious that crisis as a term has been erased for a long time from public and scientific discourse in Russia, despite a large number of cases corresponding to the definition of crises (Strovsky, 2012). Strovsky (2012) presents an historical view on the role of the Russian media in crises. According to the author, during different periods, the media were either dependent of the State or were involved in a black market of publishing *compromat* (compromising materials) on political and business rivals. Considering the scarcity of press freedoms, crisis communication required, not public relations excellence, but political or financial power to exert pressure on the media. Samoilenko (2016) said the Russian authorities are influenced by the Soviet legacy that tends toward stonewalling and repentance strategies in crises. However, he observed only the crisis communication of the government, while corporate crisis communication in Russia remains in the shade.

To fill these existing gaps, future culture-related research on crisis communication in Russia should focus on the specifics of corporate crisis communication, the problem of aversion to crisis discourse in the Russian research and practice, and the existing frameworks that substitute or supplement the crisis communication approach.

Crisis management and communication discourse in Russia

By contrast with the United States, crisis management and crisis communication in Russia are not allied fields. Crisis management (or anti-crisis management, *antikrizisnoe upravlenie*) in the Russian context means turnaround management of enterprises that face bankruptcy due to financial problems. According to the professional literature, the functions of a crisis manager are financial and organizational restructuring of a company (Barinov, 2005; Kruglova, 2010). If an enterprise is already subject to a bankruptcy proceeding, following the Federal law on bankruptcy (*Federalniy zakon o nesostoyatelnosi (bankrotstve), 26.10.2002 # 127-FZ*), a court appoints a bankruptcy trustee. Although the term "crisis manager" is not mentioned in the Federal law itself, educational institutions use it as a description of a trustee's professional competences (Moscow University of Finance and Law, n.d.). The terminological difference in the meaning of organizational crisis and the functions of a crisis manager may explain the avoidance of the crisis terminology concerning financially stable companies in Russia. To differentiate the Russian approach, it will be further referred to as anti-crisis management in this chapter.

From the standpoint of crisis discourse analysis (CDA), orders of discourses reflect and influence social orders. The discourse of anti-crisis management frames a company as a financial unit and, thus, determinates organizational crisis as a threat of bankruptcy, whereas, in crisis management, any organization is primarily a social unit: Therefore, it faces crises of physical environment, social climate, or management failure (Lerbinger, 2012). Crises are considered as threats to "the basic structures or the fundamental values and norms of a social system" (Rosenthal, Charles, & Hart, 1989, p. 10). With the definition "anti-crisis management" occupied by turnaround management and the absence of another nominalization, the profession of crisis manager is not institutionalized in Russia.

Despite the fact that organizational crises are perceived through the lens of financial performance, crisis communication (anti-crisis communication, anti-crisis PR) in Russia exists separately as a function of public relations. Crisis communication in Russia is theoretically and methodologically rooted in conflict studies (Chumikov, 2013), placing crisis in the framework of confronting interests and interpretations. The conflict-crisis communication approach is based on theories of social conflicts and research by the Center of Conflict Studies of the Russian Academy of Sciences, especially professor Alexander

Chumikov who is also a practicing PR consultant. Another scientific approach to crisis communication in Russia is rooted in sociology of management and provides three models for complex resolution of conflict, consensus, and polemic crisis types by the government (Gryzunova, 2013).

The historical context of confrontational business and political environments in the early 1990s was marked by the emergence of "black PR" (Tsetsura, 2003). This term was specific for the post-Soviet period of "wild capitalism" that was characterized by the negligence of ethical standards and even law. In the English language, the concept of "black PR" that is aimed at destroying the target's reputation is also labeled "negative PR" and "dark public relations" (International Association of Communication Activists, n.d.). Black PR strategies include manipulation, juggling with facts, and releasing compromising materials. Publications cover both "attack" and "defense" methods (Vuyma, 2005) or only focus on "defense" (Yushuk & Kuzin, 2008). The discourse of manuals based on the black PR concept (Vuyma, 2005; Sheynov, 2007) is generally characterized by: External attribution of negative events, enemy image, metaphors of conflict, communication framed as power relations, storytelling instead of case studies, propaganda theories, and folk psychology argumentation. Corporate black PR defense in the Internet (Yushuk & Kuzin, 2008) accommodated the concept of "information war" that was previously used as a synonym for hostile propaganda in geopolitical context (Panarin & Panarina, 2003). Some authors, such as Olshevskiy (2003) and Skobeleva and Shelep (2010), combined the discourses of black PR and crisis communication in their publications. However, such combination leads to ideological struggles within orders of discourses because crisis communication discourse is ideologically stakeholder-oriented, whereas black PR discourse is adversary-centered.

Future research should explore whether current professional crisis communication discourse in Russia has been colonized by black PR discourse. As far as formal features of a text are associated with social structures such as knowledge and beliefs, social relationships, and social identities (Fairclough, 1996), CDA could provide some insights into the level of institutionalization and special characteristics of the crisis communication field in Russia.

Pilot study: Critical discourse analysis of a crisis communication conference program

A critical discourse analysis method was chosen because the goal is not simply to define the current topics of professional discussions; rather, it was chosen to discover social processes and mental representations of crisis communication practitioners in Russia that are determined and reproduced by the discourse. Subject conference materials allow us to track characteristics of the professional crisis communication discourse for this pilot study.

At the time of writing, the most recent conference on crisis communication in Russia was 13–14 July 2017 in Moscow (Image media events, n.d.). The conference web page consisted of several sections, including texts directly related to crisis communication such as the conference announcement, the list of subjects for discussion, and presentation summaries.

Appendix 12.1 is the conference announcement. For the transparency of the analysis, the text is translated as closely to the original as possible to reproduce the vocabulary, grammatical features, and structures of the original Russian text when translating it into English. Readers who understand Russian may also have a look at the source.

We analyzed the text to track experiential, relational, and expressive values imbedded into the vocabulary and grammar. Experiential values coded in the text are a cue to the text producer's knowledge and beliefs: Relational values reflect social relations, and expressive values are linked to social identities. Classification schemes reflect particular ways of structuring the reality, which are ideologically based because they reflect a certain representation of that reality.

In the text are a classification of crises. One of the schemes is for conflict crises: "railroading by competitors" and "information war" directly fall into this scheme. However, this classification scheme differs from a similar one of the crises of the human climate (Lerbinger, 2012). No confrontation with activist groups is mentioned, such as protests or boycotting. The expression "railroading" (*naezd*) is typical for black PR discourse (Yushuk & Kuzin, 2008). It is metaphorically transferred from criminal jargon (Katin, 2007) and means aggressive pressure. The term "information war" is used in the singular, which usually stands for geopolitical hostile propaganda (as compared to multiple information wars in business and in other spheres). Therefore, conflict crises in the classification scheme are conflicts for power in business and politics. Conflicts based on value inconsistencies and failed expectations of stakeholders are not included. "Mergers and acquisitions" here are "ideologically contested" words (Fairclough, 1996, p. 114). They seem irrelevant to any crisis classification, but open the list followed by the conflict crises. Items that fall into one category are usually united in a text. If mergers and acquisitions are not just business as usual, but implicate conflicts of power, they are considered as a conflict-crisis type in the classification scheme. This classification scheme is closer to black PR discourse, judging by the vocabulary used and the external attribution of conflicts that are rooted in struggle for power.

Another classification scheme is for crises of the physical environment. These crisis types are briefly named. Accidents and emergencies at an industrial facility correspond to technological crises. As far as catastrophes are concerned, there is no specification whether they are of a natural or technological kind. Two additional crisis types are organizational failures: Leak of confidential information and management or employees' misdeeds. These classification schemes fit into crisis communication discourse.

Another classification represents a list of those who publish negative information online. The opponents and stakeholders are mixed in the same list, which means inferring connections (Fairclough, 1996, p. 188). There is "overwording" (Fairclough, 1996, p. 115) in description of negative comments. All the synonyms exaggerate aggressive conflict behavior of the commentators. No possible constructive critique from their part is mentioned. According to Fairclough (1996), "overwording shows preoccupation with some aspect of reality—which may indicate that it is a focus of ideological struggle" (p. 115). Here, the overwording shows a preoccupation with an adversary-centered approach to organizational problems that is typical for black PR discourse. Consumers and clients are framed negatively because they post *"repulsive comments"* the same way as do enviers or competitors.

According to Fairclough, choice between different grammatical forms may be ideologically significant (1996, p. 120). In the text are different types of sentences, such as actions, events, and attributions. Actions represent a particular interest because they reflect relations of causality and responsibility. In the sentence *"Unpleasant events happen ..."*, the "agent" is an inanimate noun. Such grammatical constructions with "crises" or "events" as agents are typical for crisis communication discourse. In general, the grammatical constructions of the whole text correspond to typical crisis communication discourse.

However, in the sentence *"Enviers, competitors ..."*, there is a list of five types and other possible agents who *"discharge flows of"* negative information. Here, the agency is stressed by the large classification and overwording mentioned above. The grammatical and linguistic features of the sentence are more typical for black PR discourse.

According to Fairclough, "relational value is a trace of and a cue to the social relationships which enacted via the text in the discourse" (1996, p. 112). Crisis communication discourse and black PR discourse are different in terms of relationships. Crisis communication discourse is focused on relations with stakeholders, such as restoring trust, caring about victims, or gaining support. Black PR discourse is centered on battles with adversaries in the information field.

In the text above, the description of stakeholders constitute negative evaluations: *"resentful employees"* and *"dissatisfied customers"* who *"discharge flows of negative messages, repulsive comments, and acerbic remarks"*. They are considered as adversaries, being put in the same list with enviers, competitors, and political opponents. *"Notable people"* is a euphemism for another possible generalization that may have direct negative value such as "malevolent actors". However, the sarcastic nature of the euphemism emphasizes its affectation. The organization for its part has to *"counter the negative"* and *"to reply to negative feedback"*. These relational values in the text are typical for black PR discourse and are represented the following way: They attack—the organization defends.

Expressive values are linked to social identities. In the texts, expressive vocabulary is used in the text only to emphasize the conflict side of crises, which is the attack on the organization: *"flows of negative messages, repulsive comments, and acerbic remarks"*. The lexical expressions here are aimed at evoking almost tangible aversion to negative messages and the commentators who sling dirt at the organization. Social identities in the discourse may be compared with those reflected by the expressive language used in a stakeholder-centered approach in

Table 12.1 Conference report summaries

Crisis communication discourse	Black PR defense discourse
Stakeholders	Adversaries
Texts # 1, 2, 6, 13	Texts # 2, 3, 4, 5
Crisis lifecycle	Information battlefield
Texts # 11, 12, 14, 15	Texts # 2, 3, 4, 5, 11, 13

another text from a prominent American crisis communication expert, James Lukaszewski: *"Management should be supportive, break down barriers, act like brothers and sisters, mothers and fathers, grandmothers and grandfathers to those who are injured or are suffering as a result of what is going on"* (2013, p. 23).

For the conference report summaries, we analyzed frames as mental representations of the world that are more typical for either crisis communication discourse or black PR defense discourse. The total number of report summaries was 15. The texts are enumerated by lines as they appear in the source, from left to right. The results are presented in Table 12.1.

Black PR defense frames in communication with the audience

The characteristics of crisis communication/black PR defense discourse in Russia reflect mental representations and actions of communication practitioners. The research needs to move forward from exploring professional discourse to analyzing messages for the audience and public relations as a social order or "network of practices" (Fairclough, 2001, p. 122). Do adversary-centered and information battlefield frames happen to appear not only in professional discussions of crisis communication, but also in communication with the media and the public? The recent cases of Rosneft and Gorky Park are provided as illustrations. However, further research is needed to make generalizations on the subject.

On June 27, 2017, the Russian oil company Rosneft faced a cyber-attack on its servers. The official Twitter account in Russian @rosneftru issued seven tweets on the subject. Six of the messages, which were also repeated in the English-language account @rosneftEN, contained general official information about the situation and the measures taken by the organization to assure business continuity. The message not translated into English was directly addressed to the media (and possibly social media users as well): "Those who release false panic messages will be considered as accomplices of the attackers and will be prosecuted together with them" (Rosneft, 2017). Rosneft had a previous history of prosecuting the media on allegations. For example, in a statement August 2, 2016, the press-service commented on the lawsuit of Igor Sechin, CEO of Rosneft, to Novaya gazeta: "In contrast with the success of Rosneft, the campaign in the media against Rosneft and its management was deliberately arranged in the context of the current market situation, including the privatization" (Rosneft, 2016).

On August 13, 2017, in Gorky Park, central park of Moscow, Stanislav Dumkin was attacked and got a head injury. On August 20, he died in the hospital. On August 25, publications about the tragedy appeared in the media, and soon the discussion went viral online. On August 26, social media users began posting critical 1-star reviews on the Facebook page of the park. The park's management was accused of absence of official reaction and lack of security. A statement from the park management, which appeared later on August 26, began with the opening line that, "due to active dissemination of information including incorrect facts in the media and social networks", and urged people not to treat the tragedy as *"profane sensation"* (Gorky Park, 2017). Another publication of the park, which presumably appeared on its official Facebook page August 26, but which was was later deleted (the screen shot was republished in the media), called the reaction of the Facebook users as a *"flash mob of hatred"* and *"wittiness competition"* (Gavasheli, 2017). The official statement and the communication policy of Gorky Park generally earned critical remarks on Facebook, including a negative reaction from Vitaliy Dumkin, the victim's father. Some comments were emotional, but many were also constructive crisis communication expectations of stakeholders who requested the information about future security-building measures and insisted on organizing a commemorative event in the park. Gorky Park did not respond to Facebook comments on the situation, regardless of the commentator sentiment (Park Gorkogo, n.d.).

Conclusions, limitations, and suggestions for future research

Previous crisis communication research was generally focused either on rhetoric of communicating with stakeholders (Benoit, 2005; Hearit, 2006) or on the perception of organizational response by stakeholders, depending on different factors (Coombs, 2014). However, it is also important, especially in cross-cultural research, to explore the specifics of professional discourse about crisis communication.

Based on the above findings, it is possible to conclude that there are traces of colonization of crisis communication professional discourse in Russia by previously the dominant discourse of black PR. Although the term "black PR" has not been widespread in recent years, the frames of black PR defense discourse are still present, not only in professional discussions but also in external communication with the audience. Although adversary-centered and information battlefield mental representations of external communicative environment used to be and may be still conditioned by objective factors, the case of Gorky Park shows that black PR defense frames influence external communication and impede mutual understanding with stakeholders.

We need to emphasize the limitations of the pilot study presented in this chapter. We primarily concentrated on a detailed qualitative study of a particular text as an example of how cognitive discourse analysis could be applied to crisis communication professional discourse. We also chose a limited number of cases to illustrate black PR defense frames in external communication. Further studies on the hybridity of crisis communication discourse in Russia can be extended to: Analyzing a larger and statistically representative corpus of texts, applying other research methods such as content analysis and interviews, and broadening the research subject by bringing in crisis discourses in the Russian mass and social media or by providing a cross-cultural view on crisis communication discourses in different countries.

Appendix 12.1: Conference announcement

About the Conference

The conference "Anti-crisis PR-2017 – reputation protection and dealing with the negative" is a two-day practical event with the series of lectures-reports.

WHY IS THE PARTICIPATION IN THE CONFERENCE VALUABLE FOR YOU?

Unpleasant events happen in each organization, and, in case of wrong actions, cause considerable harm to its reputation and can become reasons of complete collapse and termination of performance.

These are crises of all kinds: mergers and acquisitions, railroading by competitors, information war, catastrophes and accidents, emergencies at an industrial facility, leak of confidential information and its fall into the public domain, inadequate actions of management or employees made out in the open, and so on.

Practically any organization – be it governmental, municipal, non-profit, commercial one – faces with the flow of the negative in the Internet. Enviers, competitors, resentful employees, dissatisfied customers, political opponents, and other remarkable people sometimes discharge flows of negative messages, repulsive comments, and acerbic remarks to the Internet and social networking sites.

How to struggle with this? How to behave in crisis situations to come out with honor or at least with minimal damage?

How to counter the negative and how to reply to negative feedback? How to organize this work correctly?

The speakers will talk about these subjects on the conference "Anti-crisis PR-2017: reputation protection and dealing with the negative".

(Image media events, n.d.).

References

Barinov, V. A. (2005). *Antikrizisnoe upravlenie [Crisis management]*. Moscow: FBK-Press.
Benoit, W. L. (2005). Image restauration theory. In R. L. Heath (Ed.), *Encyclopedia of public relations: Volume 1* (pp. 407–410). Thousand Oaks, CA: Sage.

Chumikov, A. N. (2013). *Antikrizisnie kommunikatsii [Crisis communication]*. Moscow: Aspekt Press.

Claeys, A., & Schwarz, A. (2016). Domestic and international audiences of organizational crisis communication. In A. Schwarz, M. W. Seeger, & C. Auer (Eds.), *The handbook of international crisis communication research* (pp. 224–235). Chichester: John Wiley & Sons.

Coombs, W. T. (2007). *Ongoing crisis communication: Planning, managing, and responding* (2nd ed.). Thousand Oaks, CA: Sage Publications.

Coombs, W. T. (2014). *Ongoing crisis communication: Planning, managing, and responding* (4th ed.). Thousand Oaks, CA: Sage Publications.

Coombs, W. T. (2012). Parameters for crisis communication. In W. T. Coombs & S. J. Holladay (Eds.), *The handbook of crisis communication* (pp. 17–53). Chichester: Blackwell Publishing.

Fairclough, N. (2001). Critical discourse analysis as a method in social scientific research. In R. Wodak, & M. Meyer (Eds.), *Methods of critical discourse analysis* (pp. 121–138). Thousand Oaks, CA: Sage.

Fairclough, N. (1992). *Discourse and social change*. Cambridge, UK: Polity Press.

Fairclough, N. (2011). Discursive hybridity and social change in critical discourse analysis. In S. K. Sarangi, V. Polese, & G. Caliendo (Eds.), *Genre(s) on the move: Hybridisation and discourse change in specialised communication*. Napoli, IT: Edizioni Scientifiche Italiane.

Fairclough, N. (1996). *Language and power*. New York: Longman.

Federalniy zakon o nesostoyatelnosi (bankrotstve). (2002, October 26) 26.10.2002 # 127-FZ [Federal law on bankruptcy, 26.10.2002 # 127-FZ]. Moscow: Russian Federation.

Fink, S. (1986). *Crisis management: Planning for the inevitable*. New York: AMACOM.

Frandsen, F., & Johansen, W. (2010). Corporate crisis communication across cultures. In A. Trosborg (Ed.), *Pragmatics across languages and cultures* (pp. 543–569). Göttingen: Walter de Gruyter GmbH.

Gavasheli, M. (2017, August 28). Ubiystvo v Parke Gorkogo: versii I reakciya [Murder in Gorky Park: Versions and reaction]. *TJournal*. Retrieved from https://tjournal.ru/58715-ubiystvo-v-parke-gorkogo-versii-i-reakciya.

Gorky Park. (2017). *Oficialniy kommentariy parka Gorkogo o proishestvii 13 avgusta [Official comment of Gorky Park on accident of 13 August]*. Retrieved from http://park-gorkogo.com/news/929.

Gryzunova, E. (2013). Models of governmental crisis communications and information management. *Disaster, Conflict and Social Crisis Research Network Newsletter, 51*(14), 19–22.

Hearit, K. M. (2006). *Crisis management by apology: Corporate response to allegations of wrongdoing*. Mahwah, NJ: Lawrence Erlbaum Associates.

Image media events. (n.d.). *Antikrizisniy PR-2017 [Crisis PR-2017]*. Retrieved from http://conference.image-media.ru/category/arxiv/antikrizisnyj-pr-2017/.

International Association of Communication Activists. (n.d.). *Public relations*. Retrieved from www.iacact.com/?q=pr.

Katin, V. I. (2007). *Kriminalniy romantizm kak yavlenie kultury sovremennoy Rossii [Criminal romantism as a cultural phenomenon of modern Russia]* (PhD dissertation). Saratov State Technical University. Retrieved from https://www.dissercat.com/content/kriminalnyi-romantizm-kak-yavlenie-kultury-sovremennoi-rossii.

Kruglova, N. (2010). *Antikrizisnoe upravlenie [Crisis management]*. Moscow: Krorus.

Lee, B. K. (2004). Audience-oriented approach to crisis communication: A study of Hong Kong consumers' evaluation of an organizational crisis. *Communication Research, 31*(5), 600–618.

Lerbinger, O. (2012). *The crisis manager: Facing disasters, conflicts, and failures.* New York: Routledge.

Lukaszewski, J. E. (2013). *Lukaszewski on crisis communication: What your CEO needs to know about reputation risk and crisis management.* Brookfield, CT: Rothstein Associates Inc.

Meyers, G. C., & Holusha, J. (1986). *When it hits the fan: Managing the nine crises of business.* Boston, MA: Houghton Mifflin.

Moscow University of Finance and Law (n.d.). *Antikrizisnoe upravlenie (podgotovka arbitrazhnyh upravlyaushih) [Crisis management (education for bankruptcy trustees)].* Retrieved from http://idomfua.ru/programs/20/150/.

Ogrizek, M., & Guillery, J. (1997). *La communication de crise [Crisis communication].* Paris: Presses Universitaires de France.

Olshevskiy, A. S. (2003). *Antikrizisniy PR I konsalting [Crisis PR and consulting].* Saint Petersburg: Piter.

Panarin, I. N., & Panarina, L. G. (2003). *Informatsionnaya voyna i mir [Information war and the world].* Moscow: OLMA-PRESS.

Park Gorkogo [Gorky Park]. (n.d.). Facebook Page. Retrieved from www.facebook.com/park.gorkogo/.

Quarantelli, E. L., Lagadec, P., & Boin, A. (2007). A heuristic approach to future disasters and crises: New, old and in-between types. In H. Rodriguez, E. L. Quarantelli, & R. Dynes (Eds.), *Handbook of disaster research* (pp. 16–54). New York: Springer.

Rosenthal, U., Charles, M., Hart, P. T. (1989). *Coping with crises: The management of disasters, riots and terrorism.* Springfield, MA: Charles C. Thomas.

Rosneft (2016). *Kommentariy press-sluzhby PAO "NK "Rosneft" po povodu publikatcii v Novoy gazete [Comment of the press-service of Rosneft on publication in Novaya gazeta].* Retrieved from www.rosneft.ru/press/news/item/183141/.

Rosneft [@Rosneftru]. (2017, June 27). *Rasprostraniteli ljivyh panicheskih soobsheniy budut rassmatrivatsya...* [Those who release false panic messages will be considered...] [Tweet]. Retrieved from https://twitter.com/RosneftRu/status/879682706258440192.

Samoilenko, S. (2016). Crisis management and communication research in Russia. In A. Schwarz, M. W. Seeger, & C. Auer (Eds.), *The handbook of international crisis communication research* (pp. 397–410). Chichester: John Wiley & Sons, Inc.

Schwarz, A., Seeger, M. W., & Auer, C. (Eds.). (2016). *The handbook of international crisis communication research.* Chichester: John Wiley & Sons, Inc.

Sheynov, V. P. (2007). *Piar "beliy" I "cherniy": Technologiya skrytogo upravleniya ludmi ["White" and "black" PR: Technology of hidden manipulation of people].* Moscow: AST, Harvest.

Skobeleva, E. I., & Shelep, I. A. (2010). K voprosu o genezise I problematike antikrizisnogo PR v Rossii [Revisiting the genesis and the agenda of crisis PR in Russia]. *Trudy NGTU im. R. E. Alekseeva. Seriya "Upravlenie v socialnyh sistemah. Kommunikativnye technologii" [Transactions of NNSTU n.a. R.E. Alekseev. Series "Management in social systems. Communication technologies"], 2,* 63–70.

Strovsky, D. (2012). Crisis management and mass media in Russia: Following the historical perspectives. In B. Porfiriev & G. Simons (Eds.), *Crises in Russia: Contemporary management policy and practice from a historical perspective* (pp. 19–62). Farnham: Ashgate Publishing.

Sturges, D. L. (1994). Communicating through crisis: A strategy for organizational survival. *Management Communication Quarterly*, 7(3), 297–316.

Tsetsura, K. (2003). The development of public relations in Russia: A geopolitical approach. In K. Sriramesh & D. Verčič (Eds.), *The global public relations handbook: Theory, research, and practice* (pp. 301–319). Mahwah, NJ: Lawrence Erlbaum Associates.

Ulmer, R. R., Sellnow, T. L., & Seeger, M. W. (2007). *Effective crisis communication: Moving from crisis to opportunity*. Thousand Oaks, CA: Sage.

Vuyma, A. (2005). *Cherniy PR: Zaschita I napadenie v biznese I ne tolko [Black PR: defense and attack in business and beyond]*. Saint Petersburg: BHV.

Yushuk, E., & Kuzin, A. (2008). *Protivodeystvie chernomy PR v Internete [Countering black PR in the Internet]*. Moscow: Vershina.

13 Communication and health knowledge production in contemporary Russia from institutional structures to intuitive ecosystems

Alexandra Endaltseva

Introduction

This chapter describes the shades and composites of health communication in the Russian Federation, which could be called a procedural element of health knowledge production because the concept of "health communication", invented and developed in the context of particular Western parts of the globe, for a long time has not been compatible with Russian realities. In Russia (and perhaps in all organized collectives, from a tribe to a sophisticated nation-state), Hanisch's (2000) "the personal is the political" did not spare such an intimate and emotional, but at the same time politico-economic, field as health. Both in its biological and socio-political meanings, health, despite arduous attempts to assign it individual biomedical properties, is also comprised of state regulations, international economic structures, business strategies, affects, ontological norms, social and cultural institutions, popular myths, relationships, and communication. Therefore, the mode through which health is communicated reveals quite a bit about our histories, realities, relationships, discourses, and ways of knowing. This chapter describes the situation within which health as a concept and as a part of lifeline is being produced and communicated in contemporary Russia. It questions how the Russian situation relates to the dominant health communication discourse; the traces the transformations of health economics models in Russia, starting with the collapse of Soviet Union; and, finally, it offers an infrastructural mapping of what could be characterized as intuitive "health communication" in Russia.

When it comes to health, who is the communicator?

Health has gone global. And so has health communication. Yet what does this "global" mean? Does it suppose that the meanings of health should be reconciled across all the different regions and their specificities, or does it mean that health communication objectives, scholarship, and practice are "global" translations of the models developed in the Western countries onto the contexts in which health communication is not institutionalized. The search for epistemological status and disciplinary identities of health communication (Hannawa et al., 2015) questions the nature of research objects and interdisciplinary links. Health communication can be characterized as a system of human interactions, both face-to-face and mediated, within a health-related context. The practices of health communication have been linked to the emergence and reinforcement of social structures and to the production and reproduction of the social meanings of health, illness, and disease. These practices expose and articulate the relationship among biomedical objectives, sociocultural contexts, material and symbolic productions, and internal subjective sense-making in health-related contexts (Banks & Riley, 1993; Sharf & Vanderford, 2003).

However, health communication has been primarily explored on the basis of those nation-states that have the financial and institutional support for its research and industry implementation (Parrish-Sprowl, 2009). Russia is not present in this list (the reasons will be discussed in this chapter). Therefore, following Craig's (1999) argument that communication constitutes a practical theory or, in other words, a discursive theoretical field evoking from praxis and contributing back to the practical discourse, I propose that the situation in Russia is an opening window for critically interrogating the field of health communication per se.

In addition, the dominant reading of health communication does not include non-human entities, for example, medicaments, assistive technology, diagnostic equipment, and city infrastructures, that disregard the contexts that have a shortage of these non-human media and actors. In the early 2000s, Ratzan (2001) observed that, "today people, governments and the state interact in ways that affect health… . Health can be fully recognized as an essential component of global civil society" (p. 208), which translates health communication as a science-and-art partnership among the public, policy makers, and business sector. Nine years later, Ratzan clarified that this partnership should also be governed by "ethical employment of persuasive means for health decision making" in "public relations, advocacy, negotiation, and social marketing" (Ratzan, 2010, p. 3). This clarification brings us to contemporary Russia, which has begun to recover from its post-Soviet transition (at least, in the developed urban areas) and to expand professional communication attention toward dialogues with "power", patient-provider relations, and public health communication programs, thus forming unique intuitive health communication structures and infrastructures.

Assuming that an understanding of health communication approaches is particularly important in the attempts of global health agents to address the challenges of global mobilization and collective response to health crises (Obregon & Waisbord, 2012), this chapter invites readers to ponder the questions: Who is the communicator in health communication theories and practices; whose interest health communication should serve; and what is the benefit of the visibility and invisibility of communicators and their interests in the region in which health communication is not institutionalized?

Foundations of Russian health communication: Reforms, the reformers, and the reformed

The Russian Federation has overcome many systemic reforms in the health care sector since the collapse of the Soviet Union and its centralized Soviet Semashko public health care model. All of these reforms have been directed at the shift toward the mixed insurance-based health care provision that maintains the constitutional right to free health care and is driven by the socioeconomic and political crises in the region. This shift has been performed in the ambiance of the continuous decline of life expectancy in Eastern Europe in the late twentieth century, an unprecedented case in the history of global health in which highly industrialized nations during this peacetime have experienced rapid health deterioration despite the "health for all" motto of socialist regimes (Cockerham, 2002).

In other words, the implementation of this new system was accompanied in this region by a major socioeconomic crisis, the sociocultural trauma of the "lost generation", the increase in crime levels, and the shock economic policies. The new state has inherited a broad infrastructure of institutions and staff that had committed to universal access to care; however, this heritage has appeared to be (and remains) a burden rather than an asset. Additionally, the lack of information about how the health care system functions and what the reforms mean for the population has resulted in a more cautious behavior within this system and more questions about the reasonability of the system. These overall results shaped up to the dominating public distrust in the post-Soviet reforms.

During the crisis of the 1990s, hospitals tended to use manipulating debts and barters to overcome lack of funding (Gordeev, Pavlova, & Groot, 2011; Twigg, 1999). According to Shishkin and Vlasov (2009), the lack of governmental guarantees and poor health throughout the population, accompanied by low salaries in the state hospitals and insufficient use of the available governmental resources, are the main issues in the current state of health care in the Russian Federation. Gordeev, Pavlova, and Groot (2011) also note poor management, the impossibility of competition due to a vertical political system, and the resistance to changes from the physicians and medical personnel. All of these mentioned premises indicate the absence of explanatory, let alone persuasive, communication of the reforms in the health care sector. Thus, health knowledge production in contemporary Russia is based on the sense of lost paradise, of betrayed hope for a free democratic society, on the uncertainties, and on the necessity to pioneer innovative ways to achieve one's purposes.

In 1993, a new law implemented a system of compulsory social health insurance (OMS) for all citizens who wished to use public health care services (ambulance, out- and in-patient care, and research facilities) throughout all of Russia's regions (Gordeev, Pavlova, & Groot, 2011; Twigg, 1999). This initiative was in line with the overall transition toward the free-market system, the deregulation of the state economy, and a decrease of governmental presence in the lives of Russian citizens. During the transition to insurance-based public health care, the governmental body in charge of managing OMS, which was named the Federal Compulsory Health Insurance Fund (FFOMS) with 87 (which later was reduced to 83 and then increased to 85 to include Sevastopol and Crimea in 2014) Territorial Compulsory Health Insurance Funds, or TFOMS), collected contributions per region and redistributed these funds to the independent insurance companies that contracted care providers. The revenues for TFOMS and FFOMS derived from the United Social Tax and health premiums for the nonworking population from the municipalities.

As the independent insurance providers entered the market later, TFOMS acted as the insurers and were able to contract any provider, public or private, as long as this was in the interest of the insured patients (Gordeev, Pavlova, & Groot, 2011). This was typical for economies in transition in which former social institutions were replaced by new ones without a strategic plan and material and human resources to manage them. Even with the growing number of private and public insurers, the system did not produce the expected competition and simply redistributed the funds from OMS to the providers. Considering the socioeconomic and political instabilities in the region as well as the lack of professional training for the new administrators, high levels of corruption, and passive to negative attitudes among the public, the ineffectiveness of the reforms was quite expected.

All of these factors have affected the results of implemented reforms, which, for example, turned into a decrease in birth rates, high mortality, and a decrease in life expectancy at birth (Cook, 2015); consequently, the poor state of health has led to further reformation of the system up until today. Finally, the perpetual distrust in these social reforms among the population that were carried out as a legacy of transition times coexisted with the absence of competencies in, recognition of, and the budget for health communication on all the levels, from organizational to public relations. This created a gap between the intended objectives of the reforms and the interactions between these reforms and the population in need of health care.

Apart from the sociobureaucratic challenges, the new financial forms of health institutions and the growing sector of private health care required a change in communication strategies between doctors and patients and between health care establishments and those who require health care. In a state that has been thrown into reforms in every sector of economic, political, and everyday structures, there was no space for the professionalization of communication (or other managerial) practices of health care professionals or for organizational communication campaigns. The focus of attention has been not on the standardization of communication practices, but on the articulation of such to overcome the inconsistencies of the new system.

Zvonareva et al. (2016) have presented an account of these articulation practices in their article on the international commercial clinical trials in the Russian Federation. Zvonareva et al. (2016) said the health system after the collapse of the Soviet Union was characterized by insecurities, delays in salaries, lack of medical supplies, and the constant search for support from officials and international research grants to keep health care afloat. The illiteracy of the post-Soviet population has added to the allure of international clinical trials to Russia, which, despite ethical troublesomeness, gave a larger portion of the population access to health care.

Since the 2000s, with the improvements in the political climate in the country, Russia was no longer a recipient of aid, but had become an aid-donor in the international health arena (Twigg, 2010). After 2007, in the global health arena, Russia has been acquiring, at least on paper, the knowledge and skills of the United Nations Development Program, World Bank, and G-20 (Twigg, 2010); and, on the national scale with a more-or-less stabilized economic strategies under Putin's administration and as a response to a continuous health crisis, a new single TFOMS finance model was introduced that offered a free choice of insurance companies. However, researchers question the effectiveness of this system, especially when the choice of the insurer was mostly made by the employer and the tradition of quasi-formal out-of-pocket and under-the-table payments continued to be prevalent (Gordeev, Pavlova, & Groot, 2011; Shishkin & Vlasov, 2009). A part of such systemic failures has been—and continues to be—the lack of communication with the public; inefficient and insufficient funding; low quality of care or care technology; and overall distrust in governmental decision making.

According to the recent health reform plan, the amount of federal expenses on health is expected to be as high as 5.2% by 2020; however, according to Shishkin and Vlasov (2009), this initiative may only produce positive results when accompanied by health lifestyle promotion, specific boundaries between paid and unpaid health care, and clear standards. Although these steps have been made, the neglect to the communication practices (in contrast to a one-way information delivery) in the health care sector (from doctor-patient communication to public health campaigns) has hindered the potentiality of both the governmental initiative and the steps to contextualize it. Additionally, due to the significant income inequality in Russia, resulting in unequal access to, costs of, and quality of health care between metropolitan cities and regions, we can hardly speak of the possibility of health communication standardization and professionalization.

In the long-term socioeconomic development plan, modernization of the public health care system has been put on the priority agenda since 2008 (Shishkin & Vlasov, 2009), and, in this modernization process, "patient-oriented medicine" has been the buzzword starting only in 2016. Therefore, the question of what comprises a "patient-oriented medicine", including the role of professionalization of communication practices and the development of public engagement, is still to be determined. It becomes specifically relevant now, after telemedicine was officially recognized in the legislative documentation at the end of 2017 and the gaps in bioethical standards and the absence of choherent communication flow reappear as a public concern.

Public discontent with the quality of health care and the inefficiency of health care reforms, together with strong political influences of the Putin administration, economic insecurity, the geopolitical crisis, and budget cuts have resulted in one-way healthy lifestyle promotion by the government in order to turn the population to self-care (Pautov & Pautova, 2014). This promotion, nevertheless, is not sufficiently accompanied by careful and elaborated communication campaigns, mostly being represented by mass media, corporate social responsibility campaigns, and in the forms of grants for NGOs and social organizations, including universities and charity funds. Although multiple grant-giving bodies tackle health communication, with the recent geopolitical scandals, Russian NGOs and public institutions cannot apply for foreign funds, having to rely solely on the in-the-country funds. Among those the most prestigious and politically "safe" grant giver is the government and the system of presidential grants.

However, the number of presidential grants given each year is very limited and the maximum size of a presidential grant is 500,000 rubles (about U.S.$8,700), which makes public organizations compete for these small allocations to satisfy their visions and needs, rather than to collaborate in joint health communication programs. In contrast, pharmaceutical companies and transnational brands are successfully using this neoliberal trend for their commercial purposes, recruiting public organizations for their agenda. Recently, these marketing and communication efforts have been largely suppressed by legislation decisions, and patient organizations are slowly becoming a lead communicator in the chain of health knowledge production in Russia. Thus, a grassroots advocacy movement, which had emerged from the uncertainties of 1990s as a watchdog on patients' rights and had developed as an actor in the governmental strategy on health improvement, is mutating to be a mediator among the government, health care professionals, business structures, and the Russian population.

The absence of institutional structures or infrastructures that feed into health communication development in Russia has contributed to the appearance of a peculiar intuitive system of communication in health-related context, in which "grasstops" communication and "grassroots" communication exist in parallel realities, but in search for mediation spaces. The challenge of these emergent mediation entities, therefore, is to reconcile the gap between authoritative initiatives and public decoding of such with abundant pharmaceutical marketing campaigns; elaborate patients' communities (online and offline); municipal festivals promoting public health; growing popularity of a "healthy lifestyle" movement; shortage of resources in the regional health institutions; tensions between patients and doctors; and never-ending budget optimization reforms that are not sufficiently communicated to the concerned parties.

The plethora of communicating actors, each representing a commitment toward their social worlds with little to no alignment with the strategies of other actors, can be articulated thus:

- Governmental institutions and officials, which exercise the strategies dictated by state policies from budgets allocated to the health care field to promote import substitution due to the current geopolitical crisis.
- Patients' groups and associations, which aim for a mediator role among the health care professionals, the population in need of health care, and governmental institutions, with a commitment to patients' rights protection.
- Pharmaceutical industries, which are driven by profit-gaining strategies and which aim for a dialogue with patient communities to secure their client base and research resources.
- Private health institutions or private sectors of public health institutions, which convey a message of easier access to and better quality of care.
- Marketing and public relations firms that are outsourced by the industries, which promote professionalization of health communication practice and aim for the role of mediators between business sectors and the publics.
- NGOs and funds, which provide relief, promote self-care, and act on the discursive grounds of intersection of disability and health.
- Ministry of labor and associated formations, which communicate the intersections of health, work, and disabilities from the governmental decision makers to the publics.
- Insurance companies, which take advantage of neoliberal trends for profit-seeking strategies.
- Other commercial entities, for example, web platforms, equipment producers, and alternative practices, which promote professionalization of health communication, Western approaches to patient-oriented medicine, and self-care.
- Traditional and alternative medicine, which communicates the link between the uncertainties of the health care system, low quality of biomedical care, and self-care as a response.
- Education and research sector, which uses the current situation to communicate the topicality of medical professions, the expansion of the resource base, and adjustment to curricula (teaching how to communicate with patients).

"I am a professional patient, like many of you here ..." (Co-chair, All-Russian Patients Union, Public Speech at All-Russian Patient Congress, 2017)

While, in developed Western countries, a movement of patients began to gain power during the beginning of the twentieth century, it was not until the end of the 1980s that patients began to mobilize. European and American social scientists (Epstein, 1996, 2007; Rabeharisoa et al., 2014; Moreira et al., 2014; Akrich, 2016) discussed the various forms and contexts of patients' organizations in knowledge production in health and chronic illnesses in Western Europe and in the United States. Russian context specifies patient mobilization by introducing the dynamics of continuous reforms, distrust, and uncertainties in the entire nation-state and the lack of consistency in health communication. Patients' organizations in Russia are among the least-researched areas of Russian society, due to their work's non-political character and the lack of consolidation within the movement (Krashennikova, 2009).

However, in the making of health communication in contemporary Russia, patient organizations are the most motivated communicators. They commit a vast amount of their work to overcoming or navigating uncertainties in the health economic models; to mediating cross-sectional dialogue among patients, business, and power; and to providing access to trustworthy information in the domain of health. Furthermore, patients' organizations serve as a buffer that smoothens public and health professionals' discontent with never-ending neo-liberal reforms in the health sector, preventing this discontent from coming onto the streets and expanding into the civil crisis.

Patient organizations began to appear in Russia in the 1980s; since that time, they have evolved in their complexity and in their influence on governmental policies. Contemporary health care system in Russia, coupled with tensions on the global geopolitical arena and increasing governmental control in every sphere of social life, including internet and arts, is in constant flux and highly unpredictable. Nevertheless, the idea of a patient-centered health care is now the top priority of the national health care strategy, announced all over mass media and within the marketing slogans all across the country. So patient organizations, linking patients, the state, and health-related business, emerge as deserving attention not only to the institutional role of patient organizations in a civil society but to their collaborative creative practices, communication, and practical knowledge.

Today, there are over 40 all-Russian public patient organizations in Russia, 24 of which along with their 180 regional organizations are members of the Russian Union of Patients, the main organizational structure of the Russian patient movement, officially named "all-Russian union of public associations of patients". In 2012, patient organizations have been at their institutional inception. Shirokova (2012) cited the president of the Russian Multiple Sclerosis Society, Yan Vlasov, who also has served as a co-chair of the All-Russian Patients' Union, to demonstrate that the assessment tools for Russian health care are still based on economic determinants, rather than on the quality of patients' rights, which challenges the commitments of the patients' movement, especially since it lacks strong leaders and professionals (as cited in Shirokova, 2012).

Now, the situation has changed, driven by the Union's eduction and communication programs: Practice sharing workshops for different patient organizations, collaborative programs, peer learning, and coalition media work. Russian public patient organizations can be divided into three groups (Krashennikova, 2009; Shirokova, 2012):

- Associations committed to the legal rights protection (such as The League of Patients' Protectors).

- Patient communities based on membership and uniting people in the same nosology (type of illness)—a mixed-goal formation that deals both with rights protection and rights explanation. It can be a public organization or a public organization of invalids.
- Charity funds and NGOs dealing with explanation of patients' rights.

Having begun with almost invisible activities, which had been powered by the charisma of a few patients, lawyers, and doctors in Samara and Moscow, Russian grassroots health communication today is centralized in Moscow. Thus, it shadows the centralized governance of the state health care system and the concentration of the "receivers" of health messages, aka governmental officials and key players in the health industry as well as entities in charge of health finance. Shirokova (2012) quoted Yuri Zshulyov, president of the Russian Hemophilia Society and now also a co-chair of All-Russian Patients' Union saying that resistance to dialogue among governmental officials and the absence of transparency have traditionally challenged the work of patients' organizations in Russia. However, in his address to the participants of the All-Russian Patients' Congress, Zshulyov has mentioned that now the governmental officials are interested in and actively seeking collaborations with patient organizations (as cited in Shirokova). Such a shift in communication dynamics became a result of the communication work within the several communicative platforms. These platforms include:

- Public Councils for patients' rights protection for the Federal Bureau for Supervision in the Sphere of Health Care and Social Development in the Russian Federation and in their regional chapters.
- Public Organizations' council for patients' rights protection for the Ministry of Health Care and Social Development.
- Coordination councils for the civil rights provision and protection in the system of compulsory health insurance for the regional and territorial OMS funds.
- Congresses and conferences with governmental officials organized by the patient organizations.

While public councils serve as a platform for decision-based communication, the conferences and congresses that unite the medical personnel, patients, and health care officials are the places for establishing rapport, networking within patients' movement as well as cross-sectionally, and demonstrating intentions. All-Russian Patients' Congress, launched in Samara in 2010, is a good example of such communicative space: Right now, it is one of the most prominent platforms for the dialogue between the patients' community and the "power", including legislative and executive power branches. In 2017, this congress was held in a luxurious congress hall in Moscow City Business Center. As Zshulyov had mentioned in his address to the congress participants, the reason for choosing such location was that the movement was growing in numbers and influence, attracting more patients' groups, and, with them, attracting representatives from the Ministry of Health Care, government bureaus dealing with disability issues, and business (Shirokova, 2012).

The outlook on the Russian "grassroots" health communication infrastructure today shows an emergent intuitive ecosystem with All-Russian Patients' Union as a central communicator. The union is ruled mostly on the charisma of the leaders and the accumulated social and technological capital of the strongest Russian patients' organizations. The All-Russian Patients' Union gathers under its umbrella several federal and regional patients' organizations, including the most prominent, which include the Russian Hemophilia Society; All-Russian Association of People with Multiple Sclerosis; All-Russian public organization of invalids from psychic disorders and their families, "New Opportunities"; the Cross-regional Public Organization of Nephrologic Patients, "Nephro-Liga"; and the All-Russian Society of Oncohematology "Assistance". The central communicative hubs of this infrastructure are Public Councils to the Ministry of Health and Social Development and their regional chapters, All-Russian Patients' Congress, and the recently formed Public Councils to the Bureau of Medico-Social Expertise and their regional chapters.

These hubs, which also serve as outputs of grassroots health knowledge production, are interconnected and are powered by individuals who were at the foundation of the patients' movement in Russia in the 1980s and by their social and legal knowledge capital. The knowledge communicated to these hubs is formed primarily within the patients' organizations that represent the interests of people with chronic diseases and disabilities receiving governmental aid for treatment from the "7 nosologies" federal program. The communicative means in this passage are mixed offline and online, interpersonal and impersonal interactions, resulting in written communiques, public survey results, and allocation of expert patients for participation in events and meetings.

The deeper layer of this communicative infrastructure is the subsystems within each organization: Central leadership, regional leadership, and technological and financial resources. Finally, the base layer is comprised of individual patients or those who are affected by illness who volunteer as regional program managers on the ground, communicating with patients and their families, answering hot lines on their cellphones, and performing the everyday tasks of organizational life.

Mikhail Churakov, head of the Social Mechanics agency and one of the active participants of patients' movement in Russia since its formation, argues that the major challenge to patients' organizations now is transforming organizational communication strategies (personal communication, November, 2017). Krashennikova (2009) notes the major commitment to activism among Russian patient organizations traditionally has rested in the sphere of medicaments' provision. However, after reaching the medical provision goals by 2012 and securing generous governmental aid for expensive treatments for serious chronic illnesses ("7 nosologies" federal program), the patients' movement lost a considerable number of activists. Therefore, although major problems exist with rehabilitation and crisis prevention in Russia, it is not possible to tackle it with the same motivations, methods, and instruments as the medical treatment provision was tackled. Now, according to Churakov, the Russian patients' movement is entering a new epoch, in which communicational modes and models must be reassessed, including more extensive employment of social media to attract younger activists. As well, leaders in grassroots health communication, according to Churakov, must develop a system of retention within the movement (personal communication, November 2017).

In conclusion, Russian health communication is in the making and remains in constant flux since the fall of the Soviet Union, becoming into a unique intuitive ecosystem of health communication research and practices. This ecosystem does not mean a perfect composition of best practices—rather, it represents an alignment and simultaneous misalignment of different actors' strategies grounded in historical and cultural implications. The key feature of this ecosystem is that despite its drawbacks and misunderstandings it works. And as this chapter has tried to demonstrate, the major reason for this "working" is repair and maintenance work done by patient organizations. Based on uncertainties, inconsistencies, and the lack of trustworthy information, the Russian ecosystem of health communication is now being solidified within the Russian patients' movement, which plays as a mediator position among the governmental, business, and public sectors of health production.

References

Akrich, M. (2016). Inquiries into experience and the multiple politics of knowledge. Keynote Plenary 1: To what extent is embodied knowledge a form of science and technology by other means? 4S-EASST meeting, i3 Working Papers Series, 16-CSI-02. Barcelona, Spain.

Banks, S. P., & Riley, P. (1993). Structuration theory as an ontology for communication research. *Annals of the International Communication Association, 16*(1), 167–196.

Mikhail Churakov, M. (2017, November). Personal communication.

Cockerham, C. W. (2002). *Health and social change in Russia and Eastern Europe.* London: Routledge.

Cook, L. (2015). Constraints on universal health care in the Russian Federation: Inequality, informality and the failures of mandatory health insurance reforms. *UNRISD Working Paper, 5*, 1–31. Retrieved from www.unrisd.org/80256B3C005BCCF9/(httpAuxPages)/3C45C5A972BF063BC1257DF1004C5420/$file/Cook.pdf.

Craig, R. T. (1999). Communication theory as a field. *Communication Theory, 9*(2), 119–161. doi:10.1111/j.1468–2885.1999.tb00355.x.

Epstein, S. (1996). Introduction: Controversy, credibility and the public character of AIDS research. In *Impure Science: AIDS, Activism, and the politics of knowledge* (pp. 1–25). Berkeley and Los Angeles: University of California Press.

Epstein, S. (2007). *Inclusion: The politics of difference in medical research.* Chicago: University of Chicago Press.

Gordeev, V. S., Pavlova, M., & Groot, W. (2011, October). Two decades of reforms. Appraisal of the financial reforms in the Russian public healthcare sector. *Health Policy, 102*(2–3), 270–277.

Hannawa, A. F., Garcia Jimenez, L., Candrlian, C., Rossmann, C., & Schulz, P. J. (2015). Identifying the field of health communication. *Journal of Health Communication: International Perspectives, 20*(5), 521–530.

Hanisch, C. (2000). The Personal is Political. In B. A. Crow (Ed.), *Radical feminism: A documentary reader* (pp. 113–116). New York: NYU Press.

Krashennikova, Y. A. (2009). Rol NKO v upravlenii sistemoy zdravookhraneniya i perspektivi razvitiya patzienskogo dvizshenya v Rossii, ЖИСП, 4, 519–534. [in Russian].

Moreira, T., O'Donovan, O., & Howlett, E. (2014). Assembling dementia care: Patient organisations and social research. *BioSocieties, 9*(2), 173–193. DOI:10.1057/biosoc.2014.6.

Obregon, R., & Waisbord, S. (Eds.). (2012). *The handbook of global health communication.* Chichester: Wiley-Blackwell.

Parrish-Sprowl, J. (2009). Managing a world of problems: The implications of globalization for applied communication research. In L. R. Frey & K.N. Cissna (Eds.), *Routledge handbook of applied communication research* (pp. 257–280). New York: Routledge.

Pautov, I., & Pautova, N. (2014). Promoting a healthy lifestyle as an instrument of public health policy in modern Russia. *The Journal of Social Policy Studies, 12*(4), 493–508.

Rabeharisoa, V., Moreira, T., & Akrich, M. (2014). Evidence-based activism: Patients', users' and activists' groups in knowledge society. *BioSocieties, 9*(2), 111–128. DOI:10.1057/biosoc.2014.2.

Ratzan, S. C. (2001). Health literacy: Communication for the public good. *Health Promotion International, 16*(2), 208–2014.

Ratzan, S. C. (2010). Editorial: Strategic health communication and social marketing on risk issues. *Journal of Health Communication: International Perspectives, 4*(1), 1–6.

Sharf, B. F., & Vanderford, M. L. (2003). Illness narratives and the social construction of health. In T. L. Thomson, A. M. Dorsey, K. I Miller, & R. Parrott (Eds.), *Handbook of health communication* (pp. 9–35). Mahwah, NJ: Lawrence Erlbaum Associates.

Shirokova, Y.A. (2012). Patsientskoe dvizhenie v Rossii [Patient movement in Russia]. *Remedium, 3,* 20–27.

Shishkin, S. V., & Vlassov, V. V. (2009, June 25). Russia's healthcare system: In need of modernization. *BMJ, 338*:b2132.

Twigg, J. L. (1999). Obligatory medical insurance in Russia: The participants' perspective. *Social Science and Medicine, 49*(3), 371–382.

Twigg, J. L., (2010). Russian global health outlook: Building capacities to match aspirations. In K. E. Bliss (Ed.), *Key players in global health: How Brazil, Russia, India, China, and South Africa are influencing the game. A report of the CSIS Global Health Policy Center* (pp. 34–41). Washington, DC: SCIS.

Zvonareva, O., Engel, N., Kutishenko, N., & Horstman, K. (2017). (Re)configuring research value: International commercial clinical trials in the Russian Federation. *BioSocieties, 12*(3), 392–414. doi: http://doi.org/10.1057/biosoc.2016.11.

Part V

Conclusion

The future of communication(s) in Russia

14 The future of Russia's strategic communications

An effects-based approach

David Waterman and Katerina Tsetsura

No study of strategy should go without an in-depth review of strategic communication, given it is, and always has been, integral to the success of any strategy or campaign. And, while communication has been present in some form since history could be observed and recorded, the Information Environment of today and tomorrow is more accessible, complex, and dynamic than ever before. The Information Environment is the aggregate of individuals, organizations, and systems that collect, process, disseminate, or act on information, a heterogeneous global environment in which humans and automated systems observe, orient, decide, and act on data. (Department of Defense, 2012). Governments, organizations, state, and nonstate actors operate in an era when the global role of information is critical to success or failure. The global information environment continues to evolve rapidly, offering opportunities as well as posing threats. In today's information environment, issues such as infotainment, fake news, hate speech, bots, and propaganda negate the advantages of the internet, social media, and free, transnational information flows (Meister, 2018) and present a growing threat to the democratic process (Lewandowsky et al., 2017; van der Linden et al., 2017; Iynegar & Massey, 2018), challenging state actors and straining budgets and resources for supremacy on both the physical and cognitive battlefields.

One of the challenges is that not all state or nonstate actors utilize traditional Western models or theories of communication to engage the information environment. Yet most studies of non-Western state and nonstate actors are conducted through the lens of Western communication models or theories. This chapter discusses a heuristic communication approach to assessing state and nonstate actors who approach communication from an effects-based strategy versus a traditional Western time-driven, message-focused approach to communicating with stakeholders. This chapter discusses a nontraditional strategic communication model called *Effects-Based Communication* (EBC) as a grand strategy level model that can be used to construct and deconstruct strategic-level communication strategies in various contexts. This effects-based approach may also be applicable to various organizations, governments, and actors and can help better understand strategic communication practices of Russia.

Actors in the global information environment include nonstate and state actors, ranging from activist groups to terrorist groups as well as leading nations such as the United States, China, and Russia. With the evolution of technology and the ease of direct access to desired stakeholders, those actors who can adapt to the new speeds of engagement and who can take advantage of opportune moments are able to gain a distinct advantage in the information environment over those who cannot, or do not want to, adopt the use of *informational power* over *hard or soft power* as the primary engagement method, with soft and hard power in supporting and implementing roles.

One of the more successful state actors in the new, emerging information environment, Russia has been the focus of many studies regarding strategic communication, and, more specifically, disinformation and propaganda campaigns. Many Western diplomatic, military, and academic sources have sought to determine Russia's desires and/or intent for the future (Clunan, 2019; Herd, 2019; Casier, 2019; Kristensen & Sakstrup, 2016; Kumar, 2017; Ivanov & Kissinger, 2002). There is no shortage of explanations or speculation on the underpinning constructs of the Russian mindset of their place in world order and the use of communication to achieve that place.

Most authors, such as Clunan (2019) and Radin and Reach (2017), asserted the current and prevailing goal of Russia is to be a great power again. Radin and Reach (2017) identified five interest areas of Russian concern. These include the defense of the country and regime, influence in the near abroad, non-interference in domestic affairs, political and economic cooperation as a partner equal to other great powers, and—most important in understanding intent and strategy—a vision of Russia as "a great power" (Radin & Reach, p. 15). This is not to say it is the only great power, but one of several major powers, or, in other words, a "multipolar" version of the world (Radin & Reach, 2017, p. 15). Furthermore, Peterson (2019), argued:

> There is broad consensus among contributors that Russian President Vladimir Putin is indeed adhering to a global grand strategy, which aims to achieve the following goals: reclaim and secure Russia's influence over former Soviet nations; regain worldwide recognition as a "great power"; and portray itself as a reliable actor, a key regional powerbroker, and a successful mediator in order to gain economic, military, and political influence over nations worldwide and to refine the liberalist rules and norms that currently govern the world order.
>
> (p. vii)

Pezard and Rhoades (2020) asserted that Russia's key national interests

> which guide its foreign policy, can be summarized around three themes: defending Russia's borders and preserving the Russian regime; maintaining influence in the near aboard; and fulfilling the vision of Russia

as a great power, which include ensuring that it is being treated as such by other powers.

(p. 2)

Understanding the mindset and worldview of an actor, state or nonstate, is key when one tries to analyze communication strategies in motion. Considerable time has been spent trying to understand Russian communication activities in an effort to better understand such activities and the underpinning intent. Communicators and social scientists have long studied propaganda and how to analyze it when encountered. Such studies have focused on the message, using quantitative analysis, and trying to extrapolate it to discover its meaning and intention; however, such methods have been questioned since the 1940s (Bardach-Yalov, 2012). Sociologist Siegfried Kracauer (1952) first described a quantitative content analysis as a relevant method to use, but this method still focused on the traditional content of messages—not the underpinning intent or effect the message was trying to support. When communication strategies are assessed, it is critical to use the lens most appropriate to the source, theory, or model of communication being assessed. The most simple of analogies might be a doctor who prescribes medication based on pure observation of a patient's symptoms, without tests or examination. The more effective doctor applies the appropriate examinations and tests based on the symptoms presented and then compares test results with known characteristics or properties of potentially similar illnesses to best diagnose the presented illness.

As a result, some scholars who use traditional communication models and lens, such as Theohary (2018) and Tashev et al. (2019), argued that Russian communication appears unorganized, chaotic, and inconsistent (Paul & Matthews, 2016). This is not a unique perspective, because a Western lens has been applied to explain many nonstate and state actor communication efforts and activities in the past—if any effective communication assessment of strategy, intent, capacity, and capabilities was conducted in the first place— often resulting in erroneous observations leading to poor planning efforts and ineffective communication strategies, such as seen in NATO/Coalition communication efforts in Afghanistan (Boudreau et al., 2016).

To discuss the topic of strategic communication with some accuracy, some terms need defining for clarity. This chapter moves forward on the premise that strategic communication (singular) is a process that coordinates and synchronizes all organizational elements to achieve an organizational-defined end state. NATO defines strategic communication as:

the coordinated and appropriate use of NATO communication activities and capabilities—Public Diplomacy, Public Affairs (PA), Military Public Affairs, Information Operations (Info Ops) and Psychological Operations (PSYOPS)—in support of Alliance policies, operations and activities, and in order to advance NATO's aims.

(NATO, 2009)

A Western business definition is "strategic communication is communication aligned with the company's overall strategy, to enhance its strategic positioning" (Argenti et al., 2005). Yet another alternative strategic communication definition is presented by a 2011 Chatham House report as, "A systematic series of sustained and coherent activities, conducted across strategic, operational and tactical levels, that enables understanding of target audiences, and identifies effective conduits to promote and sustain particular types of behaviour" (Cornish et al., 2011, p. 4). Endaltseva (2015) explores a Russian view of integrated communication as:

> communication that incorporates public relations, management, marketing, political communication, media relations, and social media platforms, as reflected at all communicative levels, from corporate to personal, is a product of a capitalist consumer society with a stake in personal communication consumption choices.
>
> (p. 1)

Each definition echoes the same core theme: A process of coordinating and synchronizing organizational elements to achieve an organizational end goal. Strategic communications (plural), or integrated communication, however, has been actively used in the academic and practical contexts in Russia to indicate a variety of schools of thoughts, frames of reference, and approaches to the field of study, processes, and ways to communicate messages. Hence, sometimes the use of strategic communications (plural) in Russia can indicate the school of thought differences, in addition to the differences among approaches to mediated channels, strategic messaging, and processes.

To better understand the practice of strategic communications in Russia, one can also look at how strategic communication and information power are related. State actors have long been utilizing informational power with hard and soft power as supporting efforts. In February 2013, General of the Army Valery Gerasimov, Russia's chief of the General Staff, published, "The Value of Science Is in the Foresight," in the Russian publication Military-Industrial Kurier. Gerasimov (2013 [2016]) wrote:

> New information technologies have enabled significant reductions in the spatial, temporal, and informational gaps between forces and control organs. Frontal engagements of large formations of forces at the strategic and operational level are gradually becoming a thing of the past. Long-distance, contactless actions against the enemy are becoming the main means of achieving combat and operational goals. The defeat of the enemy's objects [objectives] is conducted throughout the entire depth of his territory. The differences between strategic, operational, and tactical levels, as well as between offensive and defensive operations, are being erased.
>
> (p. 24)

Gerasimov (2013 [2016]) concluded that, by shaping the global information environment, today's Russia in particular is creating conditions for the successful achievement of state goals using both non-military and military methods. The use of soft power and hard power is underpinned with the use of informational power across the full spectrum of the information environment. Gerasimov (2013 [2016]) noted:

> Asymmetrical actions have come into widespread use, enabling the nullification of an enemy's advantages in armed conflict. Among such actions are the use of special operations forces and internal opposition to create a permanently operating front through the entire territory of the enemy state, as well as informational actions, devices, and means that are constantly being perfected. These ongoing changes are reflected in the doctrinal views of the world's leading states and are being used in military conflicts.
>
> (p. 25)

Previous studies of Russia's communication efforts have focused on media-oriented content or media effects, which are only part of the information environment. As previously noted, while such studies are helpful in their field, they are not able to deduce the larger strategy in play. To design a grand strategy level communication program, all facets of the information environment within which the organization resides must be engaged for maximum impact. The information environment is seen in military studies as an aggregate of individuals, organizations, and systems that collect, process, disseminate, or act on information (Department of Defense, 2012). Conversely, knowing how to deconstruct any communication program is critical to not only understand intent, but to know how to engage it effectively. Some communication programs are readily understandable because they follow traditional models. Others appear chaotic, uncoordinated, or inconsistent when seen through the lens of traditional communication models.

Many scholars have studied what exactly communication is and then have defined it, usually through the lens of the writer (Cobley, 2008; Craig, 1999; Craig, 2017; Eadie & Goret, 2013; Steinfatt, 2009). While most practitioners speak of communication as an exchange of information or symbols, almost all definitions, theories, or concepts about communication revolve around three foundational elements, or the communication triangle: *A sender, through a message, aims to generate a desired response*, identified as a change in knowledge, attitude, or behavior, *in a receiver*. Much like the fire, or combustion, triangle where oxygen, heat, and fuel are needed to make fire, without one of the three elements, sender, message, and receiver, communication *with intent* is simply not possible. The concept of *with intent* means that the sender intends by design to create a purposeful effect (a desired response) and, thus, that the communication is not random, casual, or undirected communication.

In analyzing strategic communication, knowing who the senders are, why they are sending the message (intent), and why they have selected the medium for that message are arguably more critical than is the message, itself. The history of public relations in Russia, for instance, shows that messages can be placed anywhere on the spectrum from white (truthful information with an identified author) to black (false information, information communicated in a non-transparent manner, and/or misleading or unidentified author) (Tsetsura, 2011). But analyzing information that is engineered to create an effect on face value of the content of the message provides little, if any, insight into the design or intent of the message. If the goal of the sender is to create chaos or confusion, they need only send two messages that contradict each other, from the same source, and others might spend hours debating over the communication contradiction, resulting in precious resources focused on the misdirected communication, while the real intent of the sender moves forward. Strategic communication requires intent. But strategic communication is also a process of coordination and synchronization of efforts.

Most Western discussions or studies are about non-kinetic communication, strategic communication, strategic public affairs, or integrated communications and focus on media-oriented issues (Kerr et al., 2008) or refer to "the coordinated use of a variety of different promotional communication tools toward a single objective" (Hallahan, 2007, p. 299), or involve the coordination of communication messages, channels, publics, and results (Groom, 2008; Kliatchko, 2008; Zvobgo & Melewar, 2011). None address communication as a holistic, all-of-organization spanning the range of non-kinetic and kinetic effect, with kinetic effect described here as communication through physical means used to express the meaning of the message. Most studies refer to, and often assess, only the observable and tactical level (e.g., products, outputs) of communication, while none appear to study communication as a strategic-level, *wicked problem* (Radford, 1977). Design theorist and university professor Horst Rittel first coined the term wicked problem (Churchman, 1967) to describe problems associated with planning and later went on to outline ten characteristics of a wicked problem (Rittel & Webber, 1973). In short, a wicked problem isn't a measure of difficulty but a problem where traditional or common processes can't be used due to incomplete, contradictory, or continually changing elements that are often difficult to recognize. As such, non-Western communication strategies and campaigns, from both state and nonstate entities, are often mislabeled and misunderstood, resulting in misinterpretation and wasted resources in addressing a problem that does not exist or attending to engineered misdirection. As Camillus (2008) pointed out, "Not only do conventional processes fail to tackle wicked problems, but they may exacerbate situations by generating undesirable consequences" (p. 1).

So, simply put, to understand the intent of communication, it is helpful to know the strategy behind the message (again, be that any combination of action and/or rhetoric). In some way or another, strategic communication can be measured at the message or tactical level—but, without the context or the frame, the communication can only be assessed in the eyes of the receiver versus that of the sender. In the terms of Claude Shannon, the father of "a mathematical theory to communication" commonly referred to as Information Theory (of which the digital age was born), this is the challenge with corresponding and noncorresponding systems (Severin & Tankard, 2001, p. 55). "Communication takes place when two corresponding systems, coupled together through one or more noncorresponding systems, assume identical states as a result of signal transfer along a chain" (Schramm, 1955, p. 132). This simply means that the information passed between the sender and receiver must share the same code, or level of information, for the receiver to understand the information sent by the sender. If the sender engineers the information (again, action or rhetoric or a combination of both) correctly, based on the intent and the strategy behind the intent, the sender can move the receiver toward a desired effect, while receivers of the message may or may be not be aware of efforts to change their knowledge, attitude, and/or behavior. This process is a foundation of engineered information, sometimes referred to as propaganda, information operations, or psychological operations. In the corporate world, this can be labeled as a persuasive function of advertising or marketing.

If the premise is accepted that knowing the strategy, or the intent, behind communication is a key in assessing communication, a definition of strategy would now be helpful. Adopting the views of Hart (1991), *strategy* is "the art of distributing and applying military means to fulfill the ends of policy" (p. 321), while *grand strategy* is "to coordinate and direct all the resources of a nation, or band of nations, toward the attainment of the political object of the goal defined by fundamental policy" (p. 322). This view has been, more or less, adopted by militaries, and the doctrine revolves around the levels of tactical, operational, and strategic. Botan (2006) sought to bring these concepts into the field of strategic communication and public relations. According to Botan, grand strategy is "the policy-level decisions an organization makes about goals, alignments, ethics and relationship with public and other forces in its environment" (p. 225) and is very similar to the whole-of-government view by Hart. Strategy is "campaign-level decision-making involving maneuvering and arranging resources and arguments to carry out organizational grand strategies" (Botan, 2006, p. 226). Again, similar to Hart, Botan categorizes tactics as the technical or task level of accomplishing activities and outputs to support the strategy. Messages in the media are nothing more than tactics, with the concept of the strategic message dismissible under this paradigm. This is why understanding strategy is the key to understanding the message, not the other way around.

If the entity is organized, a grand strategy is where government or organizational strategic communication starts. A governing body or individual generates a grand strategy based on a desired end state—and without a clearly defined and identified timeline. The timeline during which a certain goal should be achieved is not important nor necessary. A final outcome is accepted once the strategy is complete. That governing body or individual generates a strategy based on the foundational concepts that make up the government body or individual. Time becomes poly-chronic in achieving the result of the campaign: The evaluation of a strategic communication campaign's success would happen after the goal is achieved, regardless of the time it takes to achieve it. This drastically differs from the Western notion of a strategic communication campaign that is bound by a clearly defined, time-specific process: The goal and objectives should be clearly formulated, strategies and tactics should be spelled out and defined, messages should be clearly communicated to specific stakeholders and should follow the objectives, and the effect should be measured within an identified time frame. In the Western-organized campaign, the process is central, and the timeline is clear.

In the instance of a non-Western state or nonstate actor, the governing body or even one individual might drive the strategy of the state. The intent can be identified by the governing body or an individual, without clearly specifying the timeline, process, or ways to achieve it. An idea can be strategically ambiguous and unclear on purpose. Hence, identifying that body or individual and the authority they wield might be a key to understanding the intent behind the strategy. Understanding the intent helps focus the lens of communication such that both sender and receiver can encode and decode the information or action presented at the same frequency (level of understanding). Therein lies the key to unlocking what, at times, appears to be chaos. Engaging a grand strategy without knowing the intent of the governing body or individual is the same as engaging a wicked problem and addressing the problem on its face value.

In the case of Russia, most current Western analysts (Clunan, 2019; Peterson, 2019; Pezard & Rhoades, 2020) who assess leaders in charge of Russia's future understand the value of intent. Gerasimov (2013 [2016]) helps to illustrate the point:

> In the twenty-first century we have seen a tendency toward blurring the lines between the states of war and peace. Wars are no longer declared and, having begun, proceed according to an unfamiliar template. The experience of military conflicts--including those connected with the so-called color revolutions in North Africa and the Middle East--confirm that a perfectly thriving state can, in a matter of months and even days, be transformed into an arena of fierce armed conflict, become a victim of foreign intervention, and sink into a web of chaos, humanitarian catastrophe, and civil war. ...
>
>   New information technologies have enabled significant reductions in the spatial, temporal, and informational gaps between forces and control organs. Frontal engagements of large formations of forces at the strategic and operational level are gradually becoming a thing of the past. Long-distance, contactless actions against the enemy are becoming the main means of achieving combat and operational goals.
>
> (p. 24)

Gerasimov's comments provide insight to *intent* and *effect* that is holistic in nature and implementation. He refers to the information environment and informational power over hard or soft power well before other state actors. Of note, nonstate actors long recognized the use of informational power in lieu of military strength to achieve organizational goals well before any state actors.

The information environment, a grand strategy, and wicked problems are complex and adaptive system of systems, enabling each system (i.e., functional area) to work together toward a common goal—but independently in operations, tactics, and intermediate objectives. As described by Radford (1977), *wicked problems* have several characteristics, which include inadequate information is available to decision makers, multiple and conflicting objectives are involved, several decision makers are involved, the problem environment is dynamic and turbulent, several such problems are linked together, and resolution may involve costly, irreversible commitments. Un-coding a wicked problem or grand strategy requires more than a single lens of analysis and, in the case of communication, more than the traditional lens of public relations or social science tools of study.

We introduce *Effects-Based Communication* (EBC) as an inductive method to deconstructing a grand strategy or a wicked problem as well as a method to construct a grand strategy. EBC is defined here as a *systematic approach in achieving desired effects through the holistic use of all organizational means and methods available in support of an organizational grand strategy.*

EBC is a relatively new concept, first explored by the primary author in 2005, with roots in the concept of *effects-based operations*, which can be found in more than 70 studies (Jobbagy, 2003). Effects-based operations and effects-based communication share common ground and start with an emphasis on the importance of knowledge of self and of the opposition, viewed as a complex adaptive system. This is central to the premise of knowing the organization or individual *and their intent*. For example, studies such as Feklyunina (2008), Clunan (2019), and Pezard and Rhoades (2020) provide excellent insights into the foundational concepts of Russia's strategic communications on behalf of the state. Such studies begin to reveal the strategic and underpinning intent needed to decode actions and rhetoric.

The premise of EBC is based on achieving effects through available means of the actor in support of a grand strategy. EBC enables any partner or element of the organization, regardless of culture, economic, financial, or military resources, to contribute to the desired effects and/or objectives and/or the end state, while using different communication models, functional areas, products, and outputs of the specific system or element. EBC centers around effects, speed of engagement, opportunistic engagement, economy of force, and efficiency and utilizes the end state, objectives, and desired effects as operational variables for implementation and assessment. EBC is an enduring, long-term communication model that is ultimately concerned neither with tactical products and outputs nor with messages. Products and messages are often focused on at the functional (tactical) level and are coordinated in implementation and content and synchronized in time through the process of strategic communication. EBC is solely concerned with a creation of a purposeful effect, regardless of time or process. For EBC, it does not necessarily matter how and when one gets there: what matters is that one achieves the desired effect. This freedom from coordinating outputs and products, specifically actions and messages, gives effects-based communication its speed and flexibility. Such a model does not require layers of leadership to approve tactical-level actions or messages. The effects-based model enables functional areas to be opportunistic in nature, quickly seizing moments and taking advantage of them faster than can opponents, who often need time to seek permission to engage or to clear actions and products with higher headquarters.

One key characteristic of EBC is that it is not guided by timetables or deadlines. When a strategy is pinned to a timeline, it has a built-in weakness from the beginning. Western cultures place great reliance on time, which we call *short-sighted*, whereas some cultures, such as in China and perhaps in Russia, strategies and progress are measured in generations, a *long view* of time. The pressure of time is the most intense stressor and is the most abrasive of all—it is the enemy of most strategies that are dependent on accomplishing an end state by a given date or time. We argue that the strategy with the most time flexibility would be most successful. Because EBC has no temporal restrictions, this approach can also be used to exhaust resources of the other side (e.g., a political will of the opponent).

Given the absence of a temporal restriction, it can be challenging for large corporate bodies to engage in EBC if they have no or little flexibility built into their structures. Thus, communication strategies of some Western corporations working in Russia, for instance, might be *short-sighted* in that sense, while the environment in which they operate has largely a *long view*. As a result, these entities might be burning resources and exhausting stakeholder patience by incorrectly assessing their operating environment.

In EBC, phases, and phase changes, drive a set of desired effects assigned to them. When a set of desired effects is accomplished, the next phase is implemented with its new desired effects. The absence of time enables progress to flow in either direction, regressing when needed to recreate desired effects and advancing when possible. This flexibility gives EBC its inherent ability to address wicked problems, which often do not adhere to linear timelines or schedules, but tend to live on the *edge of chaos*, where traditional analysis using the information environment would label actions and behaviors as contradictory in nature or labeled as inconsistent.

An implementer of EBC might appear to have chaotic and/or inconsistent messaging that is not connected with the parent organization. An actor can also sometimes engage in actions that do not appear to match rhetoric. But that does not necessarily mean there is a lack of grand strategy behind such communication. EBC can be used by any organization that has a strong, established, and dominant leadership, an agreed-upon organizational vision defined by the end goal, and that has the ability to disseminate intermediate objectives supporting desired effects to contributing elements and partners, and that is not overly concerned with temporal restrictions. In other words, with a strong vertical system of dissemination, the organization can effectively utilize EBC if the leadership of the organization wields power and control at the highest levels.

While it is not within the scope of this chapter to fully explicate EBC, the intent is to impart the knowledge that, to understand and successfully engage a state or nonstate actor, the correct lens must be used when analyzing the information environment and the intent of the organization or individual being observed in that environment. EBC is a nontraditional communication approach that is potentially capable of identifying the intent of a grand strategy and deconstructing engineered chaos.

The theoretical implication of EBC is that it challenges many Western views and concepts of strategic communication, which mainly operate at the message-driven tactical level. There are very few ways to understand communication that truly resides at the grand strategy level. Unfortunately, some approaches attempt this by adding the term "strategic" to imply a higher level of operation, moving from tactical to operational, or operational to strategic—yet still using a tactical-level lens, principles, and methods. EBC also presents the ability of state and nonstate actors to engage more powerful or sizeable opponents with far fewer resources or effort. As it is still a relatively new concept, EBC needs further explication and examination. Is it possible for EBC to be used by a Western entity, given the cultural requirement to adhere to timelines? If a non-Western actor uses EBC, how can a Western actor engage or counter this approach, equivalent to a twenty-first century version of a siege by informational power?

Overall, the effect-based communication approach to strategic communication in Russia provides a fresh approach to understanding how goals can be achieved in a multi-layered and dynamic environment. EBC reflects and centers around a multifaceted, complex reality of global multi-cultural public relations, which is based on fluid human practices that Rittenhofer and Valentini (2015) referred to as "swarms" (p. 12). Actors who engage in strategic communications practices in Russia should continuously recognize what they do and what they say (action and rhetoric) in light of localized shifting effect-based practices. Such "swarm conduct" (Rittenhofer & Valentini, 2015, p. 15) and public relations practitioners should seamlessly be incorporated into decision-making processes of organizations. EBC appeals to fluidity and constant change within the scope. It also allows for more accurate assessment of the importance of grand strategy within strategic communication of Russia.

Theoretical implications of EBC in Russia's strategic communications are immense. First, studying strategic communication in Russia should include a detailed analysis and examination of the intent, as well as effects and grand strategy, regardless of whether state or nonstate actors appear to communicate strategically. Understanding the intent and the connection to the end goal and/or grand strategy might also be a fruitful pursuit of novel, unique ways of understanding strategic communication in many environments beyond Russia.

Practically speaking, identifying the intent and focusing on the effects, rather than on processes, might provide additional insights into an understanding of multiple approaches to strategic communication in Russia. Identifying the intent and focusing on the effects may also encourage a more comprehensive and accurate response from global companies and other state and nonstate actors. Instead of dismissing Russia's communication as nonstrategic and chaotic, EBC can help to highlight a true meaning behind communication intended for certain stakeholders and for specific purposes. For Western companies and governments that are trying to understand strategic communication in Russia, the most critical point is to understand that Western and non-Western models of communication are expected to be present in contemporary Russia and are practiced together, sometimes simultaneously, to highlight the effects-based environment and presence of grand strategy within strategic communication. That is why we see the effect-based communication as a fruitful approach for understanding strategic communication in various environments.

References

Argenti, P. A., Howell, R. A., & Beck, K. A. (2005). The strategic communication imperative. *MIT Sloan Management Review (SMR)*, *46*(3), 83–89.

Bardach-Yalov, E. (2012). Analyzing Russian propaganda: Application of Siegfried Krakauer's qualitative content analysis method. *Journal of Information Warfare*, *11*(2), 24–36.

Botan, C. (2006). Grand strategy, strategy, and tactics in public relations. In C. Botan & V. Hazleton (Eds.), *Public relations theory II* (pp. 223–247). Mahwah, NJ: Lawrence Erlbaum Associates.

Boudreau, B., LePage, R., & Curika, L. (2016). *We have met the enemy and he is us: An analysis of NATO strategic communications: The international security assistance force in Afghanistan, 2003–2014.* NATO Strategic Communication Centre of Excellence. www.stratcomcoe.org/we-have-met-enemy-and-he-us-analysis-nato-strategic-communications-international-security-assistance.

Camillus, J. (2008). Strategy as a wicked problem. *Harvard Business Review.* May. https://hbr.org/2008/05/strategy-as-a-wicked-problem.

Casier, T. (2019). Understanding Russia's security strategy in a context of power. In R. E. Kanet (Ed.), *Handbook of Russian security* (pp. 89–96). Abingdon, UK: Routledge.

Churchman, C. W. (1967). Wicked problems. *Management Science*, 14(4), B-141 and B-142.

Clunan, A. L. (2019). Russia's pursuit of great-power status and security. In R. E. Kanet (Ed.), *Handbook of Russian security* (pp. 3–16). Abingdon, UK: Routledge.

Cobley, P. (2008). Communication: Definitions and concepts. In W. Donbback (Ed.), *International encyclopedia of communication.* Oxford, UK and Malden, MA: Blackwell. DOI: 10.1002/9781405186407.wbiecc071.

Cornish, P., Lindley-French, J., & Yorke, C. (2011). *Strategic communications and national strategy: A Chatham House report.* www.chathamhouse.org/sites/default/files/r0911es%E2%80%93stratcomms.pdf.

Craig, R.T. (1999). Communication theory as a field. *Communication Theory*, *9*, 119–161.

Craig, R. T. (2017). Definitions and concepts of communication. *Communication.* DOI: 10.1093/obo/9780199756841-0172.

Department of Defense (2012). *Information operations.* Joint Publication 3–13. Defense Technical Information Center. www.jcs.mil/Portals/36/Documents/Doctrine/pubs/jp3_13.pdf.

Eadie, W. F., & Goret, R. (2013). Theories and models of communication: Foundations and heritage. In P. Cobley, & P. J. Schulz (Eds.), *Handbooks of communication science, HOCS 1* (pp. 17–36). Berlin and Boston: De Gruyter Mouton.

Endaltseva, A. (2015). The present state of integrated communication in Russia. *Public Relations Review, 41*(4), 533–540.

Feklyunina, V. (2008). Battle for perceptions: Projecting Russia in the West. *Europe-Asia Studies, 60*(4), 605–629.

Gerasimov, V. (2013/2016). The value of science is in the foresight: New challenges demand rethinking the forms and methods of carrying out combat operations (Article in Russian published in Military-Industrial Kurier; translated). *Military Review, 96*(1), 23–29. https://jmc.msu.edu/50th/download/21-conflict.pdf.

Groom, S. A. (2008). Integrated marketing communication: Anticipating the "age of engage." *Communication Research Trends, 27*(4), 3–19.

Hallahan, K. (2007). Integrated communication: Implications for public relations beyond excellence. In E. L. Toth (Ed.), *The future of excellence in public relations and communication management* (pp. 299–336). Mahwah, NJ: Lawrence Erlbaum Associates.

Hart, B. H. L. (1991). *Strategy* (2nd revised ed.). New York: Penguin.

Herd, G. P. (2019). Putin's operational code and strategic decision-making in Russia. In R. E. Kanet (Ed.), *Handbook of Russian Security* (pp. 17–29). Abingdon, UK: Routledge.

Iyengar S., & Massey, D. S. (2018). *Scientific communication in a post-truth society.* Proceedings of the National Academy of Sciences of the USA. https://doi.org/10.1073/PNAS.1805868115.

Ivanov, I. S., & Kissinger, H. A. (2002). An overview of Russian Foreign Policy. *The New Russian Diplomacy* (pp. 7–38). Washington, DC: Brookings Institution Press.

Jobbagy, Z. (2003). *Literature survey on effects-based operations: A Ph. D. study on measuring military effects and effectiveness.* The Hague: TNO Physics and Electronics Laboratory. www.iwar.org.uk/rma/resources/ebo/Literature_survey_on_Effects-Based_Operations.pdf.

Kerr, G., Schultz, D., Patti, C., & Kim, I. (2008). An inside-out approach to integrated marketing communication: An international analysis. *International Journal of Advertising, 27*(4), 511–548.

Kliatchko, J. (2008). Revisiting the IMC construct: A revised definition and four pillars. *International Journal of Advertising, 27*(1), 133–160.

Kracauer, S. (1952). The challenge of qualitative content analysis. *The Public Opinion Quarterly, 16*(4), 631–642.

Kristensen, K. S., & Sakstrup, C. (2016). Interpreting Russian policy. Russian policy in the Arctic after the Ukraine crisis. Report. *Centre for Military Studies.* https://cms.polsci.ku.dk/english/publications/russian-policy-in-the-arctic/Russian_Policy_in_the_Arctic_after_the_Ukraine_Crisis.pdf.

Kumar, K. (2017). *The Russian and Soviet empires. Visions of empire.* Princeton, NJ: Princeton University Press.

Lewandowsky S., Ecker U. K. H., & Cook, J. (2017). Beyond misinformation: Understanding and coping with the "post-truth" era. *Journal of Applied Research in Memory and Cognition, 6*(4), 353–369.

Meister, S. (Ed.). (2018). *Understanding Russian communication strategy: Case studies of Serbia and Estonia* (ifa Edition Culture and Foreign Policy). Stuttgart: ifa (Institut für Auslandsbeziehungen). https://nbn-resolving.org/urn:nbn:de:0168-ssoar-59979-0.

NATO (2009). PO(2009)0141 (2009) NATO Strategic Communications Policy, Brussels: NATO.

Paul, C., & Matthews, M. (2016). *The Russian "Firehose of Falsehood" propaganda model: Why it might work and options to counter it.* RAND Corporation Report. www.rand.org/pubs/perspectives/PE198.html.

Peterson, N. (2019). *Russian strategic intentions: A strategic multilayer assessment (SMA).* The U.S. Department of Defense (DoD) Strategic Multilayer Assessment (SMA) program. White Paper. https://nsiteam.com/sma-publications/.

Pezard, S., & Rhoades, A. (2020). *What provokes Putin's Russia? Deterring without unintended escalation.* RAND Report. www.rand.org/pubs/perspectives/PE338.html.

Radford, K. (1977). *Complex decision problems: An integrated strategy for resolution.* Reston, VA: Reston Publishing.

Radin, A., & Reach, C. (2017). *Russian views of the international order.* Santa Monica, CA: RAND Corporation. www.rand.org/pubs/research_reports/RR1826.html.

Rittel, H. W. J., & Webber, M. M. (1973). Dilemmas in a general theory of planning. *Policy Sciences, 4* (2): 155–169. doi:10.1007/bf01405730.

Rittenhofer, I., & Valentini, C. (2015). A "practice turn" for global public relations: An alternative approach. *Journal of Communication Management, 19,* 2–19.

Schramm, W. (1955). Information theory and mass communication. *Journalism Quarterly, 32,* 131–146.

Severin, W. J., & Tankard, J. W. (2001). *Communication theories: Origins, methods, and uses in the mass media.* New York: Longman.

Steinfatt, T. M. (2009). Definitions of communication. In S. W. Littlejohn & K. A. Foss (Eds.), *Encyclopedia of communication theory* (pp. 295–299). Thousand Oaks, CA: Sage.

Tashev, B., Purcell, M., & McLaughlin, B. (2019). Russia's information warfare: Exploring the cognitive dimension. *MCU Journal, 10,* 129–147. www.usmcu.edu/Portals/218/CAOCL/files/RussiasInformationWarfare_MCUJ_Fall2019.pdf?ver=2019-11-19-093543-040.

Theohary, C. A. (2018) *Information warfare: Issues for Congress.* Congressional Research Service. https://fas.org/sgp/crs/natsec/R45142.pdf.

Tsetsura, K. (2011). Cultural and historical aspects of media transparency in Russia. In A. G. Nikolaev (Ed.), *Ethics issues in international communication* (pp. 172–182). New York: Palgrave Macmillan.

van der Linden S., Maibach E., Cook J., Leiserowitz A., & Lewandowsky, S. (2017). Inoculating against misinformation. *Science, 358*(6367), 1141–1142.

Zvobgo, M., & Melewar, T. C. (2011). Drivers of globally integrated marketing communications: A review of literature and research propositions. *Journal of Promotion Management, 17,* 1–20.

15 Conclusion

What is next for strategic communication(s) in Russia?

Katerina Tsetsura

What is next for strategic communication(s) in Russia?

This book has presented a variety of contextualized approaches and ways to examine strategic communication(s) in Russia. As the book has demonstrated, this is an exciting time of great opportunity for Russian communication scholars and educators, their students, and the nation's communication professionals. This chapter focuses on current issues that are relevant to strategic communication(s), public relations, and advertising in Russia, as perceived by Russian communication scholars and practitioners. The chapter intentionally uses the term *strategic communication(s)* to highlight the ambiguity and unsettlement among specialists in Russia on the use of the term, because it has been previously discussed and used in this book in both singular and plural forms, depending on its use in primary sources. Building on discussions of the field of strategic communication(s) in Russia that have been presented in this book, this concluding chapter summarizes the latest research and public discussions among professionals in Russia that have been published in Russian on the present and future of strategic communication(s), particularly in public relations and advertising. The chapter discusses various trends in strategic communication(s) that are prevalent in contemporary discussions about the field and the industry in public discourses among Russian professionals and highlights issues relevant to contemporary strategic communication(s) in Russia.

Finally, the chapter considers the future of theory and practice of strategic communication(s), public relations, and advertising in the country and recommends approaches that might help scholars and practitioners throughout the world to better understand the nature and functions of strategic communication(s) in Russia, today and tomorrow.

The present and the future of communications, according to the Russian Association of Public Relations

In 2017, the Russian Association of Public Relations (RASO) published a white paper on the trends and issues in communication specific to the Russian practice and market. The report, titled, "About the Future of Communications", was produced with support from the Center of Social Planning "Platform" and from the Department of Integrated Communications of the National Research University Higher School of Economics in Moscow, Russia. The report identified communication challenges and introduced an outline for successful strategic communications of the future. This report in many ways presents and recognizes challenges that the profession faces around the world. Yet, the report is unique to the Russian market and, thus, is worthy of further examination. This section presents a translated summary of the report and reflects on its conclusions.

The report begins by recognizing these communication challenges that are prevalent in the contemporary practice of communications in Russia (RASO, 2017):

1) Non-understanding among people (general lack of understanding that prevails in today's world);
2) Resistance to interact with "the others" (particularly, in light of increasing divisions and informational bubbles);
3) Differentiation of experience (the blurred boundaries of common behaviors and experiences);
4) Changes in the carrier of subject-ness (the subjects today are three equally important groups: Individual, community, and humanity as a whole);
5) New technologies (and their effect on communication);
6) Properties of the new workplace (influenced by automotization and Artificial Intelligence);
7) New management technologies (e.g., blockchain and crowdsourcing);
8) Changes in education technologies (particularly, the rise of the need for continuous education and micro-formats of educational content);
9) Localization and decentralization (specifically, distancing from official channels of communication in favor of social media forums and localization and individualization of experiences).

These identified challenges should not surprise any Western communication professionals, neither academics nor practitioners, who have been active in the field during the past decade. After all, professionals throughout the world face similar challenges and issues. The recent studies of communication practices in various regions, such as European Communication, North American Communication, and Asia-Pacific Communication Monitors, identified and highlighted these challenges throughout the years (Communication Monitor, 2019).

RASO's report also offered the future for communications by highlighting these ten trends (RASO, 2017):

1) Personalization, which means that all future communication and interaction will be further personalized.

2) Audience in Dynamics: The concept of the target audience will become dynamic, meaning that public discourse participation and geolocation will also contribute to furthering the target audience.

3) "Dear Leonid Valentinovich": A highly individualized approach will be central to all communication; naming people by their names would be a must.

4) Live Communication: As technology-centered communicated grows, the need and desire for live human interactions will be increasingly in demand.

5) Care and Help: The most valuable currency will be time. As such, people would expect from companies not only omnichannel communications but also in-depth integration into one's life through assistance with everyday problems while reflecting on emotional human reaction to every interaction.

6) Craft Content: Personalized storytelling will be at the center of communication.

7) Emotional Communications: All communications will be interactive, with a goal of evoking fast, strong emotions.

8) Elite Offline: Elites will spend less time online to clean their digital footprint and to prioritize analogue, face-to-face communication.

9) Elite and Mass Content: An important differential for the elites will be an ability to comprehend long-form content whereas mass publics would prefer mass more compact, short forms of communication.

10) Competition for Offline: Those who can find a way to get publics interested in interactions offline will win a competition for the precious minutes of attention from the individual who is increasingly shrouded in information and lives in troubled times.

As evident from these ten trends, the focus of the future among public relations professionals in Russia is centered around a growing interest in how technology affects our communication and society in general as well as on comprehensive understanding of the future of the industry as increasingly personalized, global, and, in some ways, divided. What is also evident from this report is that the Russian Association of Public Relations recognizes the need to collaborate with multiple professional associations and organizations in the country and throughout the world to address challenges effectively. At the end of the report, RASO even argues for unification of all national professional organizations into one entity to unite a self-regulatory function of the profession. It is yet to be seen whether calls for unification would bear any fruit because multiple national and international professional organizations and associations have established their strong presence in Russia in the past 30 years. For example, today Russia has seven associations that specifically position themselves as organizations for public relations professionals, and most of them are quite active and have a strong following:

1) Association of Companies and Consultancies in Public Relations, or AKOS (a Russian Chapter of ICCO);
2) Association of Communication Agencies in Russia (AKAR), which unites advertisers and other communication specialists);
3) Russian Association of Public Relations (RASO);
4) Association of Directors in Communications and Corporate Media in Russia (AKMR);
5) IABC-Russia;
6) Russian Academy of Public Relations (RAOS), which mostly is interested in developing standards of the profession and supporting educational projects;
7) Association of Educators in Public Relations (APSO).

As a result, any discussion about unification might be a bit premature. Nevertheless, the interest in self-regulation and systematic, continuous efforts to develop professional standards and, correspondingly, to influence educational programs and requirements, clearly demonstrates an ample endeavor to professionalize the occupation of public relations in Russia. A broader area of strategic communication(s), however, remains more elusive and all-encompassing as a field.

Trends in communications and advertising, according to Russian advertising professionals

Association of Communication Agencies of Russia, or ACAR (formerly known as a Russian Association of Advertising Agencies), is another leading professional association in Russia that unites advertising specialists and communication professionals. ACAR also systematically organizes professional conferences and workshops and publishes trend and research reports that examine various aspects of the Russian advertising and communication market. ACAR covers a large area of activities and produces several reports and white papers, ranging from crisis communications recommendations to companies to sports sponsorship trends and effectiveness of advertising on TV and online media, as well as on brand monitoring. According to ACAR, the volume of internet-only advertising in Russia was 203 billion rubles, or approximately 3.2 billion USD, in 2018, which was larger than any other media segment, including TV, radio, and print, and accounted for 43% of the total advertising in the media (RBK/ACAR, 2020). Understandably, current efforts of professionals are centered around Internet-based advertising practices. Recognizing that the Russian advertising market differs from those in the United States and Europe, a group of advertising professionals recently attempted to identify trends in media advertising in Russia. After interviews with several leading advertising and communication experts, the authors offered these trends (AdIndex, 2019a):

1) The growing popularity of programming and the expansion of advertising inventory and formats, including expansion of automated advertising purchasing and native advertising.
2) Development of brand media and personalized content.
3) Media as a data generator, which further allows advertisers to segment the audiences and customize messaging.
4) Growth of data-driven advertising campaigns.
5) Growth of the e-commerce sector.
6) Continuing popularity of video.
7) Continuing confrontation between the media and news channels.
8) Text-only communication no longer works.

Advertising leaders in Russia unanimously named digitalization and specialized content development as two major trends for advertising in 2019 (AdIndex, 2019b). Overall, despite many claims that the Russian market has its own, unique particularities, Russian professionals tend to cite the same trends and developments affecting the industry that are discussed by the international professional organizations and associations, such as the Native Advertising Institute, among others (see Native Advertising Institute, 2019). It is yet to be seen whether Russian advertising practitioners can clearly articulate those unique national differences, beyond simple cultural adaptation.

One possible explanation of the difficulty to articulate challenges might be anticipatory socialization, a process in which out-of-group members, through social interactions, learn to take on values and standards of the group they aspire to join (Jablin, 1987). An ever-growing pressure of newcomers to socialize into the profession, particularly in this field that is relatively new and that still continues to establish its boundaries as a professionalized occupation, is typical for public relations (Taylor & Kent, 2010). Taylor and Kent demonstrate how anticipatory socialization, for instance, influences conversations about the importance of social media among public relations professionals in the United States, even if no undisputed evidence of the effective use of social media in public relations was available. It is quite possible that the public relations and advertising professionals in Russia also experience anticipatory socialization pressures, not only inside their own country but also on the global arena, as they seek to establish themselves as experts in the eyes of international clients and fellow professionals globally.

A desire to adapt to expectations of global clients and to demonstrate an understanding and reflection on global market challenges can also contribute to global view on trends and issues that are relevant to contemporary strategic communication(s). Such inadvertent colonization of strategic communications, public relations, and advertising practices by the Western models and ideas have been present in Russia since the early dawn of the industry (Tsetsura & Kruckeberg, 2004). A wish to espouse the Western view on the industry, however, can be seen as increasingly problematic, given the tensions between

Russia and the West. Hence, a longing to articulate a unique Russian way of thinking about and acting upon strategic communication(s) might also drive some discussions about the distinctiveness of Russian communications.

Strategic communication(s) of the future, according to Russian educators

Much of this book introduced perspectives of Russian-speaking scholars and educators on strategic communication(s) as a field and as an industry. A growing number of scholars, educators, and practitioners in Russia actively discuss the present and the future of strategic communication(s), specifically public relations and advertising, at multiple regional, national, and international conferences. There is no shortage of opportunities to exchange knowledge and ideas inside and outside the country, although many of the regional experts and academics are geo-bound due to limited funding that is available to travel outside their regions. A growing presence of Russian-speaking communication educators at international academic and practical conferences, including annual events organized by the International Communication Association and by the Global Alliance's World PR Forum among others, certainly enriches academic discussions.

Additionally, an increasingly large number of academics and practitioners are able to share their points of view online and through various public forums. Although some exchanges happen in English, sometimes misunderstandings may occur because of cultural or language barriers. Still, it is crucial for the global community to be exposed to the ideas and discussions of Russian-speaking professionals about the future of the field and the industry. Although this chapter does not attempt to present an all-encompassing view on the future of strategic communication(s) in Russia, some novel, fresh ideas from Russian-speaking scholars who recently publicly shared their visions of the future are worthy of mentioning to illustrate the breadth of thinking about the future among educators, many of whom often also work in the industry.

Many Russian scholars demonstrate a continuous focus on the critical evaluation of the field and the industry as a whole. For instance, Gavra and Dekalov (2018), in their recent research, expanded the use of *communicative capitalism*, a meta-theoretical model that examines a contemporary stage of societal development as a novel format of neoliberalism (Dean, 2010), to the context of political economy of attention and to the examination of the subject of the automotive digital environment. They argued that the possession of information and of technical powers in the future is destined to become a basis for a new social stratification. That means that, in the future, according to Gavra (Stratcom, 2018), at least in business communication, interpersonal communication would be replaced by the inter-bot communication and the work of the future public relations specialist will be centered on consulting and, perhaps, communication therapy and communicative animation (entertaining).

In turn, Artemieva, a director of external communications of the large retail company Ashan and an adjunct at the Moscow Advanced Communication School (MACS), believes that the focus on individual human communication will continue to grow and dominate (Artemieva, 2018). She argued that people are at the epicenter of communication and that news and communication about companies and organizations should focus around news about people. Cogitating on the future of public relations, Artemieva noted that, on the one hand, a rapid digitalization and robotization affect the industry; on the other hand, the necessity in simple human communication is still relevant. She continued that, in the optimistic scenario, the profession of communication specialist would become more imperative and would occupy a leading position in the company; in the pessimistic version, it would be broken up into pieces and would be divided into narrow specializations. She summarized her ideas by alluding to what Tsetsura (2011) called a co-construction of the public relations field, "Whether communicators will lead key processes in business and reputation management or dissolve in niche tasks depends on us and our actions" (Artemieva, 2018).

Trubnikova, an area head of advertising and business communications at the Institute of World Economy and Law in the RUDN University, agreed that strategic communication would depend on the future generation of professionals (RUDN, 2019). Speaking at the 2019 conference on future directions of advertising, Trubnikova said that the new realities require a new understanding of modern communications. Public relations or advertising on its own would not be able to succeed, and a comprehensive impact on the minds and feelings of stakeholders would need to be supported by event-based activities. According to Trubnikova, the young professionals who just enter the industry would have to realize this trend and act upon it.

A comprehensive Russian-based understanding of what the field of strategic communication(s) encompasses is also visible from the description of the program offered by one of the leading universities in Russia, MGIMO University (Moscow State Institute of International Relations, an official higher education institution of the Ministry of Foreign Affairs of Russia). The official website of MGIMO, a university that offers a Master's program in "New Media and Strategic Communications", defines strategic communications as "establishing long-term relations of the organization—state, political, public, commercial—with society" (MGIMO, 2020, online). The description continued:

> Strategic communications form the image and reputation of the organization and the individual, increase competitiveness and profitability, and ensure political, social and economic success. Finally, strategic communications as the most important component of 'soft power' are aimed at solving the problem of informational support of the foreign policy of the modern state. (MGIMO, 2020, online)

This understanding of strategic communication(s) brings us to one more way of thinking about the future—the future (or, some might argue, the present) in which strategic communication(s) is understood as a process to define a national strategy and pursue state interests.

Future of strategic communications as a way to influence foreign audiences

Any discussion of the present and future of strategic communication(s) in Russia needs to include perspectives of those who see strategic communication(s) through the lens of political and government communication and national strategy. Recognition of public affairs and government relations (GR) as one of the main areas within public relations, and more broadly political strategic communication(s), has had a long history in Russia. After all, the very first Russian public relations and strategic communications agency, "Nikkolo M", started as a political consultancy agency in early 1990s (Tsetsura, 2004).

Since then, a history of political consulting has been intertwined with public relations and strategic communications practices in Russia. Much of the propaganda-based critique has also been based on the very idea that strategic communication (and certainly public relations) is a fancy word for *good, old political propaganda*. Russian communication scholars, as well as international relations specialists and military and security analysts, often use the term strategic communication to describe measures that the Department of Defense and other U.S. government agencies implement to influence foreign audiences (Burlakov, 2016). In other words, the concept of strategic communication has been used by some Russian scholars to describe a new trend that increasingly influences public diplomacy (Tsvetkova, 2015). It has been labeled as "a dialogic propaganda, which was used by the United States during the Cold War, but today has returned into practice of the American foreign policy in a slightly modified form" (Tsvetkova, 2015, p. 122). Tsvetkova continued:

> The introduction of the concept of 'strategic communication' leads to changes in the work of the departmental mechanism, financing, regional priorities, target audiences and the content of public diplomacy. As a result, Washington's behavior in the international arena is also evolving.
>
> (p. 122)

Strategic communication is often discussed in relation to other related terms, such as soft power, smart power, digital diplomacy, and informational power, introduced by Western (e.g., Armitage & Nye, 2007; Ross, 2011) and interpreted by Russian scholars (Bogdanov, 2017; Philimonov & Tsaturyan, 2012; Tsvetkova, 2011; Yudin, 2015). As a result, an increasing number of academic articles, published in Russian, focuses on strategic communication(s) as a tool, process, or concept as it relates to public diplomacy and foreign policy, with its roots in the use of strategic communication by the U.S. government toward foreign audiences (Burlakov, 2016). Such interpretation, reasonably so, takes the field of strategic communication(s) into the trans-disciplinary universe and expands its boundaries well beyond Western, business-focused understanding of public relations and advertising. A few chapters in this book incorporated, or at least alluded to, this approach toward strategic communication(s) of Russia. The future of such understanding, however, would largely depend on continuous co-construction of the field among Russian communication scholars, educators, and practitioners, who will be the ones to determine whether such adaptation and interpretation of the term strategic communication(s) is pertinent, relevant, and applicable to Russia's communication efforts.

Final thoughts

Based on the examination of discussions among Russian communication professionals, it is clear that the future of strategic communication(s) in Russia can be classified into three distinct areas: (1) strategic communications in the context of business; (2) strategic communications in the context of society; and (3) strategic communications in the context of the information environment and global security.

Trends and issues in Russian strategic communication(s) in the context of business largely follow overall global trends and issues. That can be explained by the global market dominance and, thus, dominance of the functional approach to global public relations and advertising. The second area, strategic communication(s) in the context of society, has a distinctive interpretation and understanding of the field, largely based on the global trends and issues related to technology and increasingly fragmented society. The use of strategic communication(s) practices and techniques to achieve specific goals is becoming more automated and personalized. A managerial approach to understanding changes in the society dominates a public relations discourse among Russian scholars and practitioners. What is largely missing from this Russian discourse, however, is recognition of a societal function of public relations that allows for civic participation in the fully functioning society (Heath, 2018). It is no surprise then that some academics and practitioners still see strategic communication(s), or public relations, simply as another fancy word for propaganda.

Finally, the third approach to understanding strategic communication(s) is largely connected with the informational environment and global security and is based on public diplomacy and security studies in the West. This approach is sometimes driven by studies of informational power, informational warfare, and psychology of manipulation on the global scale. As such, strategic communication(s) focuses on understanding the strategy of communication as an end goal and considers communication as a tool for achieving a desired action. It is still a very functional approach to strategic communication(s), which is based on the a priori idea that the roots of strategic communication(s) are in propaganda and in psychological and socio-psychological manipulation of masses, magnified and elevated to the novel era of sophistication, thanks to the modern technologies and transformation of global online communications.

That brings us to a unique perspective, a distinctive understanding of strategic communication(s), that is manifested by some Russian communication scholars and practitioners. Juxtaposition and confrontation of Russia and the West are quite typical for explaining and interpreting actions of Russia in the West (see, for instance, Anno, 2019; Glaser, 2019; Martinez, 2013; Patomaki & Pursiainen, 1999). Strategic communication(s) is no exception. Although some Russian strategic communication(s) academics and practitioners focus their discussions on such confrontation (e.g., Panarin, 2018), it would not be accurate to label this view as dominant. A more accurate way would be to distinguish among the three aforementioned areas in which strategic communication(s) operate: Business, society, and global politics. Each of these areas has an important function and role to play in Russian communication(s) and needs to be justly recognized and further examined.

This book has scrutinized Russian strategic communication(s) as a concept, discipline, and area of scholarly inquiry. This book also has discussed Russian models of communication education and professional practice. We hope that this book can be a catalyst to discussions and dialogues among Russian-speaking scholars, educators, students, and practitioners and their counterparts elsewhere throughout the world. This volume has recognized paradigmatic commonalities and has identified and attempted to reconcile Russian communication paradigms that are incongruent with those that had originated and have evolved elsewhere. However, in twenty-first-century global society, globally applicable theories, normative models of education, and benchmark professional practices should be sought. Russian scholars, educators, students, and professionals are eager to participate in this quest, and, as this book has demonstrated, they can certainly contribute significantly to global discussions, dialogues, and collaborations. The future of strategic communication(s), in Russia and throughout the world, will be co-constructed through these ongoing pursuits, and rightly so.

References

AdIndex. (2019a, February 27). *8 trendov reklamy v media 2019* [Eight trends of advertising in the media 2019]. Online post. Retrieved from https://adindex.ru/publication/opinion/media/2019/02/26/270206.phtml.

AdIndex. (2019b). *Reklamnye* itogi 2019 [Advertising results 2019]. Online post. Retrieved from https://adindex.ru/specprojects/industry/index.phtml.

Anno, T. (2019). *National identity and great power status in Russia and Japan: Non-western challengers to the liberal international order.* New York: Routledge.

Armitage, R., & Nye J. (2007). *CSIS Commission on Smart Power: A smarter, more secure America.* Washington, DC: Center for International and Strategic Studies.

Artemieva, S. (2018, September 13). *PR buduschego: Vse zavisit ot nas* [PR of the future: Everything depends on us]. Online post. Retrieved from https://exlibris.ru/news/pr-budushhego-vse-zavisit-ot-nas/.

Bogdanov, S. V. (2017). Strategicheskie kommunikatsii: Kontseptualnye podxody i modeli dlya gosudarstvennogo upravlenija [Strategic communications: Conceptual approaches and models for government management]. *Gosudarstvennoe Upravlenie. Elektronnyj Vestnik* [Government Management. Electronic Vestnik], *61*, 132–152.

Bulakov, V. (2016). Strategicheskaja kommunikatsija kak metod sovremennoj geopolitiki [Strategic communication as a method of modern geopolitics]. *Ojkumena. Regionovedcheskie issledovania* [Ecumene. Regional Studies], *2*, 7–15. Retrieved from https://cyberleninka.ru/article/v/strategicheskaya-kommunikatsiya-kak-metod-sovremennoy-geopolitiki.

Communication Monitor (2019). Official website. Retrieved from www.communicationmonitor.eu/.

Dean, J. (2010). *Blog theory.* Cambridge, MA: Polity Press.

Gavra, D. P., & Dekalov, V. V. (2018). *Tsifrovaja elita vs analogovaja elita: Tranformatsija sotsialnoj stratifikatsii v setevuju epokhu* [Digital elite vs analogue elite: social stratification transformation in the networked age]. Proceedings of the VI International scientific conference "Strategic Communications in politics and business" (pp. 118–128). St. Petersburg: St. Petersburg State University.

Glaser, M. (2019, October 31). Globalization: A Russian perspective. *Global-E, 12*(48). Online. Retrieved from www.21global.ucsb.edu/global-e/october-2019/globalization-russian-perspective.

Heath, R. L. (2018). Fully functioning society. *The International Encyclopedia of Strategic Communication.* Wiley Online Library. Retrieved from https://doi.org/10.1002/9781119010722.iesc0078.

Jablin, F. M. (1987). Organizational entry, assimilation and exit. In F. M. Jablin, L. L. Putnam, K. H. Roberts, & L. W. Porter (Eds.), *Handbook of organizational communication*(pp. 679–740). Newbury Park, CA: Sage.

Martinez, F. (2013). On the peripheral character of Russia. *Novos Olhares Ssobre o Espaço Pós-soviético, 19.* Retrieved from https://journals.openedition.org/eces/1562.

MGIMO (2020). New Media and Strategic Communications Program. Official website. Retrieved from https://mgimo.ru/study/master/smm/.

Native Advertising Institute (2019). *39 predictions for native advertising.* Online report. Retrieved from https://nativeadvertisinginstitute.com/wp-content/uploads/2019/01/NAI-ebog_Trends_2019.pdf.

Panarin, I. (2018). Strategic communications and world politics. *Communications. Media. Design, 3*(3), 23–34.

Patomaki, H., & Pursiainen, C. (1999). Western models and the "Russian idea": Beyond "inside/outside" discourses on civil society. *Millennium: Journal of International Studies, 28*(1), 53–77.

Philimonov, G. Y., & Tsaturyan, C. A. (2012). "Myagkaja sila" kak forma nepryamoj applikatsii "natsionalnogo interesa" ["Soft power" as a form of indirect application of the "national interest"]. *Vestnik Rossijskogo Universiteta Druzhby Nadorov. Serija: Mezhdunarodnye Otnoshenija* [Vestnik of Russian University of Friendship of the People. Series: International Relations], *2*, 21–30.

RASO (Russian Association of Public Relations) (2017). *O buduschem kommunikatsiij.* [About the future of communications]. White paper. RASO with support from the Center of Social Projection "Platforma" and the Department of Integrated Communciations at NRU HSE. Retrieved from www.raso.ru/news/24128/.

RBK/ACAR (2020). *Reklama 2020. Kak menyaetsja mirovoj rynok reklamy i chrm 'to grozit biznesu* [Advertising 2020. How the world advertising market changes and what it means for business]. Online post. Retrieved from https://plus.rbc.ru/news/5db96d287a8aa9b7f54096bd.

Ross A. (2011). Digital diplomacy and US foreign policy. *Hague Journal of Diplomacy, 6*(3–4), 451–455.

RUDN (2019). *Vektory kommunikatsij buduschego obsudili v RUDN* [Vectors of communications in the future were discussed at RUDN]. News release online. Retrieved from www.akarussia.ru/press_centre/news/id8781.

Stratcom (2018, November 28). *Mir kommunikatsij cherez sto let posle "1984"* [The world of communication a hundred years later after "1984"]. Online post. Retrieved from http://jf.spbu.ru/index/146–13203.html

Taylor, M., & Kent, M. (2010). Anticipatory socialization in the use of social media in public relations: A content analysis of PRSA's Public Relations Tactics. *Public Relations Review, 36*, 207–214.

Tsetsura, K. (2004). Russia. In B. van Ruler, & D. Verčič (Eds.), *Public relations and communication in Europe: A nation-by-nation introduction to public relations theory and practice* (pp. 331–346). Berlin: Mouton De Gruyter.

Tsetsura, K. (2011). Is public relations a real job? How female practitioners construct the profession. *Journal of Public Relations Research, 23*(1), 1–23.

Tsetsura, K., & Kruckeberg, D. (2004). Theoretical development of public relations in Russia. In D. J. Tilson (Ed.), *Toward the common good: Perspectives in international public relations* (pp. 176–192). Boston, MA: Pearson Allyn & Bacon.

Tsvetkova, N. A. (2011). Publichnayaj diplomatija SShA i revolutsija v arabskom mire [Public diplomacy in the USA and revolution in the Arab world]. *Mir i Politika* [The World and Politics], *4*, 45–53.

Tsvetkova, N. (2015). Publichnaja diplomatija SShA: Ot "myagkoj sily" k "dialogovoj propaganda" [Public diplomacy in the USA: From "soft power" to "dialogic propaganda"]. *Mezhdunarodnye Protsessy* [International Processes], *3*(42), 121–133.

Yudin, N. V. (2015). Sistemnoe prochtenie fenomena myagkoj sily [Sistemic reading of the phenomenon of soft power]. *Mezhdunarodnye Protsessy* [International Processes], *13*(2), 95–105.

Index

Printed in the United States
By Bookmasters